NOTES FOR THE FUTURE

NOTES FOR THE FUTURE

An alternative history of the past decade

edited by ROBIN CLARKE

THAMES AND HUDSON · LONDON

Printed Offset Litho and bound in Great Britain by
Cox & Wyman Ltd,
London, Fakenham and Reading

Contents

Part Four THE TECHNOCRACY CHALLENGED

Part Five WAYS AHEAD

Part Six THE HUMAN FUTURE

Acknowledgments

The editor and the publishers are grateful to the following copyright owners for permission to reprint the articles named: 'New tools for democracy', Peter van Dresser; 'A generation in search of a future', Prof. George Wald and the MIT Press; 'Resource needs and demands', Prof. Harrison Brown, the Nobel Foundation, and Almqvist & Wiksell Förlag AB; 'Food – the great challenge of this crucial century', Georg Borgstrom and the Macmillan Publishing Co. Inc.; 'Population control or Hobson's choice', Prof. Paul R. Ehrlich and The Academic Press; 'A look at the future', Dr Donella H. Meadows; 'The tragedy of the commons', Prof. Garrett Hardin, the Editor of *Science*, and the American Association for the Advancement of Science; 'The economics of permanence', Dr E. F. Schumacher and the Editors of *Resurgence*; 'The technological flaw', Dr Barry Commoner, Alfred A. Knopf, Inc., and Jonathan Cape Ltd; 'The historical roots of our ecologic crisis', Prof. Lynn White Jr, the Editor of *Science*, and the American Association for the Advancement of Science; 'The sacramental vision of nature', Prof. Theodore Roszak, and the Editor of *New Humanist*; 'Ravings of a fatigued, drunken, young ex-scientist', Peter Harper; 'The scientist as shaman', Malachi Martin; 'Does science control people or do people control science?', Henryk Skolimowski; 'Science, technology and poetry', Robert Graves, and the Editor of *New Scientist*; 'The second Dark Ages', Prof. Jerome Y. Lettvin, and the Director-General of Unesco; 'Ode to Terminus', Faber & Faber Ltd, and Random House Inc.; 'Ecology and revolutionary thought', Murray Bookchin, Times Change Press, and Wildwood House Ltd; 'A modest proposal: science for the people', John Todd; 'Self-sufficiency: what is it? Why do it?', John and Sally Seymour, Faber & Faber Ltd., and Schocken Books Inc.; 'China: a new society in the making', Derek Bryan, and the Editors of *Futures*; 'Passage to more than India', Gary Snyder, New Directions Publishing Corporation, and Jonathan Cape Ltd; 'Community and city planning', Murray Bookchin, and Harper & Row; 'The new consciousness', Judson Jerome, and the Twentieth Century Fund; 'Where the wasteland ends', Theodore Roszak, Doubleday & Co. Inc., and Faber & Faber Ltd.

Introduction

This is a history book – a history of the past ten years of Western society. You will find nothing in it on industrial unrest, the boom in pornography, the problem of Israel, the undoing of Mr Nixon. Nothing on the conquest of the Moon, on the advertising industry or Malcolm Muggeridge. Nothing on the affluent society.

Such things are a poor guide to the future. They are but the last gasps of a society conditioned to view everything through the darkened spectacles of the present. In every death a rebirth. And in the midst of our civilization's struggles to survive to an unnatural old age, we can detect, if not a rebirth, then at least a new conception. This book is an attempt to write a history of that conception and, in so doing, to provide a guide to understanding the offspring of the future which will result from it.

The story starts – as do so many – with war. And for our generation the Vietnam war marks the end of the old and the beginning of the new. Like many wars, it was one not universally acclaimed. Without question it produced the largest and most vociferous anti-war movement in human history. It solidified the ranks of the young, not only in America but in Europe as well, against a common enemy whose coat bore no particular political colour. It was the war of the largest nation against the smallest. The war of the computer against the bicycle. The war of the rich against the poor. The war of man against the land.

In all these ways, Vietnam stood for more than the first American defeat. It was also the victory of people over machines and of belief over affluence. A conquering of the West by the East. It was the end of an era.

The initial protest was ordinary enough, save for its size. The issues of imperialism, aggression, torture and massacre are common to all wars. But attention soon turned to the techniques of war – to napalm and chemical weapons, to laser-guided bombing, defoliation and ecological devastation. To the use of anthropologists to advise on the proper techniques for 'pacification' of the ignoble savage of the south-east Asian jungle. To the use of social scientists to advise on methods of maintaining a world-wide *status quo*. And to the use of computers to simulate war games whose naïveté would make Napoleon groan in his grave.

Thus was the attention of the protest diverted to novel areas. The uses to which Western man could put his technology were questioned. The role of the universities, particularly in the United States, was exposed. The scholar turned out to be dressed in military uniform and, worse, to be wearing the general's stars. It had taken three centuries for us to realize what Bacon had meant when he claimed that 'knowledge is power'. The ethic of reason, rationality, science, knowledge, technology and progress was in the melting-pot. Materialism had lost out to the mysterious East.

The New Enlightenment began to stir even before the carnage in Asia reached its agonizing end. In the United States the students shut down their universities – first for a day (4 March 1969), then for weeks and months. Finally, many left altogether, never to return. Instead of the techniques of technocratic specialization, they chose to ask the big questions. What was man doing to man? What was man doing to his planet? What was technology doing to man? And why was it necessary? Were there alternatives? Not subjects to be found in any university syllabus in the 1960s.

From the bomb-ripped chemical wasteland of Vietnam to the polluted stench of our great cities was not such a big step. The twisted metal wreckage of a car junk yard looks much like an old battleground; the lethal 'side-effects' of radiation from a nuclear reactor are not so different from those of the bomb itself, except in scale. And to the disenchanted, pollution in the name of progress soon seemed as evil as pollution in the name of war. But though pollution stuck with the media for many years, the real debate soon moved on. To many of the young, our industries did not produce pollution as an unfortunate side-effect. Its products were themselves garbage – garbage deliberately produced in the name of economic growth, capitalism and the quick profit. Now consumerism was under attack.

Of course, it had been since World War II. But the grounds were novel. Calculations could easily be made to show that the United States, with 7 per cent of the world population, used nearly 50 per cent of world resources. The Western model for democratic progress was found wanting. It was no model at all. If such a standard of living were extended it could, at most, provide for 15 per cent of the world population, providing no one minded that the other 85 per cent be robbed of even their meagre lot. There was not enough to go round, and for the first time doubt was cast on those scientists and technologists who airily claimed that 'means would be found'. As far as food was concerned, means had not been found; more people die daily from starvation and its side-effects now than ever before in the history of the planet. The technical utopia became more remote. Scientists looked at the glass and pronounced it half full. The rest pronounced it half empty.

Characteristically, for a technical society whose main aim was to replace people by machines, the first reaction was to blame people. Far too many of them, with the promise of more, many more, to come. The planet was too small for such a crowd, particularly in the developing countries. And so the debate moved towards its 'crisis era'; the prophets of doom predicted eco-collapse and preached enforced population control as the means of salvation. The 'limits to growth' were publicized, in archetypal style, by a grand computer study which demonstrated the end of the world through the interacting variables of capital investment, pollution rate, population growth, available food and depletion of natural resources. Garrett Hardin, the biologist, explained that the tragedy of the commons was that through being forced to share resources the individual could gain at the expense of the public.

To the older culture, conditioned, as Murray Bookchin argues, to the idea of scarcity, these neo-Malthusian philosophies were adequate enough. The young flirted with them, took to macrobiotic food, and found beauty in the cultivation of the earth. A few went further. Why, they asked, was there an ecological crisis at all? If there were too many people, what caused their explosion in numbers? 'Be fruitful and multiply', says the Bible, and one eminent historian captured many hearts with his thesis that Judaeo-Christian myth lay behind our ecological downfall. Others saw eco-doom as the inevitable death-agony of capitalist society – and tried to prove that Marx predicted it. Gradually the debate homed-in on the nature of technology and the relationship between man and nature which it camouflaged. Theories of knowledge were tested – and found wanting. The analytical, reductionist style of our society, hitherto universally accepted as the only legitimate means to truth, was challenged. What gave rise to the idea that finer and finer examination of smaller and smaller particles would reveal the true nature of the universe and all therein? Yet that is precisely the unwritten credo of our science, for which there appears to be no logical or philosophical justification. In challenging this, the counter-culture thrust nearer to the heart of Western man than any of the eco-doomsters, Malthusian or otherwise.

The cases against both the technocracy, and the scientific philosophy on which it is based and by which it was originally inspired, are by no means complete. Perhaps they never will be, for the arguments already available have been sufficient to convince many that an alternative – and preferably many alternatives – should be found. Yet blueprints are themselves products of the technocracy, so the models of the alternative which have driven this argument forward are hard to find. There are no grand schemes for the rearrangement of the world, along the lines of Thomas More and Fourier in earlier times. In their places appear some 'modest proposals' – a plan to experiment with a science which is human in scale, has well-defined ethical boundaries and is devoted to the protection of the earth. Ideas for technologies which will reunite men with each other, and with nature. Sketchings of how 'economics' would be if it were not economics as we know it. A cookery book for those who want to solve the world food problem. In short, a whole contrast of style and philosophy with the aim of dealing with a world in chaos.

The last chapter of this history is at once the least developed and the most important. For as our recognition of the nature of the crisis draws nearer home, we see much that was formerly thought to be the cause – the nature of our technology, the fashion for ecology – as symptoms of a diseased society. The real *malaise*, as Theodore Roszak writes, is within the amorphous mass the technocracy has substituted for human community. So it is within ourselves, and within our friends, that many now seek their solutions in what amounts to a religious renewal of faith in people and their imagination. In the commune, in the thirst for eastern religious experience, in the search for new vision – these are the hunting grounds of a new society. What is to be found there none can say, but it certainly seems a happier place to search than in the wilderness of a failed experiment in urban-industrial living. The post-industrial era is upon us, and the history of the past decade is the story of the switch from an old paradigm to a new one.

In keeping with this new paradigm, I do not claim either that the switch has been thrown or that it was thrown in the way in which I have seen and experienced it. As one who hops uncomfortably between the old culture and the new, I am aware that others have come through different metamorphoses. My view as a science writer is partial, and the same story as seen for example by an architect or a lawyer, a mountaineer or a teenager, would read differently. The end, however, would look much the same.

Much of what really lies in any new movement lies underground. I have chosen, however, to tell this story through the writings of those above ground – with one or two exceptions. It is a terrain I know better and one which I also know carries more weight. So the writings I have selected are those for the most part of scholars, not hippies. The only extraordinary thing, to my mind, is that the story could be told by either and, except for allowances for language and style, would be essentially the same.

Part One

BETWEEN THE WARS

'Is there anything new under the sun?' asks Peter van Dresser in this first article in this anthology – and goes on to show that there is. Yet his article is included to show that nothing is really that new. Van Dresser touches on all the hot issues of our time: big business, the inhumane power of scientific technology, the need for decentralization, for re-population of the countryside, for new technologies, and the insane course which the technocrats seem intent on setting for the whole world. With a few changes here and there, his article has been written and published somewhere a score of times every year for the past decade.

But van Dresser's piece is unique: the date of publication was March 1939, the eve of World War II. To those of us who think they may have discovered at least a little of the reason for today's global chaos, this is a sobering thought. If the movement to put science and technology back in their rightful place was so clearly articulated thirty-six years ago, what happened?

The answer, of course, is World War II – the war in which both might and right triumphed through the blunderbuss use of the technology to end all technologies – atomic power. After such a vindication, who could dare to question the course on which our explosive science had been set? The age of the atom was clearly so preferable to the age of fascism that even the doubters were silenced. For a time.

It took another war and another generation to rekindle the flame. And what happened in Vietnam was the exact opposite of the previous bout of global carnage: might lost and right won, and the fat was in the fire. George Wald, with dove-like innocence, takes us to the heart of the military state now called America. And within his prose it is easy to spot the new mood. Not for him the sophisticated argument, complicated verbiage and tedious abbreviations of the technocracy. Instead, a cry from the heart full of confidence in the correctness of the human instinct. He does not urge his students to write doctoral theses on some aspects of the impenetrability of anti-ballistic missile systems; instead he urges them not to accept what is not acceptable. And without saying so, he is telling them to relegate their science and technology to a position subordinate to human desires and emotions.

In the 1960s this was heresy. Wald's speech was written off as the meander-

ings of a simpleton, despite the thunderous student applause that greeted his words. A year later Theodore Roszak was to begin the job of articulating the reasons behind the revolt of the young which is Wald's main concern in this piece.

New tools for democracy

PETER VAN DRESSER

Tiberius Gracchus could sympathize with Roosevelt's problems; Manco Capac could give Stalin pointers on state communism; Lycurgus the Spartan would understand Hitler's policies. There were million-cities while New York and London were still trailheads; there were exploited proletariats while Europe was yet a wilderness; there were lands soil-mined to eroded deserts by industrial farming before America was dreamed of.

Is there anything new under the sun? Militant imperialism, 'exploitation of the masses', urban congestion, and rural devitalization – problems such as these which face us today seem identical repetitions of pathological patterns into which human activity has fallen since time immemorial.

But hydroelectric plants and giant power lines, airplanes and radio networks and Diesel engines *are* new under the sun. For the first time in the entire history of our planet, so far as we are aware, people possess such tools, instruments, and machines as these. In the long view, what is to come of this mutation in the habits and powers of the human species? Merely further repetitions and intensifications of the same old behavior-patterns? Cities vaster and more dehumanized than imperial Rome or Samaria? Caesaristic exploits more formidable than those of Caius Julius? National cult-communism more perfectly enforced than that of the Incas? Provinces more efficiently subdued and drained than those of the Ottomans? Is our civilization actually destined to approximate these super-mechanical utopias which are now the popular fashion, with their arrogant towering cities, their mighty systems and engines for the mass-exploitation of the earth?

Already the 'modern' world has gone far in this direction, in fascist nations especially with a deliberate and desperate mimicry of antique

Extracts from an article in *Harper's Magazine*, March 1939.

glories. And here in America, by just so much as our States and regions have become provinces culturally and economically enslaved, by just so much as men and women have become state or big-business protégés incapable of economic self-determination – by so much have we drifted back toward an age-encrusted way of life, and away from the urgent new American ideal, which is still new, desperately new, after a century and a half, and by no means assured of a permanent existence.

We have one facile, all-embracing explanation for this drift. It is all due, we say, to 'modern science'. Things are not what they were in the frontier society of Jefferson's and Washington's day. Railroads and telephones and motor cars have interconnected the nation; mass production and automatic machinery have drastically altered industrial methods.

Phrases such as 'modern science has remade America' and 'We must adapt ourselves to the march of technical progress' are constantly on our lips – so constantly, in fact, that we cease to take them in a metaphorical sense. We talk, and think, as if Scientific Technology were a kind of willful genie whose gifts we must gratefully accept while we accommodate ourselves as best we can to his bad habits.

But not for one instant will we question Scientific Technology itself; will we examine it to see if by chance its evolution might be modified to accord with our ethical and moral and political ideals.

Is this sensible? External form without underlying reality cannot be expected to maintain itself. If we have permitted something to destroy the unique economic structure of the original United States, that structure which, however imperfect, made possible the growth of a self-dependent citizenry which could conceive and put into execution the idea of self-government, then how can we expect to wage anything but a losing fight for democracy? How can we expect in the long run to achieve anything but some such *ersatz* government as plutocracy, bureacracy, technocracy?

For the entire pattern of organizing society implicit in the ideal of the technological superstate is utterly hostile to the democratic way of life. These towering 'cities of the future', these titanic mills and factories and engineering works are of the very soul and essence of imperialism, dwarfing and collectivizing the men who dwell within their shadow – or within a thousand miles of them, for that matter.

But by what right do we assume so complacently that these are new forms created out of the necessities of scientific technology? It is much more likely that they are primitive forms sprung from the ambitions of aggressive, power-loving men. For technology, scientific or otherwise, is *not* a self-determined entity; it is the child of the wishes and intentions of the men who form it. And it was most certainly not the inventors and pure scientists who controlled the development of technics during the past century; it was the entrepreneurs, the rising industrialists, the empire-builders. Why did the early manufacturers who bought Watt's new steam-engines for their plants refuse to let him improve their operation so that they would run more smoothly and quietly? *Because they liked the sensation of power that went with ownership of immense snorting and clanking engines!* Small wonder that such men and their successors have left us with a heritage of mighty industrial baronies; small wonder that the machinery they have forged thrives best in an atmosphere deadly to humanitarian democracy!

Glance for an instant at the effect, from the humanitarian point of view, that this machinery has had on America in the course of its lavish production of material wealth. It has overcentralized our industries, overbuilt our cities. It has debased our farms and farmers with one-crop agriculture. It has replaced the American yeoman with a growing landless, toolless proletariat. It has robbed our communities, villages, natural regions of all semblance of economic autonomy. It is driving our government (along with those of all other highly industrialized nations) each year deeper into a policy of oil-imperialism, raw-material imperialism, foreign-market imperialism, to supply fuel for a hypertrophied transportation system and justification for our great centralized mass-production industries. It has drafted half our man power into parasitical occupations of salesmanship, packaging, 'servicing'. It has left much of 'provincial' America spiritually and culturally bankrupt, has overstimulated a few great centers to a point of intellectual hysteria. Simultaneously and quite automatically it has steam-rollered democratic methods out of existence wherever possible.

All this we could endure and hope to remedy if we were sure, quite sure, that only through machinery of this general type can we continue to put into effect the indisputable advantages of scientific technology. *But this is a question we have never faced point-blank.*

Now it is true that in certain departments of its operation modern technology implies on strictly functional grounds the advantages of a high degree of centralization and socialization. These departments are concerned with the production of certain raw materials which occur in concentrated points and can be processed only by large machinery, and for which there is no satisfactory substitute. Giant power is one of these commodities, and the sooner the Federal Government succeeds in harnessing every important hydraulic power site available and covering the nation with transmission grids the better from an engineering point of view. Coal is another such commodity, and the sooner all coal mined is converted to electricity in large ultra-efficient plants at the minehead the better it will be for the total efficiency of the nation's utilization of such power and the conservation of human and natural resources.

There are a few other basic materials in this class, as, for instance, iron and steel, lumber, even heavy transportation. But if we examine the whole body of modern technics, with particular regard for the most advanced practices and the most significant potentialities, the surprising fact stands revealed that its present evolution is in a direction precisely contrary to the current doctrine of ever-waxing complexity, size, and regimentation! How does it happen that while inventors, researchers, engineers are unanimously striving – and succeeding amazingly well – to make machines and processes more refined, more flexible, more versatile, we find it necessary to construct a social order more rigid, top-heavy, and complex?

Look, for example, at the entire field of applied science which is coming to be known as 'electrotechnics'. Aluminum, magnesium, alloys and iron with tungsten and vanadium and molybdenum and other metals are now produced in small, clean, effective electric furnaces and cells, and used to fabricate the lightweight, rustless modern machinery. Other types of cells and furnaces produce from coke, water, brine, air, lime the endless compounds of carbon, nitrogen, and other elements that are needed in the useful arts. Arc-welding and electro-forming processes furnish new and adaptable means for handling metals. Electric machine tools of all types combine extraordinary versatility and efficiency with compactness and mobility.

This entire family of tools and methods – and their use is growing very rapidly – point toward an organization of industry essentially different from the nineteenth-century pattern. They can be set up and operated wherever a transmission line can run; they can operate as efficiently in small units as large.

Chemical engineering, which is also one of the fastest growing applied sciences, is another disrupter of respected industrial patterns. To the chemist there are raw materials galore on every American farm. His plastic materials synthesized from agricultural sources are already shouldering their way into the strongholds of metals and minerals. An airplane built entirely of plastics has been successfully flown in England, and our own Forest Products Laboratory has developed material which can be produced from sawdust and is superior to metal for many purposes, including bathtubs!

In agriculture, experts advocate more and more insistently the need for the scientific diversified farm as opposed to the mammoth one-crop agricultural factory. Agrobiology points the way to quadrupled yields per acre. Humus-building biological technics of soil enrichment replace wholesale chemical fertilization.

Urban improvements become constantly more adaptable to the country home. Sanitary plumbing and the septic tank displace the rural privy. Broadcasting networks end isolation. Aero-electricity, from wind-driven plants, lights and pumps for the most remote farm homes.

What changes could be expected in our economic organization if these more advanced tools and concepts of modern science – *as distinct from finance and industry* – were applied functionally? We should undoubtedly witness a widespread growth of small and moderate-sized factories and plants scattered throughout the various regions and communities of the nation. These establishments would be equipped with the most modern machinery and apparatus, and would make the utmost use of local and regional raw materials. They would produce a wide range of goods necessary for a civilized society, from processed foods through chemicals, textiles, utensils, electrical apparatus, and machine tools – everything, in fact, except the few basic concentrated raw materials and the heaviest machinery.

We should witness a decline in the number of big plantations and industrial farms devoted to soil-mining monoculture and an increase in the number of smaller, diversified farms supplying local markets and maintaining soil fertility through crop-rotation and organic composting, as practiced successfully in Holland and Switzerland.

We should witness a dispersive movement from the great cities, a gradual building up of 'greenbelt' and 'broadacre' communities in rural sections, a development of types of modern country dwelling constructed scientifically of regional materials and adapted to the climate of the locality.

We should witness a decline in the importance of the great coal and steel centers, brought about by the increasing use of hydroelectricity, of plastics and non-corrosive alloys and metals, of more effective methods of reclamation, and by the dwindling importance of heavy transportation and construction coincident with the diminution in the size of cities. This trend would effect enormous savings in coal, oil, and other resources.

We should witness the rapid growth of the conservation movement and the socialization of certain basic resources, made possible with the replacement of an imperialistic, exploitative industrial technic by a functional technic.

It is unnecessary here to discuss the endless obstacles in the way of such an evolution, the vested interests which oppose it, and so on. The point is that this economic order which modern technics is making constantly more logical is infinitely better adapted to the democratic way of life than the mechanized, socialized, economic superstate which seems to be the ideal, in one guise or another, of each of the great modern industrial nations.

In his two brilliant volumes, *Technics and Civilization* and *The Culture of Cities*, Lewis Mumford has attempted a broad survey of the future possible for America if these potentialities of modern science are allowed to develop and mature according to their own inner logic. His concept of *biotechnics*, the applied science of the age that might thus be brought into being, is inspiring. He pictures its technic as vastly different from the nineteenth-century technic of brute power and size, of mass-operations and mass exploitation, of endless multiplication and concentration and aggrandizement, under whose influence our ideas are still molded. It is a technic which, as the name implies, is adjusted to the needs and rhythms of human life rather than to the formation of industrial empires; which makes far ampler use of biological processes of growth, of the clean energy in falling water and wind and sunlight than we do at present.

Out of the application of this technique springs a pattern of civilization totally new on the face of the earth – as new as American democracy, as new as electronics. It is an order in which the age-old pattern of all previous high civilizations – arrogant Megalopolis reared on exhausted Province – may be at last displaced. It is an order in which an entire nation – region by region, community by community, dwelling by dwelling – may be developed as carefully and fruitfully as a garden; in which industries are decentralized and functional, designed to fill local and regional requirements rather than to augment the wealth of centralized industrial dynasties. It is an order in which cities are cultural and co-ordinative centers rather than seats of despotic economic power; an order whose citizens, the vast majority, live in the garden-surrounded homes natural to civilized man.

This is the pattern for the future, *based on purely technical and functional considerations*, which is gradually displacing the nightmare visions of supermechanical, super-urbanized Utopias. And it is obviously a pattern far friendlier to the democratic ideal.

America's intellectual liberals, of all people, should be most keenly concerned with action leading toward a realization of this concept. They are the ones who have lamented most loudly the forces of reaction and imperialism associated with Big Business and Big Industry. They are the ones who feel most acutely the loss of independent security, the dwindling rights of the individual, the proletarization of the nation.

Yet it seems a tragic truth that our liberal intelligentsia are still constitutionally blind to the possibility of this course of action. Embattled farmers, Mrs Roosevelt, and even Henry Ford may have gleaned some inkling of the technological jacquerie underfoot – but not America's intellectuals. Essentially urban or suburban in conditioning, they seem actually to resent any implication that the cause of democracy may be aided by anything remotely resembling what they refer to contemptuously as 'back to the land movements'. Long ago they deserted the land for the hothouse environments of the great cities, choosing the fancied security of corporation jobs rather than the discomfort of individual effort in the hinterland. The very thought that they should forego their 'careers' in New York or Chicago for a life's work in the provinces is abhorrent to them. America beyond the frontiers of suburbia has now become for them an unfamiliar land peopled by taciturn sharecroppers, militant Farm Unionists, and small-town Babbitts; a region to be penetrated occasionally on slumming trips in search of material for reports and surveys. Irresistibly their attention focusses on the centers of 'big time' activities, on the spectacular duels of the Big Fellows, on the maneuvers at Washington, on the latest brilliant book exposing capitalism or the shocking conditions in Germany.

It is urgently necessary that somehow, and soon, men and women of this class should become generally aware of the technic for the reconstruction of a democratic nation which research is creating. Political action, collectivist action, in which they still trust, alone cannot preserve democracy – there must be an underlying economic structure which permits the survival of the self-dependent citizen.

That such a structure can be built in terms of the highest of today's and tomorrow's science is now certain. That there is an immense task of pioneering before the building can be begun is also certain. And it is finally certain that this is pioneering which cannot be done in Metropolis with talk. It must be done in America, with tools.

A generation in search of a future

GEORGE WALD

All of you know that in the last couple of years there has been student unrest breaking at times into violence in many parts of the world: in England, Germany, Italy, Spain, Mexico, and needless to say, in many parts of this country. There has been a great deal of discussion as to what it all means. Perfectly clearly it means something different in Mexico from what it does in France, and something different in France from what it does in Tokyo, and something different in Tokyo from what it does in this country. Yet unless we are to assume that students have gone crazy all over the world, or that they have just decided that it's the thing to do, there must be some common meaning.

I don't need to go so far afield to look for that meaning. I am a teacher, and at Harvard I have a class of about 350 students – men and women – most of them freshmen and sophomores. Over these past few years I have felt increasingly that something is terribly wrong – and this year ever so much more than last. Something has gone sour, in teaching and in learning. It's almost as though there were a widespread feeling that education has become irrelevant.

A lecture is much more of a dialogue than many of you probably appreciate. As you lecture, you keep watching the faces; and information keeps coming back to you all the time. I began to feel, particularly this year, that I was missing much of what was coming back. I tried asking the students, but they didn't or couldn't help me very much.

But I think I know what's the matter, even a little better than they do. I think that this whole generation of students is beset with a profound uneasiness. I don't think that they have yet quite defined its source. I think I understand the reasons for their uneasiness even better than they do. What is more, I share their uneasiness.

What's bothering those students? Some of them tell you it's the Vietnam War. I think the Vietnam War is the most shameful episode in the whole of American history. The concept of war crimes is an American invention. We've committed many war crimes in Vietnam; but I'll tell you something interesting about that. We were committing war crimes in World War II, even before the Nuremberg trials were held and the principle of war crimes stated. The saturation bombing of German cities was a war crime. Dropping atom bombs on Hiroshima and Nagasaki was a war crime. If we had lost the war, some of our leaders might have had to answer for those actions.

I've gone through all of that history lately, and I find that there's a gimmick in it. It isn't written out, but I think we established it by precedent. That gimmick is that if one can allege that one is repelling or retaliating for an *aggression* – after that everything goes. And you see we are living in a world in which all wars are wars of defense. All War Departments are now Defense Departments. This is all part of the double talk of our time. The aggressor is always on the other side. And I suppose this is why our ex-Secretary of State, Dean Rusk – a man in whom repetition takes the place of reason, and stubbornness takes the place of character – went to such pains to insist, as he still insists, that in Vietnam we are repelling an aggression. And if that's what we are doing – so runs the doctrine – anything goes. If the concept of war crimes is ever to mean anything, they will have to be defined as categories of acts, regardless of alleged provocation. But that isn't so now.

I think we've lost that war, as a lot of other people think, too. The Vietnamese have a secret weapon. It's their willingness to die, beyond our willingness to kill. In effect they've been saying, you can kill us, but you'll have to kill a lot of us, you may have to kill all of us. And thank heavens, we are not yet ready to do that.

But that Vietnam War, shameful and terrible as it is, seems to me only an immediate incident in a much larger and more stubborn situation.

Part of my trouble with students is that almost all the students I teach were born since World War II. Just after World War II, a series of new and abnormal procedures came into American life. We regarded them at the time as temporary aberrations. We thought we would get back to normal American life some day. But those procedures have stayed with us now for more than twenty years, and those students of mine have never known anything else. They think those things are normal. Students think we've always had a Pentagon, that we have always had a big army, and that we always had a draft. But those are all new things in American life; and I think that they are incompatible with what America meant before.

I say the Vietnam War is just an immediate incident, because so long as we keep that big an army, it will always find things to do. If the Vietnam War stopped tomorrow, with that big a military establishment, the chances are that we would be in another such adventure abroad or at home before we knew it.

As for the draft: Don't reform the draft – get rid of it.

A peacetime draft is the most un-American thing I know. All the time I was growing up I was told about oppressive Central European countries and Russia, where young men were forced into the army; and I was told what they did about it. They chopped off a finger, or shot off a couple of toes; or better still, if they could manage it, they came to this country. And we understood that, and sympathized, and were glad to welcome them.

Now by present estimates four to six thousand Americans of draft age have left this country for Canada, another two or three thousand have gone to Europe, and it looks as though many more are preparing to emigrate.

A few months ago I received a letter from the Harvard Alumni Bulletin posing a series of questions that students might ask a professor involving what to do about the draft. I was asked to write what I would tell those students. All I had to say to those students was this: If any of them had decided to evade the draft and asked my help, I would help him in any way I could. I would feel as I suppose members of the underground railway felt in pre-Civil War days, helping runaway slaves to get to Canada. It wasn't altogether a popular position then; but what do you think of it now?

But there is something ever so much bigger and more important than the draft. That bigger thing, of course, is the militarization of our country. Ex-President Eisenhower warned us of what he called the military-industrial complex. I am sad to say that we must begin to think of it now as the military-industrial-labor union complex. What happened under the plea of the Cold War was not only that we built up the first big peacetime army in our history, but we institutionalized it. We built, I suppose, the biggest government building in our history to run it, and we institutionalized it.

There's another feature of this that disturbs me very much. In recent years, in our innocence, almost every scientific society in the country was sold the idea of establishing a Washington office. We were going to have lobbies like everybody else. So now we've got ourselves a secretariat in Washington attached to practically all of the major scientific societies. Those secretariats are full of bureaucrats just like all the other

Washington bureaus. They look for things to do, for more influence, for more money, and there's that Department of Defense with money to burn.

So, one has some very peculiar manifestations. I'm a biologist. The AIBS, the American Institute of Biological Sciences, about a year ago, in a nauseating display of hypocrisy, announced that they were staging two scientific meetings under the sponsorship of Fort Detrick. The first of those meetings – a symposium – wasn't called 'Defoliation'. No, it was called 'Leaf Abscission'. The second of those meetings had nothing to do with biological warfare and virus infections – Oh, no – it was called 'The Introduction of Foreign DNA'.

I was called by a man in Washington some months ago who told me to my enormous surprise that he was the Director of Biological Research for, of all things, the Federated American Societies for Experimental Biology. I didn't know they had a Director of Biological Research, and I haven't the least idea what such a person might conceivably do. But what he was on the phone for was to tell me that the Department of Defense had asked him to organize a new committee to go into visual problems connected with the use of some new weaponry.

I'm sorry to say that the worst offender in this regard has been the National Academy of Sciences. The outgoing President of the National Academy of Sciences – and I, for one, as a member, find this a shocking thing – has been simultaneously the chairman of the Scientific Advisory Board of the Department of Defense.

I don't think we can live with the present military establishment and its $80 billion a year budget and keep America anything like we have known it in the past. It is corrupting the life of the whole country. It is buying up everything in sight: industries, banks, investors, universities; and lately it seems also to have bought up the labor unions.

The Defense Department is always broke; but some of the things they do with that $80 billion a year would make Buck Rogers envious. For example: the Rocky Mountain Arsenal on the outskirts of Denver was manufacturing a deadly nerve poison on such a scale that there was a problem of waste disposal. Nothing daunted, they dug a tunnel two miles deep under Denver, into which they have injected so much poisoned water that beginning a couple of years ago Denver began to experience a series of earth tremors of increasing severity. Now there is a grave fear of a major earthquake. An interesting debate is in progress as to whether Denver will be safer if that lake of poisoned water is removed or left in place. (*N.Y. Times*, July 4, 1968; *Science*, Sept. 27, 1968.)

Perhaps you have read also of those 6,000 sheep that suddenly died in Skull Valley, Utah, killed by another nerve poison.

The only point of government is to safeguard and foster life. Our government has become preoccupied with death, with the business of killing and being killed. So-called Defense now absorbs 60 per cent of the national budget and about 12 per cent of the Gross National Product.

A lively debate is beginning again on whether or not we should deploy antiballistic missiles, the ABM. I don't have to talk about them, everyone else here is doing that. But I should like to mention a curious circumstance. In September 1967, or about 1½ years ago, we had a meeting of MIT and Harvard people, including experts on these matters, to talk about whether anything could be done to block the Sentinel system, the deployment of ABMs. Everyone present thought them undesirable; but a few of the most knowledgeable persons took what seemed to be the practical view, 'Why fight about a dead issue? It has been decided, the funds have been appropriated. Let's go on from there.'

Fortunately, it's not a dead issue.

An ABM is a nuclear weapon. It takes a nuclear weapon to stop a nuclear weapon. And our concern must be with the whole issue of nuclear weapons.

There is an entire semantics ready to deal with the sort of thing I am about to say. It involves such phrases as 'those are the facts of life'. No – they are the facts of death. I don't accept them, and I advise you not to accept them. We are under repeated pressure to accept things that are presented to us as settled – decisions that have been made. Always there is the thought: let's go on from there! But this time we don't see how to go on. We will have to stick with those issues.

We are told that the United States and Russia between them have by now stockpiled in nuclear weapons approximately the explosive power of 15 tons of TNT for every man, woman, and child on earth. And now it is suggested that we must make more. All very regrettable, of course; but those are 'the facts of life'. We really would like to disarm; but our new Secretary of Defense has made the ingenious proposal that now is the time to increase greatly our nuclear armaments so that we can disarm from a position of strength.

I think all of you know there is no adequate defense against massive nuclear attack. It is both easier and cheaper to circumvent any known nuclear defense system than to provide it. It's all pretty crazy. At the very moment we talk of deploying ABMs, we are also building the MIRV, the weapon to circumvent ABMs.

So far as I know, the most conservative estimates of Americans killed in a major nuclear attack, with everything working as well as can be hoped and all foreseeable precautions taken, run to about 50 millions. We have become callous to gruesome statistics, and this seems at first to be only another gruesome statistic. You think, Bang! – and next morning, if you're still there, you read in the newspapers that 50 million people were killed.

But that isn't the way it happens. When we killed close to 200,000 people with those first little, old-fashioned uranium bombs that we dropped on Hiroshima and Nagasaki, about the same number of persons was maimed, blinded, burned, poisoned, and otherwise doomed. A lot of them took a long time to die.

That's the way it would be. Not a bang, and a certain number of corpses to bury; but a nation filled with millions of helpless, maimed, tortured and doomed persons, and the survivors of a nuclear holocaust will be huddled with their families in shelters, with guns ready to fight off their neighbors, trying to get some uncontaminated food and water.

A few months ago Sen. Richard Russell of Georgia ended a speech in the Senate with the words: 'If we have to start over again with another Adam and Eve, I want them to be Americans; and I want them on this continent and not in Europe.' That was a United States senator holding a patriotic speech. Well, here is a Nobel Laureate who thinks that those words are criminally insane.

How real is the threat of full-scale nuclear war? I have my own very inexpert idea, but realizing how little I know and fearful that I may be a little paranoid on this subject, I take every opportunity to ask reputed experts. I asked that question of a very distinguished professor of government at Harvard about a month ago. I asked him what sort of odds he would lay on the possibility of full-scale nuclear war within the foreseeable future. 'Oh,' he said comfortably, 'I think I can give you a pretty good answer to that question. I estimate the probability of full-scale nuclear war, provided that the situation remains about as it is now, at 2 per cent per year.' Anybody can do the simple calculation that shows that 2 per cent per year means that the chance of having that full-scale nuclear war by 1990 is about one in three, and by 2000 it is about 50–50.

I think I know what is bothering the students. I think that what we are up against is a generation that is by no means sure that it has a future.

I am growing old, and my future so to speak is already behind me. But there are those students of mine who are in my mind always; and there are my children, two of them now 7 and 9, whose future is infinitely more precious to me than my own. So it isn't just their generation; it's mine too. We're all in it together.

Are we to have a chance to live? We don't ask for prosperity, or security; only for a reasonable chance to live, to work out our destiny in peace and decency. Not to go down in history as the apocalyptic generation.

That is the problem. Unless we can be surer than we now are that this generation has a future, nothing else matters. It's not good enough to give it tender loving care, to supply it with breakfast foods, to buy it expensive educations. Those things don't mean anything unless this generation has a future. And we're not sure that it does.

I don't think that there are problems of youth, or student problems. All the real problems I know are grown-up problems.

Perhaps you will think me altogether absurd, or 'academic', or hopelessly innocent – that is, until you think of the alternatives – if I say as I do to you now: we have to get rid of those nuclear weapons. There is nothing worth having that can be obtained by nuclear war:

nothing material or ideological, no tradition that it can defend. It is utterly self-defeating. Those atom bombs represent an unusable weapon. The only use for an atom bomb is to keep somebody else from using one. It can give us no protection, but only the doubtful satisfaction of retaliation. Nuclear weapons offer us nothing but a balance of terror; and a balance of terror is still terror.

We have to get rid of those atomic weapons, here and everywhere. We cannot live with them.

I think we've reached a point of great decision, not just for our nation, not only for all humanity, but for life upon the earth. I tell my students, with a feeling of pride that I hope they will share, that the carbon, nitrogen, and oxygen that make up 99 per cent of our living substance, were cooked in the deep interiors of earlier generations of dying stars. Gathered up from the ends of the universe, over billions of years, eventually they came to form in part the substance of our sun, its planets, and ourselves. Three billion years ago life arose upon the earth. It seems to be the only life in the solar system. Many a star has since been born and died.

About two million years ago, man appeared. He has become the dominant species on the earth. All other living things, animal and plant, live by his sufferance. He is the custodian of life on earth. It's a big responsibility.

The thought that we're in competition with Russians or with Chinese is all a mistake, and trivial. Only mutual destruction lies that way. We are one species, with a world to win. There's life all over this universe, but in all the universe we are the only men.

Our business is with life, not death. Our challenge is to give what account we can of what becomes of life in the solar system, this corner of the universe that is our home and, most of all, what becomes of men – all men of all nations, colors, and creeds. It has become one world, a world for all men. It is only such a world that now can offer us life and the chance to go on.

Part Two

TOO SMALL A PLANET

Men have always found fault with their planet. At various times, and in different places, they have found it too hot, too cold, too wet, too dry, too salty, too overgrown, too savage. What led them to the idea in the 1960s that it was too small, perhaps none can say. Because we saw it for the first time as a globe from the Moon? Because we learnt to fly from anywhere to anywhere on it in less than a day? Because our dreams of further imperialisms were finally vanquished? Or because an American politician hit on that happy term 'spaceship Earth'?

But the discovery of the Earth's smallness was more serious. Wet places can be made drier, dry ones irrigated. But not even the most lunatic of our technocrats promised a means of expanding the Earth. And, historically, this was what was important in the doomy years of the late 1960s. Rational men, many of them pillars of the scientific establishment, went into print claiming they had come up against an obstacle decidedly unamenable to scientific progress: there was not enough to go round, and there would be less in the future.

The President of the International Council for Scientific Unions, Professor Harrison Brown, alerted a group of world experts in Stockholm to the resource crisis. Georg Borgstrom thundered into print with some appalling statistics concerning our shortage of food, and the rapidly worsening situation that could be expected. And Paul Ehrlich, who in the 1960s could out-doom anyone, predicted nothing but catastrophe both globally and, in the article reproduced here, even for Britain herself.

Finally, of course, mechanistic society mechanized the whole doom business by running a computer simulation of the future of the globe under various assumptions about pollution levels, food availability, population and capital investment. The result, the famous book The Limits to Growth*, held the attention of the media for many months. I have chosen not to reproduce an extract from it here because in fact it was little more than a device to impress upon an unbelieving world that there really was a problem. Donella H. Meadows's 'A look at the future' was given as testimonial evidence long before the Club of Rome became famous, and really tells us all we need to know.*

These four articles give a very characteristic flavour to a period of great historical interest. To be sure, they all say much the same thing: too many people chasing too few resources, with the number of people increasing as fast as the resources disappear. And in the background the concept of the presumptive affluence of the few extorted from the misery of the many. The link that couples the two themes is economic growth and international trade. But for the time being no one looked too closely at exactly how the whole exploitive system worked. No one was really trying to discover whether growth or population or the type of technology used was the real culprit. For the moment all was held responsible but, as we shall see in Part III, the day was not far away when generalized doom would be replaced by a more detailed searching for the key issue which had produced the concept of the dwindling future.

Resource needs and demands

HARRISON BROWN

When man-like creatures first appeared upon the earth some two million years ago, individual needs for resources were very modest. Man needed food, water, protection and shelter, which he could obtain using the simplest of technologies. But as increasingly elaborate technologies were developed, aimed at better satisfying these needs, demands for raw materials increased. The development of stone tools and weapons necessitated access to supplies of rock of the right kind for tool manufacture. The development of the controlled use of fire for cooking and warmth created the need for supplies of wood. The invention of agriculture created demands for land particularly suited to cultivation. The emergence of the great ancient urban civilizations led to the development of increasingly elaborate technologies and to the need for increasing *per capita* quantities of raw materials, notably stone, wood, clay, fibers and leather.

Copper was the first metal to come into widespread use on a substantial scale, not because it is particularly abundant (actually it is fairly rare), but rather because it can easily be reduced to the metal from its ores. Reduction temperatures are rather low, with the result that the technology of producing the metal can be quite simple.

Talk given at a Nobel Foundation symposium, 'The Place of Value in a World of Fact', held in Stockholm, 15–20 September 1969.

Metallic gold is actually easier to produce from its ores than is metallic copper, and indeed it often exists in nature as the metal. But gold is orders of magnitude less abundant than copper. Indeed, it is so rare in nature that it could never come into practical use on any truly substantial scale.

Iron is considerably more abundant than copper, but it is much more difficult to produce in metallic form. Higher temperatures are required and this necessitates in turn the development of fairly elaborate technology. As a result, many centuries were required following the first substantial use of copper before the technology of producing metallic iron was developed.

The use of copper became widespread in the ancient urban civilizations and demands for the ore grew rapidly. Egypt, for example, quickly depleted her own local ore resources and began importing ore, primarily from Europe including the British Isles. Elaborate trade routes were developed for the purpose. But so rare is copper in nature, the price of the metal prevented it from coming into general use outside the cities. The peasants, who represented by far the greater part of the population, continued to depend upon the availability of rock and wood for their tools.

Once iron technology was developed, the use of metals could become truly widespread. The availability of new metal tools permitted Europe to be transformed from a vast forest to a fertile cropland. The great demand for metallic iron led to the emergence of a large iron industry in England where iron ore is plentiful and where there were ample trees for the production of charcoal.

Throughout the seventeenth century metallic iron was produced from the ore using charcoal as the reducing agent. Charcoal is obtained by heating wood at a sufficiently high temperature to denature it and drive off the volatile ingredients, leaving the carbon residue (or charcoal) behind.

Originally Britain had plenty of trees, but so great did the demand for wood become that in the latter part of the seventeenth century a serious wood shortage developed. Indeed, the iron industry of the island came close to shutting down. Attempts were made to substitute coal, abundantly available, for charcoal but the impurities in the coal gave rise to a product which was unusable for manufacturing purposes. Little progress was made until the eighteenth century, when by 1709 Abraham Darby had learned to drive off the volatile fumes from coal and produce 'coke'. By mid-century the right kind of coke could be produced in quantity for the blast furnaces.

Increased demand for coal led to the development of the steam engine and triggered a succession of technological developments. Demands for iron in the UK increased from 70 thousand tons per year in 1788 to 250 thousand tons per year in 1806. British coal production rose from 4.5 million tons in 1750 to 10 million tons in 1800 and to 16 million tons in

1829. Demands for many other metals increased equally rapidly. As the new technology spread to Europe and to North America, world demands for resources leapt upward and international competitions for their control developed, eventually to become severe.

The new technology was characterized by a sequence of technological competitions each of which gave rise to increased human productivity, but which inexorably gave rise to increased resource demands. As an example, in the middle of the nineteenth century the horse was the primary source of power on US farms and the horse population grew about as rapidly as the human population. One horse was added to the population for every four persons. If this trend had persisted there would now be about 50 million horses in the United States, but the introduction of steam power to the farm about 1875, followed by the introduction of the internal combustion engine shortly after the turn of the century, produced a precipitous decline in horse population which is now little more than one million. Associated with this development we see greatly increased *per capita* demands for energy, steel and other metals. We also see greatly increased productivity, and mass migration of workers from the farms to the cities.

Some of these changes which resulted from technological competitions proceeded with unprecedented rapidity. In a period of but thirty years (1870–1900), for example, the composition of the merchant marine of the United Kingdom was transformed from 90 per cent wooden sailing ships to 90 per cent iron ships powered by steam. In the process, of course, there was developed a greatly enhanced capability for transporting large quantities of materials and goods and greatly increased consumption of raw materials, in this case iron ore and coal.

In the nineteenth century, England became the dominant industrial power, eventually to be replaced by Germany. Following World War I, the United States quickly became the giant industrial power. Today, the USSR and Japan are rapidly moving toward this position.

During the first half of this century steel production in the United States increased rapidly both on an absolute and on a *per capita* basis. By 1900 steel production was about 0.14 metric tons *per capita*. By 1910 it had reached about 0.3 tons *per capita*. For the past quarter century, however, although total steel production has continued to rise, *per capita* production has remained on the average virtually constant at about 0.55 metric tons per person per year. Only about 40 per cent of this steel is generated from recycled scrap; the remaining 60 per cent must be made up with new iron produced from ore.

The question as to why *per capita* production has flattened at this particular level is an interesting one. Studies of the consumption figures in other major steel-producing countries suggest that for complex reasons this might represent the maximum rate at which new steel can be effectively absorbed by a highly industrialized society. In 1968 *per capita* steel production in Japan, Belgium, West Germany and Czechoslovakia were all higher than that of the United States but a considerable proportion of the steel produced in those countries is exported.

Were all of the metallic iron which has been produced in the United States in the last century still in existence, there would be in use some 15 tons per person. Actually a great deal of this has been lost as the result of production losses in the recycling of scrap, corrosion and other irrevocable losses. The figures suggest that we actually have in use some 10 metric tons of steel per person.

With respect to other metals which are essential to industrial civilization, some of the more important of them are used in remarkably constant proportions to steel. In spite of dramatically changing technologies, copper has been consumed during the last one-half century at a rate corresponding to 17 kilograms per ton of steel; zinc at a rate corresponding to 11 kilograms per ton and lead at a rate of 16 kilograms per ton of steel. By contrast, the proportion of tin to steel has been decreasing steadily, in part as a result of the rarity of the metal and in part as a result of technological developments which have given rise to substitutes. Also, by contrast, the proportion of aluminum to steel has been increasing steadily, in large part as a result of its abundance, its usefulness and rapidly changing technology.

These figures suggest that we now have in use in the United States for every person some 160 kilograms of copper, 140 kilograms of lead, 100 kilograms of zinc, 18 kilograms of tin and 110 kilograms of aluminum. Similar accumulations have been attained or are being approached in other industrialized parts of the world.

In order to meet our needs for steel and other metals together with the products derived from them in the United States, we transport each year for every person nearly 15,000 ton-kilometers of freight. Each person travels on the average each year some 8500 kilometers between cities, makes over 700 phone calls and receives nearly 400 pieces of mail. The population of private automobiles has reached 85 million, corresponding to more than 0.4 cars per person. About 0.3 tons of packaging materials are produced and sold each year for every person, most of which enters the solid waste system, to be collected and disposed of.

Consumption of non-metallics in the United States is increasing considerably more rapidly than is that of metals. Since 1950 alone *per capita* consumption of stone, sand and gravel has increased from 3.2 tons to 7.7 tons, a factor of 2.4. *Per capita* consumption of cement has reached 350 kilograms and that of common salt has reached 175 kilograms.

In order to take care of all of the mining, production and distribution in the United States, we expend energy at a rate equivalent to our burning about 10 tons of coal annually per person. In contrast to steel, this level of *per capita* consumption is increasing at a rate of about 15 per cent per decade.

Where are we heading?

Clearly man has become a major geological force. The amount of rock and earth he moves each year in the industrialized regions of the world, a process which I have termed 'technological denudation', is already prodigious and will continue to grow, in part because of the spread of industrialization and in part because the demands of the industrialized nations of the world will continue to increase. When we add to this the fantastically high potential demand which would come into existence were the development process to be accelerated in the poorer countries, the total potential demand staggers the imagination. If by some magic the *per capita* inventory of metals in the world as a whole were to be brought up to the average level of the ten richest nations, all of the present mines and factories in the world would have to operate for more than sixty years just to produce the capital, assuming no losses. If we were to assume a world population of 10 billion persons (which I suspect is conservative) and a *per capita* steel inventory of 20 tons, some 200 billion tons of iron would have to be extracted from the earth. At the current rate of extraction, 400 years would be required.

With our present anarchical system of competing nation-states such levels of demand would place enormous strains upon the resources of the earth and would greatly intensify rivalries between nations. The richer nations already find it necessary to import increasing quantities of raw materials. Japan is virtually completely dependent upon imports. In 1950 the United States imported only 8 per cent of her iron ore; today she imports over 35 per cent. A large proportion of these imports come from the poorer countries.

From a purely technological point of view man can in principle live comfortably off the leanest of earth substances. He has always done the easiest things first. The first copper he used came from pure crystals of malachite which he picked up off the surface of the earth. This source gone, he dug deeper, went farther afield and processed ore of lower grade. Even so, by the turn of the century we were still processing ore containing 5 per cent copper. A few years later the average grade was 3 per cent, then 2 per cent, then 1 per cent. Today we are processing ore which averages but 0.4 per cent copper.

There are no technological barriers to our continuing this process and indeed it can be shown that man could, if need be, live comfortably off ordinary rocks. A ton of granite contains easily extractable uranium and thorium equivalent to about 15 tons of coal plus all of the elements necessary to perpetuate a highly technological civilization. Indeed, it would appear that we are heading for a new stone age!

Were I a cosmic gambler looking at the earth from afar, asking where mankind is heading, I would probably write the following scenarios:

The affluent nations will continue to become more affluent; the gap between the rich nations and the poor will continue to grow and mankind will eventually be completely divided into two groups. The smaller group will be well fed and rich and will live comfortably by applying technology to the leanest of earth substances. The larger group will be poor, hungry, and permanently miserable. It will have no advanced technology and will long before have been stripped of its high-grade resources.

But the rich groups, too, will face grave dangers. Being completely dependent for survival upon the perpetuation of its technology, it will be extremely vulnerable to disruption. And being made up of heavily armed nation-states, disruption will be highly probable. Sooner or later a nuclear war will take place and technological civilization will crumble. The poor will then inherit the earth and will live miserably ever after. With the earth's high-grade resources long ago having disappeared, technological civilization will be gone, never to rise again.

My second scenario is really a special case of the first. Here the disruption takes place before high-grade resources have disappeared, the poor inherit the earth but eventually technological civilization once again emerges, preparing itself to experience the first scenario.

My third scenario is the least probable one. Indeed, it verges on the miraculous. In this one, the rich nations arrive at a series of rational decisions. They eliminate vast nuclear weapons systems, thus lessening vulnerabilities. They control the flow of arms and develop effective procedures for the peaceful resolution of conflict. Even more important, they embark on a major programme aimed at eliminating poverty in the world. A world-wide civilization emerges which can perpetuate itself indefinitely and in which all people can live comfortably and in peace with each other.

In the long run the two keys to the world's resources problems are politics and energy. Our present system of nation-states is not conducive to a healthy world resource economy, perpetuating as it does gross inequities and inefficiencies.

Perhaps the greatest tragedy of the human experience is that our understanding of man and his behavior has not kept pace with our knowledge of how to control nature. We have now reached the point where from a technological point of view starvation and misery in the world are inexcusable. We can mobilize our genius to fly to the moon. But somehow we are unable to mobilize that same genius to build a world in which all people who care to do so can lead free, abundant and even creative lives.

Food – the great challenge of this crucial century

GEORG BORGSTROM

American and Soviet scientists, asked by the French weekly *l'Express* in 1962 about mankind's future and how it will shape up in the year 2000, concluded that voyages to the moon and also inhabited artificial satellites will then be commonplace. These experts were selected from among Nobel Prize winners, members of scientific academies, and other notables whose qualifications were beyond dispute. Among their predictions were the following:

> By the year 2000 all food will be completely synthetic. Agriculture and fisheries will have become superfluous. The world's population will by then have increased fourfold but will have stabilized. Sea water and ordinary rocks will yield all the necessary metals. Disease, as well as famine, will have been eliminated; and universal hygienic inspection and control will have been introduced. The problems of energy production will by then be completely resolved.

Reading about those hilarious excursions into our future dreamlands, one gets seriously concerned about our academic education, but still more, profoundly worried about this almost dimensionless flight from reality.

The fact is that the world in all likelihood, and this on the basis of most available evidence, is on the verge of the biggest famine in history – not, to be sure, the world *we* live in, but the poor world, the countries of Asia, Africa, and Latin America. Such a famine will have massive proportions and affect hundreds of millions, possibly even billions. By 1984 it will dwarf and overshadow most of the issues and anxieties that now attract attention, such as nuclear weapons, communism, the space race, unemployment, racial tensions, Vietnam, the Middle East, the Congo, the Dominican Republic, Cyprus, etc. These current issues will fade into the background as the enormous task of feeding mankind impresses itself on the Western world.

Extracts from Chapter XIV of *Too Many* (Macmillan, New York, 1969).

The scientist's role

The main function of the scientist in a modern society – besides accumulating, discovering, and disseminating facts and knowledge – is to be a lookout on mankind's vessel, constantly interpreting the radar signals picked up and warning of dangers lurking ahead. The mapping of the future course to pursue is a joint undertaking in which the politicians have prime responsibility. The most disquieting aspect of this particular food issue is the fact that with few exceptions the scientific and technical community has been signaling green light to mankind, when red signals are far more appropriate. With semantic exercises and iffy proposals mankind has been made to believe we could take care of almost any number of people, at any rate for the foreseeable future. An analysis of statements and pronouncements made by leading Western scientists of almost all disciplines reveals a shocking disregard for the abject conditions prevailing for almost four-fifths of the human race and a corresponding lack of awareness of the plight of man. Whatever happens, whatever urgent measures we may take, food is going to be the overriding issue of this crucial century. Let us briefly review some relevant facts pertaining to this calamity.

The population upsurge

Human numbers are rapidly reaching unmanageable proportions. Our resources are in most respects, possibly with the temporary exception of energy, grossly inadequate. The gap between the rich and the poor nations is rapidly widening and threatening within this very century to engulf the few remaining oases. At a breathtaking speed, mankind in this twentieth century doubled in numbers by 1960, thereby passing the three billion mark. There is every sign that another three billion will be added within little more than thirty years, and yet this figure is predicated on a gradual universal practice of birth control within this brief period. If no efficient control is applied, which is the more likely alternative, this crucial century will see the world population zoom above eight billion, barring a major catastrophe.

It is nevertheless almost macabre to witness the present auction in human numbers. The bidders are specialists of various categories. They delve into the futile game of calculating how many the world could nourish; 15 billion, 25 billion, 40 billion. The bids go still higher: 100 billion, 270 billion, 900 billion. Even among humanists, few raise their voices in defense of human dignity and values, although it should be self-evident that such numbers would by their very size annihilate anything worthy of being called civilization. And if there were a trace of realism in these armchair exercises, it is a superscandal that the world looks in the direction it does. It has failed to provide satisfactorily for more than half of its present population of 3.5 billion. A doubling of world food production is called for to give everyone now living his minimum needs.

This increase in human numbers is indeed of grave concern to the modern world, particularly as it affects demands for space, water, and food. We are presently adding seventy million to the world population each year. Do we recognize the true magnitude of this added board-and-lodging burden? Do we realize that the greatest exodus in human history, the big European trek to all continents, comprised in all seventy million people, and yet this one event shaped human history for almost 400 years? It brought about the Europeanization of the world and is also the great epic of the North American continent. Never did man collect a greater booty than the vast forest lands of the northeast and the rich soils of the prairies. Hardly any other people has been more fortunate in the great lottery of mankind. This accident of history constitutes the foundation for our firm conviction in universal abundance and in the supremacy of technology.

World War II brought an end to this era in human history. But as late as 1939 shipload after shipload of peanuts left starving India to fatten the cows of the distant empire rulers of the British Isles. More than 1.5 billion people in Asia and Africa have since then attained independence. World food markets have adjusted to this new scene: annually more than 2.5 million tons of grain are now moving from the rich world to feed the hungry, as against the latter part of the 'thirties when eleven million tons of grain were dispatched from the hungry to provide for the well-fed.

The monopoly of the European race, however, is sustained. Public attention is focused on grain, but when we direct the searchlight to other commodities and the key nutrient of protein, the scene changes radically. The 2.5 million tons of grain protein delivered annually by the rich and well-fed are counterbalanced by a flow to the Western world of no less than 3.5 million tons of other proteins of superior rating in the form of soybeans, oil-seed cakes, and fish meal. We in the Western world are actually making what amounts to an almost treacherous exchange.

The privileged West

A completely new technology is needed which respects the basic laws of ecology and tackles the fundamental grave contradiction of pursuing an economic and technological advancement, aiming at making man superfluous, in a world that has only one true surplus, man himself. This new technology has further to make a complete accounting for total costs including basic resources. It can be safely asserted that our particular form of civilization with regard to the use of energy, water, forests, and soils cannot be copied on a global scale.

We should never lose sight of the historical fact that in the Western world the Golden Age lies behind us and in effect never was anything more than the privilege of a minority. Due to its power position the West tapped an unreasonable part of the resources of the globe. Currently, about 450 million enjoy affluence and abundance. Five to six times that number live in parsimony, scarcity, or serious shortage. This is basically the reason why our high-handed projections into the future may not materialize at all, even when seemingly well founded.

A new global trade pattern is urgently needed. We in the Western world not only have greater soil and water resources, but we are intruding on the meager subsistence basis of this other world. Hundreds of millions in the tropics are forced to shrink their food production to raise peanuts, cotton, bananas, coffee, tea, cacao, etc., for export, in order to accrue foreign currency. This is particularly explosive, as such cash crops are now enjoying high priority with regard to credit, fertilizers, irrigation, etc. Yet their hard-won currency is dwindling in relative value. Since 1952 the deliveries of agricultural products from the poor to world markets have increased by one-third in tonnage, but in value only 4 per cent.

By changing over from food production for domestic consumption to food production for export crops, cultivation could in most instances provide a subsistence wage. Increasing numbers of the rising populations in underdeveloped countries therefore took to the cultivation of such crops. It is highly debatable if this pattern can be sustained in a world desperately short of food, water, and land. Cash crops as earners of coveted currency have a vanishing role, as a growing percentage of this money has to be devoted to the buying of food. Before long, food protein will presumably have to be installed as the new gold standard of world trade.

There are innumerable things we can do. We can repeat our mistakes as long as possible and in the short run provide for more millions. By and large we *prefer* to look to such immediate returns in most of our actions. The pressing needs and humanitarian imperatives are in several instances so overwhelming that we have no longer a reasonable margin of choice. As a human race, however, we must start to think in strategic terms. We must learn to weigh short-range benefits against long-range goals.

Sooner or later we must come to a recognition of the self-evident fact that our spaceship is limited, and accommodate ourselves to this obvious condition. Do we ever give this irrevocable fact serious attention in our planning? Do we recognize that a single generation has taken for itself the benefits of farm mechanization? By this one-time trick we have freed the farm soils from producing energy. Some 250 million people in our luxury world are today provided with food thanks to the replacing of the horse with the tractor; the next generation has no such trick up its sleeve.

How far are we prepared to go in jeopardizing the millions by placing them in direct dependence on the chemical industry and thereby greatly increasing their vulnerability? At least 500 million people today depend on fertilizer plants for their survival. If all were to be adequately fed, this figure would in effect exceed one billion. Looking ahead at the prospects of this crucial century, we see that it is highly unlikely that present soils can be made to yield more than twice as much food as they now do. In excess of 120 billion dollars will be needed in investment for this purpose alone. On the basis of these considerations one can seriously question whether future chemistry is not already committed to a seriously oversized burden, yet we encounter glib talk about moving the entire feeding burden to chemical plants, in effect reducing agriculture and fisheries to hobbies. The truth is that the fertilizer industry is already facing the tortuous and herculean task of providing for at least 1.5 billion additional humans within thirty years. Railroads, road trucks, airlines, and the merchant navy of the world will encounter an additional transportation load far exceeding the weight of the human population as such.

More food

Seventy million more mouths to feed – the present annual growth – mean that thirty to forty million new acres are needed each year simply to keep the world's people at their current malnourished level. To improve nutrition throughout the world, a doubling of world food production is required by 1980 and a quadrupling by the year 2000. It is both feasible and imperative to produce more food, but it is not self-evident that this is feasible where it is needed most. We have taken it for granted it could be done and that we know the techniques.

The impression is frequently conveyed that past and present efforts to produce more food have been negligible, while future undertakings in this respect are sure to meet with great success. On the contrary, in many places in Asia and Central America an astonishingly efficient use is being made of available land. In Taiwan and Guatemala the mountainsides have been painstakingly terraced high up in a series of gradations. Thousands of acres of tidelands have been reclaimed in Asia. The degree of double-cropping whenever feasible has mounted and at a rather rapid rate, as in Burma, Malaysia, Thailand, Taiwan, China, and Japan.

The hungry people live in the tropics and are governed by a rice market economy and small feeding plots. The feasibility of large-scale production is questionable in terms of available land. Yet we expect these people to double and quadruple their production over a short time span, something we in the Western world never have been able to do, even with our enriched soil and ample land. One can in all seriousness raise the quite opposite issue: are there not good reasons for *not* trying to farm some areas? Several Latin American experts anticipate that thirty or forty million people will have to be removed from their impoverished, impossible lands, which never should have been broken into cultivation.

The agricultural history of this century is replete with serious incidents where the excessive zeal of colonizers or the technical aid programs have caused disasters and detrimental rebuffs. Mention may be made of the Dutch deep-plowing of the rice paddies in Java, the corresponding operations by the British in Burma, and excessive fertilizing, which destroyed crops by accelerating water depletion and reducing drought or frost resistance.

The most spectacular failure is the Tanganyika Groundnut scheme. Many thousand acres were turned into dust bowls, the end result of an ambitious, 2.64-million-acre project, costing in excess of 100 million dollars. This failure cannot be blamed on the backward indigenous population, nor on the British Socialist government. It was Western technology and agricultural techniques that failed in this fateful encounter with African realities.

How many Mekong projects – around ten billion dollars for two million acres – would available development funds support? How many are, in geographical terms, really promising? In too many cases they are a big gamble with high stakes, as we do not know how the involved soils will stand up to irrigation and its long-range consequences. What is the life-span of the dams? How many Mekong projects would be required to keep up with the current population growth?

Presently, it costs on an average about fifty dollars to bring an acre of new land into high productivity, which means that 3.5 billion dollars – 2.6 billion of this in underdeveloped countries – are needed per year, merely to keep up with present population growth.

In theory it is possible to produce, by means of rational exploitation of natural resources, enough food to nourish five billion human beings. But this can be accomplished only at the price of forced labor, a new kind of slavery, and tremendous investments – presumably pricing still more food than presently out of the markets of the poor.

Resources and technology

Although industrialization unquestionably would help to solve part of the economic woes of some poor countries, it is highly unlikely that it could come fast enough to overtake an unregulated population expansion. Very few countries have the investment capital required to employ gainfully the swelling numbers entering the labor forces. Even with a very low investment figure of 2,000 dollars per person, few budgets of Latin American countries could afford to accommodate these entrants and are presently very far from doing so.

The most serious fallacy of all is to believe that the world's resources are abundant and are limited only by man's ingenuity. It is commonly thought that man is capable of substituting technology for resources.

This is feasible only to a very limited degree. Furthermore, the basic distinctions between renewable and nonrenewable resources are woefully neglected. The world's nonrenewable resources have lasted as long as they have principally because so few of the world's people have been using them. The United States, with 6 per cent of the world's population, is consuming more than one-third of the world's production of raw materials. Quite aside from the moral aspect of our right to this kind and degree of voracity, there is a much more far-reaching question. Will not the 2.5 billion poor people, multiplying within thirty years to more than four billion, demand their share?

It is sobering to keep in mind that in this very century, when the United States population doubled from 1900 to 1950, the 'rising expectations' of the American people resulted in an eight-fold increase in the use of minerals and a thirteenfold increase in the use of fuels. The total remaining resources of the globe are grossly inadequate to allow a similar extravagance among the have-nots; the meeting of even legitimate and reasonable demands will mean an unprecedented and devastating drain. In this light we have to examine our own blueprints for this other world. The average investment in machinery and equipment required on the farm in present-day United States agriculture exceeds 30,000 dollars per farm worker. This is in effect two to three times above that required for an average industrial worker. Even when recognizing chances for somewhat lower costs (in absolute figures) in poverty-ridden countries, it is still this disproportion that raises doubts whether this kind of capital-devouring agricultural operation is on the whole feasible in this hungry, poor world.

We are currently moving from the chronic hunger crisis of the postwar years into an acute starvation crisis, which in all likelihood will be permanent if drastic long-range countermeasures are not implemented. Despite our wheat deliveries to India in 1967, exceeding one-fourth of the United States crop, the situation was grave. Our mass media only casually reported on the African tragedy – the eastern part of its tropics experienced in 1966–7 a sixth consecutive year of drought. Cattle died by the thousands every week, and many thousands had to be moved to water. Men, women, and children were in despair. Food had to be airlifted to Bechuanaland. These happenings were described as 'scourges' or 'temporary setbacks', but we forget that in all instances recurrent drought is part of the regular climatic pattern of these regions. Drought is in effect a normal, almost intrinsic feature on the Indian, South American (northeast Brazil in particular), and east African scene. Even rain-rich Uruguay experiences years almost devoid of rain.

Despite the extensive irrigation of India, some 80 to 85 per cent of the tilled land is exposed to the vagaries of the monsoons which through the centuries have shown a great degree of fluctuation in regularity. This also indirectly affects irrigation efficiency. Even at a future time when most of the average runoff may have been fully harnessed for irrigation,

India will retain this kind of vulnerability; two-thirds of the tilled land will remain at the mercy of the monsoon. Eastern tropical Africa is in a far more critical dilemma. During most of this century, water use has been such as to create a negative water balance. The hydrological cycle has rarely ever been able to compensate the losses.

Failures

We have seen in our generation more than the colossal failure of Western education, in which the West has proclaimed an abundance merely waiting for man's ingenuity and resourcefulness to provide for all. We have also witnessed a serious emasculation of all religion; the basic belief in the universal brotherhood of man has become empty phraseology. We have further evidenced the failure of technology to assert its human aims. In a world where less than 500 million have satisfactory water facilities, where 2,000 million lack homes, sanitation, clothing, and beds, we are engaging in an armaments race and the maintenance of a terror balance costing more than the total gross national product of all the developing countries. And, as the climax of absurdity, we are deserting the globe for celestial adventures of highly questionable value to man's future.

The aims of technology, which were clear enough a century and a half ago, have gradually disappeared from view. Humanity seems to have forgotten the wherefore of all its travail, as though its goals had been translated into an abstraction or had become implicit, or as though its ends rested in an unforeseeable future of undetermined date. Everything today seems to happen as though the ends had disappeared, as an outflow of the magnitude of the very means at our disposal.

Futile armchair exercises, guessing or calculating future human numbers, or *mañana* promises are of little help in the greatest crisis ever to hit the human race. We can ill afford our present childish armaments and space race. We need to mature and show some degree of responsibility to our own future as well as to that of all humankind. The world has become one whether we like it or not. Four hundred years of Western leadership carry many glories but much disgrace; the spearhead of progress no longer rests in our hands and is now pointed against us. If we do not take our place among the forces that mold destiny, our civilization may well vanish. To achieve this end, the priority lists of mankind need a drastic and urgent revision. The educational failure to acquaint ourselves with reality, and the bankruptcy of religion both point to the need of a revival and renewal in the form of a new religion and a new education.

The sobering 'sixties

The conspicuous contrast between rhetoric and reality has become almost offensive. Today we find a world where the surpluses, once given the absurd designation 'eternal', are almost at an end. Chinese and Soviet purchases have taxed the grain stocks of Australia and Canada to the limit. India and to some degree tropical Africa and the Middle East are quickly emptying the grain bins of the United States, and we are close to a danger point.

John F. Kennedy went in person to the UN in 1961 to proclaim the 'sixties as the United Nations Decade of Development – 'to enablc all nations, however diverse in their systems and beliefs, to become in fact as well as in law, free and equal nations'. The results so far are deeply discouraging. Harsh realities have not only created stagnation but in the needy world severe retrogression. There are, however, some glimmering rays of hope in the rapidly growing recognition of the indispensability of population control. There are, furthermore, many signs of a more realistic appraisal of regional resources, as well as of the shortcomings in our technology and methods and their limited universal applicability. Most essential is the growing awareness of the urgency of these matters. The notion is also gaining ground that our own spaceship Earth needs an overhaul, is clearly defined as to its size, and cannot take on any number of additional dwellers. Many compartments are already seriously overfilled.

The business community, largely supported by science and technology, gave to the 'sixties the designation 'Soaring'. It is to be hoped that future history will rather describe this decade as the 'Sobering 'sixties' which put an end to the rhetoric and laid a more solid foundation for man's future. Thus once again we would assert the viability of man's mind by mobilizing science and technology for great new endeavors to the benefit of *all* mankind, in support of the only war mankind can still wage, that of human survival. Our future is at stake in this very century, and food is the key issue.

Population control or Hobson's choice

PAUL R. EHRLICH

There is a growing consensus of opinion that the fate of Western civilization will be sealed by events of the next decade or so; this makes writing about the effects of world conditions on Britain in the year 2000 quite a challenging assignment. The first question which must be considered is whether the situation at the turn of the century can be predicted by extrapolation of trends now obvious, or whether major discontinuities will occur that will make such projections rubbish. Judging from events of the first two-thirds of the century, discontinuities will be the rule, not the exception. Indeed, many of the trends developing today seem to lead directly to such discontinuities. It would be extremely foolhardy, therefore, to expect accuracy in predicting thirty years into the future; it would be equally foolhardy, however, not to take a critical look at the major possibilities. The first four possibilities below assume, among other things, that there will be no effective world-wide population control. If there is not, Britain will be in the position of the patrons of Mr Hobson's famous stable, who had to accept whichever horse was standing nearest the door. There will be little opportunity for some 60 million island people to select a future. It will be a question of taking what you get – Hobson's Choice.

Thermonuclear war

There is a tendency for laymen and scientists to suppress thought or discussion of the possibility that a thermonuclear war might intervene in the 'orderly' march of world events (Frank, 1967). For instance, even a supposedly systematic projection such as Kahn and Wiener's *The Year 2000* (1967) tends to discount the possibility. This is in part a tribute to the authors' faith in the efficacy of nuclear deterrence, a faith

Extracts from Chapter 12 of *The Optimum Population for Britain* (proceedings of a symposium held at the Royal Geographical Society, London, on 25 and 26 September 1969), edited by L. R. Taylor and published for the Institute of Biology by The Academic Press, 1970.

that is not surprising as Kahn was one of the major architects of deterrence theory. Unfortunately, deterrence theory depends on demonstrably false assumptions about human behaviour (Green, 1966), non-existent systems analysis, and inapplicable games theory.

In spite of the psychological need to discount the potential for thermonuclear war, such a conflict is clearly possible before the year 2000, and if one should occur before then it would be the major determinant of world conditions at the end of the century. At the moment the probabilities of general war seem to be rapidly increasing. There is, indeed, every reason to believe that every person added to the world population adds ever so slightly to the odds favouring Armageddon. Systematic studies done by my colleague, Professor Robert North of Stanford's Department of Political Science, have added to the mass of anecdotal evidence that over-population is a factor leading to war. Professor Georg Borgstrom of Michigan State University has recently argued (1969) that the continuing growth of competition for water is a source of international tensions, involving the basins of the Mekong, Indus, Jordan, Nile, Euphrates-Tigris, Amur, Danube, and other rivers. Needless to say, demand for water is just one of the sources of conflict which can be traced in large part to population growth. Land shortage alone may be a major factor, as it was in the recent war between El Salvador and Honduras. Another factor, which is bound to escalate in importance over the next decade, is competition for fisheries. Unquestionably, generalized competition (in the biological sense*) will continue to increase as the population of the world increases. Access to petroleum, copper, wheat, beef and many other commodities will become critical problems for nations without ample domestic supplies. The over-developed and generally resource-poor countries such as the United States, Great Britain, Western Europe and Japan will find it increasingly difficult to maintain the favourable trade positions so necessary for their continued affluence, especially when they will be unable to offer food in exchange for the goods they need. People of the under-developed countries are acutely aware, for instance, that the prime commodity of all, protein, flows not from the well-fed to the hungry nations, but vice versa.

A final potential population-related source of international tensions must be mentioned. It is clear that man's polluting activities, especially those of the developed countries, are going to have increasingly profound effects on the lives of all humans. One needs only to think of the chlorinated-hydrocarbon eco-catastrophe, and the great Rhine fish-kill of June 1969 to see the trend. But most severe are the possible consequences of pollution-caused weather modifications. As dust, CO_2, contrails, and other pollutants change the climate of the Earth and

* Biologists say that two organisms are in competition when they both are utilizing a resource which is not abundant enough fully to satisfy both, or where the presence of one organism impedes the access of the other to the resource.

gradually begin to make our planet uninhabitable, some nations will feel the pinch first, and will call for drastic action. One might guess that less affected nations will be reluctant to do much, and another major area of international conflict will develop.

So, unpleasant as the prospect may seem, there are many reasons, both in conventional politics and on the population–food–environment front, for considering a thermonuclear war as possibly the major determinant of Britain's AD 2000 environment. If it is, almost any rational analysis makes it seem likely that little of interest to the Briton of 1969 would remain. Immediate effects, of course, would vary with the size, nature, and timing of the attack. How many megatons targeted on the United Kingdom? Are they detonated at ground level or above (an important variable affecting the amount of fall-out and the size of fire storms and conflagrations)? Are they aimed at military facilities or population centres or both? Is the attack carried out before or after the harvest is gathered? These and many other questions would have to be answered before any semi-precise estimate of total damage could be made. In general, however, in any situation (barring a possible, carefully limited air-burst strike against military facilities) the prognosis for the survival of British civilization as we know it is negative.

In the unlikely event of a major thermonuclear war *not* involving Britain the outlook still would be grim. Britain's viability would depend on the kinds of factors enumerated above. Should, for instance, huge amounts of smoke and debris be added to the already overburdened atmosphere, then cooling comparable to that accompanying the 1815 eruption of Tomboro (in what is now Indonesia) could occur, destroying, at least temporarily, England's agricultural production. If trade were heavily disrupted, the United Kingdom might well face starvation. If sufficient dust were added to the atmosphere, a vicious cycle of cooling could set in, leading to greater snow corridors, increase of the Earth's albedo, further cooling, and so on. If enough of the North Atlantic were to freeze over, the Gulf Stream could be deflected (Humphreys, 1940; Stonier, 1963), altering the climate of England and Europe more or less permanently. There is considerable current controversy over the causation of ice ages, but the consensus seems to be that one may be brought on quite precipitously.

Similarly, increased silting of the North Sea and chemical run-off from ruined cities (assuming the European continent was hit) might seriously damage crucial fisheries, and fishing in general might suffer from a lack of fuel oil. And, of course, there would be the general health hazards of increased environmental radiation, to say nothing of the plagues which would almost certainly develop in a war-ravaged world, even if biological warfare were not used.

In short, world population growth is almost certainly contributing to the chances of a thermonuclear war. In the absence of population control it may be the 'Hobson's Choice' that England ultimately confronts; and her chances of surviving it, as something resembling the nation she is today, are slim.

World-wide plague

At the present time the world has the largest, densest population of human beings that it has ever seen. And every year an additional 70 million souls are being added to the approximately 3.6 billion already present. In addition to the densest population, it is also the weakest. Some 1–2 billion people are now under-nourished or malnourished and their situation seems likely to deteriorate. Add to this our great capacity for transporting sick people rapidly around the world, and you have the potential for an epidemic unparalleled in human history. Even without further environmental deterioration the health hazard is great; a mutant flu virus could readily decimate mankind. Furthermore, there is a grave threat of accidental escape (or deliberate use) of biological warfare agents. Superviruses, constructed 'to order', give even poor nations the possibility of creating doomsday weapons. There are already rumours, for instance, of a pneumonic form of rabies, which, if it were transmissible before symptoms appeared, could wipe out most of mankind. And, if the world faces the kind of breakdown anticipated in the next section, many of mankind's ancient scourges, plague, typhus, cholera, malaria, and so forth, may again become preponderant.

Because of Britain's insular position and relatively high quality of medical care (in infant mortality, a good indication of the quality of such care, the United Kingdom in 1966 ranked number 10 in the world, the USA number 15), she would be in a better position than most countries to ward off infection. But, again, her dependence on trade makes her position vulnerable. If we can infer from the history of past catastrophes (Langer, 1958; Stonier, 1963; Frank, 1967), it seems likely that world trade would suffer serious derangement, and that Britain, for purposes of quarantine, would stringently have to limit access to English ports of those ships still operating.

Should a major epidemic hit England, its effects would be likely to change British attitudes and behaviour for centuries, even if the other disasters dealt with in this paper are avoided. Such relatively minor events as the Irish potato famine have had long-lasting consequences for the societies involved. A plague killing perhaps one-half or more of the population could easily cause the collapse of British society. Disruption of food supplies, riots (especially among those attempting to flee from affected areas), breakdown of garbage collection, disruption of water supplies, cessation of fire-fighting and police protection, and so forth would probably create horrors beyond even those experienced in England during the Black Death of the fourteenth century (to say nothing of the London blitz). If nothing else, the degree of change in the life of the average citizen would be much greater now than then. But the over-all consequences of a world plague for the England of the year 2000 would depend on the state of so many variables that any kind of detailed prediction would be reckless. About the most that can be said is that, if Mr Hobson's horse is plague, the results may be less severe than in the case of thermonuclear war, but they hardly present a pleasing prospect.

Eco-catastrophe

A final type of gross discontinuity in projections of the world future must be mentioned – eco-catastrophe. An eco-catastrophe is a widespread, strongly deleterious change in the human environment. Signs of past, rather minor eco-catastrophes are easily seen in such places as the Tigris and Euphrates valleys, the Sahara desert, and Angkor Wat. Today we seem to be witnessing the start of a global eco-catastrophe caused by the action of chlorinated hydrocarbons released into the environment. The nature and current extent of this disaster is so well publicized (summary in Ehrlich and Ehrlich, 1970) that I need not deal further with it here. The chlorinated-hydrocarbon situation *could* lead to the loss of virtually all food from the sea, and a great reduction in the amount which may be obtained from terrestrial agriculture. It also may lead to greatly reduced life expectancies world-wide. Hopefully, however, the manufacture and dissemination of these compounds will be halted before it is too late (unless, of course, we have unknowingly passed the point of no return already).

If population is controlled, it should be possible to stop air pollution before the entire planet becomes uninhabitable. Pollution increases gradually, and is more or less reversible, although its reversal may mean great expense and hardship. The greatest danger of a generalized eco-catastrophe originating in air pollution lies in the possibility of dramatic changes in the weather. There are, for instance, several ways in which a new ice age could be rapidly generated – one of which already has been mentioned in connection with thermonuclear war. Even in the absence of such a war the veil of pollution which now encircles the Earth might create sufficient cooling to start the downward spiral. On the other hand there are those (Wilson, 1964; Hollin, 1965; Haas, 1968) who feel that ice ages may start with the Antarctic ice cap slipping rapidly outward. The increase of the albedo resulting from a large increment in the area occupied by ice creates the necessary cooling effect. Most Britons, however, would be spared the after-effects of an ice age brought on in such a manner, since its initiation would create great tidal waves which would sweep over much of the British Isles.

On the other hand, an over-all warming trend created by increased carbon dioxide in the atmosphere might cause the planetary 'heat engine' to turn over more rapidly, perhaps producing dramatic cooling in England or changing her weather for the worse in some other way.

Another possibility is that the course of the jet streams will be altered, perhaps indirectly as a result of contrails of high-flying jet aircraft. The contrails form the nuclei of cirrus clouds which, in ways not fully understood, deflect jet streams. And, of course, there are always the possibilities of dramatic changes wrought by the contrails of high-flying supersonic transports (SSTs). The SST, even without considering its ecological effects, must surely be viewed as a major competitor for the prize of 'most ridiculous non-military technological development of all time'. But when possible ecological problems related to its contrails and exhausts are considered, it has the potential for becoming a major threat to humanity. The exact meteorological consequences for the weather of SST effluents deposited above the tropopause do not seem to be predictable at this time; we shall have to wait for this most interesting experiment to be run.

The climate of the Earth is, of course, changing gradually all of the time, and man already has had considerable influence on it, especially through deforestation and the creation of deserts. In the last century, for instance, man has increased the amount of the Earth's land surface that is desert or wasteland from less than 10 per cent to about 25 per cent (Doane, 1957). Further acceleration of change, no matter what the direction, cannot but adversely affect the carrying capacity of the planet, at least in the short run. The reason for this is simple: agriculture is extremely dependent on climate and agricultural practices are slow to change. Any substantial reduction in the amount of available food will be bad for Britain, dependent as she is on imported food. Should, for instance, changes in the course of the jet stream create an 'instant desert' in the mid-west of the United States and freeze the plains of Canada, the United Kingdom will be in deep trouble. For, instead of drawing on these two countries for food, she would find herself in competition with them for sustenance.

It seems quite likely that one of the horses close to the door of Mr Hobson's stable is named 'Eco-catastrophe', but his breed is uncertain. As the human population grows, so do man's polluting activities, and so (at least so far) does his dependence on ecologically ignorant agricultural practices. Without population control, or even with it (since at least several decades will pass before it could be effective), mankind will have to face a series of difficult-to-grasp but very potent threats to the life-support systems of the planet.

Current trends continue – the downward spiral

What if there are no drastic discontinuities between now and the year 2000? What kind of year will Englishmen face then? Assuming current trends continue, some reasonably certain statements can be made. All resource-poor countries, those whose standard of living depends heavily on imports, will suffer declines in their standard of living. The United

States and Great Britain both will suffer, the latter more severely because of its less favourable resource position. As the population of the world grows, it will be impossible for England to maintain her present level of imports. The proportion of the world's people who are hungry will escalate rapidly, and the flow of protein from under-developed countries (UDCs) to developed countries (DCs) will slow or cease. Political turmoil will be the rule over much of the world, and the starving UDCs will be attempting to get food in exchange for their hard resources. Under these circumstances, England may find it extremely difficult to import the materials that her industrial plant requires. A partial list of these resources which must be obtained from outside the British Isles includes petroleum, iron, chromium, copper, tin, lead, manganese, molybdenum, mercury, magnesium, tungsten, vanadium and zinc (United Nations, 1967). It is interesting to note that projections of the United States' cumulative demand (1960–2000) indicate that the United States alone *plans* to use virtually all of the non-Communist world's reserves of some of these minerals – especially tungsten and copper – and far more than her 'fair share' of most of the rest (Landsberg *et al.*, 1963). Furthermore, both phosphate rock and potash, critical to British agricultural production, must be imported. According to the 1966 UN figures, Britain produces only 49 per cent of the wheat she consumes, 71 per cent of the other cereals, 97 per cent of the potatoes, 37 per cent of the sugars, 13 per cent of the pulses, nuts, and seeds, and 65 per cent of the meat. It would appear that even if the fertilizers were available to keep production up, a Britain unable to obtain imports of food would be in deep trouble.

Britain, then, by the turn of the century, probably will be extremely hard-pressed to feed her population. A general decline of world fisheries, from over-exploitation and pollution and increased competition from other nations (especially Russia and Japan), will have greatly reduced the amount of food which Britain can extract from the sea. Expansion of her terrestrial agriculture is virtually impossible. That lesson was learned during the First and Second World Wars when the government had to stop the ploughing of marginal land and over-grazing, in order to prevent massive soil erosion (Borgstrom, 1969).

Even in the absence of clear-cut eco-catastrophe, Britain probably will suffer heavily, both directly and indirectly, from world ecological conditions by the year 2000. Global air pollution will affect the health of all citizens, regardless of whether they live in the industrial Midlands or the mountains of Scotland. Chlorinated-hydrocarbon loads will likely be increasing the death rates from various nervous disorders, hypertension, cirrhosis of the liver, hepatic cancer, and so on. Death rates from emphysema, bronchitis, and other respiratory diseases will have sky-rocketed. As diseases such as plague, cholera, and various 'flu's' create vast epidemics, Britain will find it more and more difficult to isolate and protect her increasingly malnourished population.

Finally, there will be the psychological trauma for the British population engendered by decades of economic decay and loss of world influence. If current trends continue, by the year 2000 the United Kingdom will simply be a small group of impoverished islands, inhabited by some 70 million hungry people, of little or no concern to the other 5–7 billion people of a sick world. No – if the horse that Britain gets from Mr Hobson's stable is named 'Downward Spiral' the British will have little to cheer about. But neither will anyone else.

Current trends dramatically changed

Is there any way that Britain can avoid Mr Hobson's choice of one of those four nags, 'Thermonuclear War', 'Worldwide Plague', 'Eco-catastrophe' or 'Downward Spiral'? Can Hobson's stable be by-passed completely? There is a possibility, but it would involve a series of changes in human attitudes and behaviour that must be labelled Utopian. An obvious first step is to recognize the relationship between science and war. As the French scientists, Fetizon and Magat (1968) put it: 'We must either eliminate science or eliminate war. We cannot have both.' The super-powers must face the utter bankruptcy of the theory of nuclear deterrence (Green, 1966) and start replacing the gross risks of continuing the arms race with the lesser (but still perhaps serious) risks of disarmament. Such a move is essential, not just to avoid the ultimate disaster of a thermonuclear war, but also to free the resources needed for an attempt to avoid a 'crash' in the human population – an end to civilization as we know it through a combination of famine, plague, and eco-catastrophe. The need for such a change has been clearly recognized on both sides of the Iron Curtain – it has been articulated recently by Academician Sakharov (1968) and Lord Snow (1969). Both feel that expenditures of the order of 20 per cent of the gross national product of the rich countries will be necessary for the next decade or so if the growing UDC–DC gap is to be closed, and such figures are probably unrealistically low if the entire problem of arresting environmental deterioration is to be tackled. A basic problem, then, is a refocusing of the developed world's energies from unrealistic and eventually lethal arms races to an attempt to preserve civilization. This seems like a well-nigh hopeless task, but perhaps with the help of growing knowledge about human conflict and its resolution (*see* Frank, 1967, for summary) we might have a chance.

If the resources became available and the people of the DCs decided seriously to try to avoid the approaching disaster, what then? Population control in both DCs and UDCs is a *sine qua non* of success. It is not, of course, a panacea for all human problems, but, if achieved, would at least give mankind the opportunity of trying to solve the others. It is abundantly clear, for instance, that mankind will have great difficulty providing an adequate diet for 3.5 billion people by the year 2000, and that providing a proper diet for 7.0 billion by that time is out of the question (President's Science Advisory Committee, 1967; Paddock and Paddock, 1967; Borgstrom, 1969; Ehrlich and Holdren, 1969; Ehrlich and Ehrlich, 1970). Only the most determined disregard for biology, physics, human behaviour and economics permits any other conclusion (e.g. Clark, 1958). If we are lucky and if we initiate population control measures immediately, we might hope for some amelioration of the world food situation shortly before the turn of the century (there is a built-in time lag of decades before any programme of birth control can show results).

One factor working in mankind's favour is that population control should be easier to achieve in the developed countries, where, in at least one sense, population growth poses the greatest threat. These countries are the major wasters of protein and non-renewable resources. They are the source of the most threatening environmental decay. If the money to try and save civilization becomes available a great deal of it will be spent in the developed countries, helping to cure their over-development, clean up the environment, train ecologically knowledgeable agricultural technicians, plan population control programmes and train personnel to carry them out, and so forth. The problems of how to help the UDCs achieve population control and a reasonable level of agricultural development are especially complex and will require the co-ordinated efforts of a trained manpower pool which does not exist at present.

The question always arises as to whether population control can be achieved by voluntary action. If by 'voluntary action' is meant the standard family planning approach of 'every child a wanted child', the answer is clearly no. The idea that the population problem can be solved by eliminating unwanted births has been thoroughly discredited (Davis, 1967). It is clear that governments, including eventually a world body, must undertake the task of regulating the population size just as they now attempt to regulate economies. There are many different ways in which this might be attempted beyond providing family planning programmes which include access to abortion and voluntary sterilization. For instance, any policies which affect marriage ages, employment opportunities for women outside the home, and economic advantages or disadvantages for large families are likely to influence reproductive behaviour. Tax systems which favour single people and small families, preferably without penalizing the poor, and bonuses and lotteries for late marriage, delayed childbirth or childlessness are among the economic possibilities. Encouragement of adoption and stringent measures against illegitimate pregnancy, such as compulsory abortion and/or placement for adoption could be relatively direct policies against births. Provision of outside employment for women may be particularly helpful, and giving such assistance as paid maternity leave (perhaps limited to two babies) and day care would still probably encourage outside work more than it encouraged maternity.

Social climates also can be influenced by governments. Disapproval of more than two children per couple can be fostered, as can alternate life styles, such as easily dissoluble marriages for the childless. At present there is strong social pressure in many countries on people both to marry and to have children. This pressure could be reversed, and status become attached to the free and single individual and to childless couples.

There is little doubt in my mind that, given the necessary changes in human attitude, a successful attempt could be made to pull us through what is clearly the most dramatic crisis *Homo sapiens* has ever faced. Certainly there will be an escalation in suffering before an amelioration is achieved. As Professor Borgstrom (1969) has said, 'There are not many oases left in a vast, almost world-wide network of slums.' Even with the most dramatic programmes, the general deterioration of the planet and of the human condition cannot be halted instantly. But, if the effort is made, it is possible that by the early part of the 21st century the *quality* of the average human life could far surpass that of today.

I would be less than honest if I expressed the conviction that such a change will occur. If I were a gambler, I would take even money that England will not exist in the year 2000, and give 10 to 1 that the life of the average Briton would be of distinctly lower quality than it is today. I am afraid that they and all the peoples of the world are going to end up, figuratively, at Mr Hobson's stable.

REFERENCES

Berelson, B. (1969). 'Beyond family planning.' *Science, N.Y.* **163**, 7 February, 533–43.

Borgstrom, G. (1967). *The Hungry Planet*, rev. ed. Collier Books, New York.

Borgstrom, G. (1969). *Too Many*. Macmillan, New York.

Clark, C. (1958). 'World population.' *Nature, Lond.* **181**, 1235–6.

Davis, K. (1967). 'Population policy: Will current programs succeed?' *Science, N.Y.* **158**, 10 November, 730–9.

Doane, R. R. (1957). *World Balance Sheet*. Harper, New York.

Ehrlich, P. R. and Holdren, J. 'Population and panaceas,' *Bioscience*.

Ehrlich, P. R. and Ehrlich, A. H. (1970). *Population, Resources, Environment*. Freeman.

Fetizon, M. and Magat, M. (1968). 'The Toxic Arsenal' in *Unless Peace Comes* (Nigel Calder, ed.), p. 146. Viking Compass, New York.

Frank, J. D. (1967). *Sanity and Survival*. Vintage, New York.

Green, P. (1966). *Deadly Logic*. Schocken, New York.

Haas, E. (1968). 'Common opponent sought . . . and found?' *Bull. Atomic Scient.* November, 8–11.

Hollin, J. T. (1965). 'Wilson's theory of ice ages.' *Nature, Lond.* **208** (5005), 12–16.

Humphreys, W. T. (1940). *Physics of the Air*. McGraw-Hill Book Company, New York.

Kahn, H. and Weiner, A. J. (1967). *The Year 2000*. Macmillan, New York.

Ketchel, M. M. (1968). 'Fertility control agents as a possible solution to the world population problem.' *Perspect. Biol. Med.* 687–703.

Landsberg, H. H., Fischman, L. L. and Fisher, J. L. (1963). *Resources in America's Future. Patterns of Requirements and Availabilities 1960–2000*. Johns Hopkins Press, Baltimore.

Langer, W. L. (1958). 'The next assignment.' *Am. Hist. Rev.* **63**, 283–304.

Paddock, W. and Paddock, P. (1967). *Famine – 1975*. Little, Brown and Co., Boston.

President's Science Advisory Committee. (1967). Panel on World Food Problem, *World Food Problem*. Washington, D.C.
Sakharov, A. D. (1968). *Progress, Coexistence, and Intellectual Freedom*. New York Times Book, New York.
Snow, C. P. (1969). *The State of Siege*. Charles Scribner's Sons, New York.
Stonier, T. (1963). *Nuclear Disaster*. Meridian, Cleveland.
United Nations (1967). *International Trade Statistics Yearbook*. New York.
Wilson, A. T. (1964). 'Origin of ice ages: an ice shelf theory for Pleistocene glaciation.' *Nature, Lond.* **201** (4915), 147–9.

A look at the future

DONELLA H. MEADOWS

I would like to look with you into the future, to the problems and the issues that our children – the children we are educating now – will have to deal with. I hope that by doing this, I can show you *what* an environmental education program might teach our children and *why* it is important that they learn these things.

You are certainly aware that life is not getting any easier as we approach the 21st century. We as voters and you as legislators are faced with difficult decisions every day. Our children will have even more difficult decisions to make. Today I am going to discuss the probable future outlook in four vitally important areas – natural resources, energy supply, food production, and population. I have not come here to scare you, but I must say that I myself am a little scared, because I am convinced that if our generation and the generations to come do not make wise and informed decisions in these areas, the consequences will be very serious indeed.

You may wonder where I have put my crystal ball and what my qualifications are for making dire predictions about the future. I am a member of a research team at MIT, employed to calculate, as scientifically as possible, the future trends in world population, industrial growth, pollution, food production, and natural resource depletion. We are working closely with a number of national and international organizations to gather the vast amount of information we need.

From testimony given before the Education Committee of the Massachusetts Great and Central Court on behalf of House Bill 3787, on 31 March 1971.

Natural resources

You may have heard the statement that the United States has 6 per cent of the world's people and uses 40 per cent of the world's irreplaceable natural resources. It is a true statement, but it isn't very impressive, if we have an infinite supply of those resources. Do we?

Table 1 lists some of the natural resources which are vital to modern industry. The static reserve index gives the number of years our known world reserves will last at our present rate of usage. The dynamic index shows how long they will last if the usage rate increases by 2.5 per cent per year. The actual present growth rate is also listed. You will notice that nearly all these resources are due to 'run out' within our lifetime or within the lifetime of our children.

Now, we are not really going to completely 'run out' of any of these substances. Long before we reach the end of our reserves, we will have to mine poorer and poorer ores and transport them from more and more inaccessible places. The price of each material will increase, at first gradually, and then rapidly. As an example, the price of mercury, which, you will notice, has a current reserve index of only fourteen years, has increased by a factor of *ten* since 1948. We can expect similar price increases in at least nine other basic materials in the next few years. And the inevitable effect of that will be higher prices and a slowdown in business growth, since more money will have to be spent on raw materials.

There are several things we can do to counteract this very real threat to our economy. We can recycle used products and reclaim some of the resources they contain. We can remove depletion allowances that encourage increased resource usage. We can design products that last longer. We can look for new reserves or substitute a more abundant resource for one in short supply. None of these policies is free and some of them are extremely expensive. Who should pay for them? Which policy is cheapest? Which one will be most effective in preserving resources? We are going to have to answer these questions very soon. And we can't possibly come up with good answers without knowing the facts.

There are some even harder questions attached to the natural resource problem, and those are environmental ones. We are told that if we want oil for the 1980s, we have to build a pipeline across the whole state of Alaska. If we want copper, we have to create a huge open pit mine in the middle of Cascades National Park. What should we do? Is it important to leave wilderness areas for our children and grandchildren? Or is it more important to give them oil and copper? Can we get along without that oil and that copper? We Americans have to make *those* decisions *this* year, and every year from now on, since the pressure to build the pipeline and the mine will only increase as other sources are depleted. And such decisions will be even more frequent for our children. What will they do if someday someone wants to mine titanium from the sands of Cape Cod or uranium from the granite of the White Mountains?

TABLE 1 *World reserves of minerals and energy sources, 1971*

Resource	*Static reserve index (years)*	*Dynamic reserve index (years) at 2.5% increase*	*Current rate of increase*
chromium	560	110	4.0
iron	400	98	
manganese	160	65	
cobalt	160	65	
aluminum	160	65	7.0–8.0
nickel	130	59	
molybdenum	100	51	5.0
tungsten	45	31	5.0
copper	40	28	
tin	25	19	6.0
silver	23	18	6.0
zinc	20	17	
gold	19	16	
platinum	19	16	
lead	18	15	2.0
mercury	14	13	3.0
oil	33	25	6.9
coal	800	200	3.6
natural gas	20	17	6.6
uranium-235	66	40	6.0

REFERENCES

M. King Hubbert, in *Resources and Man*, W. H. Freeman and Company, San Francisco, 1969.

P. T. Flawn, *Mineral Resources*, Rand McNally, Chicago, 1966.

P. R. Ehrlich and A. H. Ehrlich, *Population Resources Environment*, Freeman and Company, San Francisco, 1970.

J. Randers, 'The Dynamics of Solid Waste Generation', System Dynamics Group, MIT, 1971.

Energy

The last four resources listed in Table 1, oil, coal, gas and uranium, are the source of 96 per cent of the energy we use in the world today. That energy, of course, is the entire basis for all industrial development, and without it we would be forced to revert to a simple agricultural society. The reserve lifetimes listed in the table make it clear that we shall have to learn to do without oil, gas, and conventional nuclear reactors very soon. However, I am very hopeful about the energy situation. We *can* solve our energy problem, *if* we make the right choices. These are our alternatives:

1 We can use coal. Our coal reserves won't last for ever, but they can carry us through until another solution is available. Coal is not an ideal answer to the energy problem. When it is burned, like all fossil fuels, it creates smog. The city of London banned the burning of coal in 1952 after 4000 people died in a lengthy, smoggy thermal inversion. Since the ban, they estimate that 50 per cent more sunshine falls on London. To reduce air pollution, we must process coal to remove sulfur and other substances. That costs money, of course. We must treat it in liquification or gasification plants before we can use it for many industrial and transportation purposes. Europe has a coal gasification plant, but we do not. Should we? Should we pay the necessary cost to make coal a clean fuel?

2 We can develop fast breeder nuclear reactors. This is the course the US Government has chosen, and we are funding the fast breeder program at a rate of $200 million a year. Fast breeder reactors essentially create their own fuel – once they are going, they will never run out. Unfortunately, fast breeder reactors can be terribly dangerous. They run essentially at the point of near-explosion. That doesn't mean that a fast breeder reactor is likely to blow up like an atomic bomb, but it does mean that breeder reactors are subject to 'excursions' – sudden bursts of energy which could possibly crack a containment vessel and release truly catastrophic amounts of radioactive isotopes, which are about the deadliest substances known to man. Such an excursion actually happened at the Fermi plant, thirty miles from Detroit, in 1966. I have been told by an AEC employee that it was only *luck* that there was no public exposure to radiation during that meltdown. If the containment vessel had cracked and if the normal weather patterns had held, at least 133,000 people could have been killed.

It is possible to make breeder reactors safe, but only by making them costly. The AEC, at the moment, does not seem inclined to pay that cost. Will the American public insist on safety, or will we prefer cheap power? How can we make that choice, if we are not even aware of the alternatives?

3 We can develop fusion reactors. A successful fusion reactor has not yet been built anywhere in the world. The best guess is that one will not be built for another twenty to thirty years. The technical problems are tremendous, but the possible payoff is great. Fusion reactors will run on a component of sea water – we have at least a billion-year supply. Fusion reactors tend to run at the point of shutting down, rather than at the point of explosion. Therefore they are much safer, and even if one should be opened somehow (by a 747 jet landing on it, for instance), it would contain far less dangerous nuclear fuel than a breeder reactor. The government has just cut the budget for fusion research – we are spending six times as much for the fast breeder program as for fusion research. That budgeting decision will be re-evaluated every year during the 1970s and probably during the 1980s. Should American citizens have a stronger voice in that decision? I believe they should, if they know the facts.

4 We can investigate solar radiation. Man uses about 1/46,000 of the energy which falls on the earth each year in the form of sunlight. The rest is reflected or radiated away. Solar radiation is a perfectly safe, pollution-free power source. Several responsible scientists have suggested that a large part of our energy requirements could be met by making better use of sunshine. Since it falls everywhere, it might even eliminate much of our need for power lines – the roof of every house could be made into a solar collector. With present technology, solar power costs ten times as much as conventional power. If we put serious research into it, it could be cheaper. This year the federal budget for solar power research is zero.

5 We can decrease our use of power. Since, by *any* of the above alternatives, power will be more expensive, we must find ways of using it more efficiently. Our total power consumption is increasing by 3 per cent every year, our electrical power consumption by 7 per cent. That means that we must double our electric power-producing capacity every ten years. Already we have brown-outs because we can't keep up with demand. Why is demand for power increasing so rapidly? Mainly because up until now it has been so cheap that we have learned to squander it. Why has it been so cheap? Because we have assigned no cost to environmental pollution and no cost to the fact that we are burning fossil fuels which cannot be replaced. We may never have to pay these costs, but our children will.

If we think about it, and understand the options available to us *and their costs*, we can think of many relatively painless ways to conserve power. We need not use electricity, one of the most inefficient power sources, to heat improperly insulated houses. We do not need a 200-horsepower engine to transport a single person to work every day. The average European uses about half as much power as the average American, yet Europeans have a comfortable living standard and better health than we do. Our children will have to be much wiser than we are in their use of power, and the more we go on using energy as frivolously as we do now, the sooner they will need to employ their wisdom.

Food

You have undoubtedly heard that millions of people are starving to death in the underdeveloped countries of the world each year. Does that mean that we have reached the limit of food production on this planet? The answer to that question, fortunately, is no, not yet.

There is an absolute upper limit of 8 billion acres of arable land on the earth. At present we cultivate 3.6 billion acres. We could produce more food if we utilized the rest of the land, but we must realize that farming that land will be more expensive. We have used up the easily cultivated acres – the rest will have to be cleared or heavily fertilized or extensively irrigated. In fact the UN Food and Agriculture Organization has suggested that, considering the costs of opening new land, our efforts should be directed instead to improving yields on the farmland we already have.

Improving yields is also not free. It involves irrigation, pesticides, fertilizers, tractors – in other words, money. Increased yields have environmental costs too. The Green Revolution, which is the agricultural modernization program supposed to feed Asia's growing population, is based on fertilizers that kill lakes and pesticides that kill fish, birds, and maybe people. You probably realize that the money for the Green Revolution is not coming from the starving Asians. They can't possibly afford it. You may not realize that the environmental effects of the Green Revolution are also not absorbed only by the Asians. Whenever DDT is sprayed anywhere in the world, it runs into the oceans and it evaporates into the air. It circulates around the globe and falls down in the rain. It has been found in Alaskan Eskimos, in Antarctic penguins, and in the milk of Swedish cows and Swedish mothers. We have calculated as part of our research that even if we start decreasing DDT use all over the world, starting tomorrow, it will continue to increase in animals and man for ten more years, and it won't get *back down* to its present level until 1995. I am not at all suggesting that we ban DDT tomorrow, or that we let Asians starve. I am just pointing out some of the facts that we all need to know about future food production. We *can* feed a lot more people, if we are willing to lower the standard of living and the environmental safety of everyone. And now, since I've mentioned more people, let's look at the population situation.

Population

The present population doubling time of the world is thirty-two years and decreasing. We have every reason to expect that, if we stay ahead of the food problem, we will have twice as many people around by the year 2000. All the other problems I have mentioned here are very much related to this population growth rate. Let me show you why.

I have included in this testimony a simple diagram, which I believe

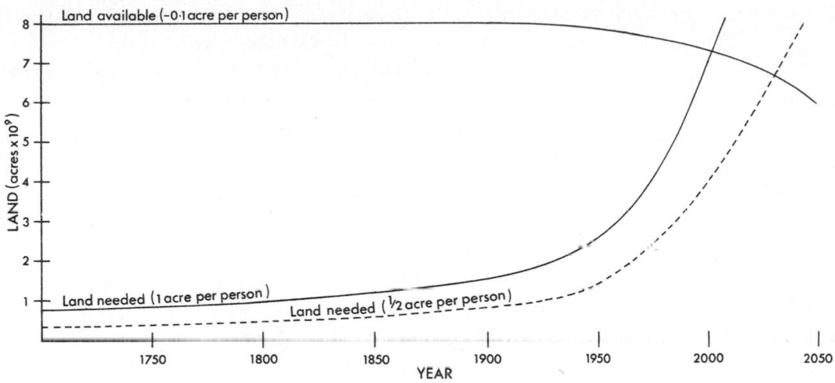

is one of the first things a child should learn about the environment. It illustrates the very tricky nature of exponential growth. I have drawn it here for land resources, but its message is the same for *any* resource we care to discuss on this finite earth, from oil to fresh water to space in national parks. The top line indicates the amount of land we have for cultivation in the world. I have chosen the most optimistic value possible, 8 billion acres, although we use less than half that amount now. The lower line indicates the amount of land *needed* to feed the world's population. I'm assuming that one acre per person is required, which is the amount of land we cultivate per person today. We could get by with less than that, if we decide not to produce any meat, because meat is about ten times more expensive in terms of land than plants are. But I have supposed that the world's population would prefer to keep about the same amount of meat in its diet as it has today. The lower curve is rising exponentially exactly as the world's population has risen up until now, and I have assumed that the same growth rate will continue into the future. The upper curve is decreasing slightly, because each new person takes up some agricultural land for the house, roads, airports, garbage dumps, and so on that he uses. Each American uses about 0.2 acre of farmland for these purposes. I have assumed in this graph that each person removes just half of that, or 0.1 acre.

You can see from the graph that exponential growth can go on for a long time with almost no effect, and then, within one or two doubling times (thirty to sixty years for the human population) the situation can get completely out of control. You can see how we may have had an incredible surplus of land (or resources or clean air) for 200,000 years, and then within a few years we can suddenly have an incredible shortage. You can also see that the conclusion you reach from the graph is almost independent of the assumptions I have made. If we make each acre twice as productive, we only gain thirty years before the two curves cross. If we decide that no agricultural land is lost to houses, so that the top curve is flat, we gain even less than thirty years. That is what exponential growth means, and we have today an exponentially growing population with exponentially growing consumption habits.

Many Americans think that the population problem is limited to the underdeveloped countries. It is true that their population is growing three times faster than ours, but that does not mean that ours is not growing. In many ways, our population growth is a more serious problem, because *we* are the ones with exponentially growing demand for the world's resources. To give you an idea of what that means, I have given you a list of some of the things that the average American baby born in 1971 will consume, spend, or throw away during his lifetime. In terms of spoiling the environment and using world resources, we are the world's most irresponsible and dangerous citizens. The birth rate of America is twenty-five times more important than the birth rate of India in determining whether our world has any ecological future at all.

TABLE 2

One American will require:

26 million gallons of water
28 tons of iron and steel
1200 barrels of petroleum
13,000 pounds of paper
50 tons of food
$10,000 in public expenses

He will throw out:

10,000 no-return bottles
17,500 cans
27,000 bottle caps
2.3 automobiles
35 rubber tires
126 tons of garbage
9.8 tons of particulate air pollution

The choices ahead

I am convinced that we can support twice as many people on this earth as we have now – and we will have to thirty years from now. We can probably even support four times as many people, sixty years from now, when our children reach old age. But it will cost a great deal to do so. Our children, and their children, will have less personal freedom, because greater densities of people always interfere with individual freedom. They will have less natural beauty around them. Their environment will be more polluted, and their standard of living will almost certainly be lower than ours.

Whether all this will happen depends on the choices and decisions that we and our children must make. They are very, very difficult choices and decisions, and they are coming at us very quickly. The birth rate in 1971 will have an effect for the next seventy years. The pesticides we spray today may be with us for twenty-five years. The oil we burn now will never be ours to burn again. Even doing *nothing* about the matters I've discussed here is, in effect, doing something, and in general it is doing something bad.

REFERENCES

Paul Ehrlich, *The Population Bomb*, Ballantine Books, New York, 1968.

John G. Mitchell, in *Ecotactics*, Pocket Books, Inc., New York, 1970.

Senator Joseph Tydings, in *The Congressional Record*, S9243, June 18, 1970.

J. Randers, 'The Dynamics of Solid Waste Generation', System Dynamics Group, MIT, 1971.

American Almanac, Statistical Abstract of the United States, US Department of Commerce, Grosset and Dunlap, New York, 1970.

Part Three

CAUSES OF CHAOS

In many ways the ecological 'crisis' was, and is, a cover-up. Throughout the 1960s the New Left, particularly in the United States, sought to expose it as a liberal plot to divert attention from the real problems – those of social injustice, war and the evils of capitalism. The truth is, of course, that the ecological crisis was not a diversion from these things but a result of them. The crisis mankind was facing was not simply the problem of pollution: biological weapons, racialism, urban breakdown, technomania, poverty, and exploitation of man, the environment and other species all featured in the agenda, jostling for priority as the most urgent of all the problems.

So those who looked for solutions were led away from partial ones. An ill-defined malady seemed to be lurking unidentified in the wings of the stage, and the race was on to expose it to the global audience. Of course, for many years the sickness had seemed clear enough to those who thought the planet too small: there would have to be fewer people. Behind all the articles in the last section lies the haunting figure of the population explosion as the cause of all our ills. With remorseless logic, Garrett Hardin, Professor of Biology at the University of California, Santa Barbara, pushed hard at the implications of there being too many people. They yielded, and revealed a planet big enough to house more people, but people with a lot less freedom.

In the end, the over-population theorists did not get away with it. Many economists tried their hand at the idea that it was not the number of people that mattered so much as what those people thought they needed – or were told by the advertisers that they needed – to live a fulfilling life. Two cars and a yacht seemed a trifle excessive to many, and affluence and economic growth were a good pair of villains on whom to attach the blame. Dr E. F. Schumacher made the soundest job of demolishing the fad of growth. But his success sounded like a threat to the poor, and particularly to the underdeveloped nations who saw in the industrialized world's new mood of material puritanism yet another neo-colonialist plot.

It was left to Barry Commoner, of Washington University in St Louis, to destroy both arguments. By calculating pollution levels in the United States over a 25-year period, he showed that the increases were far greater than could be accounted for either by the much smaller growth in population or in the economy. The problem, he claimed, was the sweeping changes in the nature of the technology that had come about in that time. In this, he found hope: the social and political changes needed to rectify the ecological situation would, he argued, also give men – all men – a chance to live a decent life free from exploitation and the risk of global catastrophe. Subsequently a famous debate developed between Commoner and Paul Ehrlich on the subject of population growth, with Commoner vehemently attacking the neo-Malthusians on political grounds.

A few years after the storm, hindsight gives us a clearer picture of what all these words implied. Ours is a society dedicated to replacing people by machines, one in which the last forms of social communion are fast disappearing. Small wonder, then, that such a society faced suddenly with future bankruptcy should look to people as the first cause of the problem. In the West we have always found people too aggressive, too dishonest, too ambitious – forgetting, of course, that behaviour is largely conditioned by the social constraints and imperatives of the society in which it takes place. It was natural for us to blame people – too many of them – for any real global problem. In the West people have always been the problem, rarely the solution.

And of course ours is less a society than a market place. Economic criteria do rule the day in the life of the average Westerner, and if as a result his life appears to be wanting, it is to those economic criteria that one is tempted to look first. So many economists did just that, although few did it with much subtlety. But it is not growth per se which creates the problems, for who would wish to control the growth of love, of well-being, of social cohesion?

Two things need to be said about Commoner's thesis. First, there is a confusion between pollution and the environmental crisis: the two things are not the same, and the more limited forms of pollution with which Commoner deals do not describe the whole of the environmental debate. Second, even Commoner's apparently revolutionary approach is still one that lies entirely within the Western rationalist tradition. Isolate the problem, examine the relevant statistics, frame the hypothesis, expound the solution. And what Commoner never tells us is 'why?' Why did technology go the way it did? And without knowing that, it seems difficult to try to make it go any other way.

But there were plenty who did want to delve deeper. Lynn White, the historian, develops here his remarkable thesis that it is our Judaeo-Christian heritage which compels us to walk the Earth with that arrogant swagger which is but the prelude to ecological collapse. A bitter pill for a society as unreligious as ours to swallow, although certainly the idea that the Earth and all the species on it were created for Man's benefit is not one to be found in most of the world's religions.

Theodore Roszak takes us yet deeper into our philosophical origins. Having championed, in his book *The Making of a Counter-Culture*, the cause of youthful unrest, he begins to ask whether the exclusive scientific/rationalist *approach to the world is not the key to all the problems. What we lack, he claims, is a proper respect for mystery and hence for life and for our planet. His search for that takes him back much farther than the origins of Judaeo–Christianity; it returns to the philosophy of those primitives whose nature-poems have survived to this day; and it questions the meaning of knowledge itself.*

The tragedy of the commons

GARRETT HARDIN

At the end of a thoughtful article on the future of nuclear war, Wiesner and York[1] concluded that: 'Both sides in the arms race are . . . confronted by the dilemma of steadily increasing military power and steadily decreasing national security. *It is our considered professional judgment that this dilemma has no technical solution*. If the great powers continue to look for solutions in the area of science and technology only, the result will be to worsen the situation.'

I would like to focus your attention not on the subject of the article (national security in a nuclear world) but on the kind of conclusion they reached, namely that there is no technical solution to the problem. An implicit and almost universal assumption of discussions published in professional and semipopular scientific journals is that the problem under discussion has a technical solution. A technical solution may be defined as one that requires a change only in the techniques of the natural sciences, demanding little or nothing in the way of change in human values or ideas of morality.

In our day (though not in earlier times) technical solutions are always welcome. Because of previous failures in prophecy, it takes courage to assert that a desired technical solution is not possible. Wiesner and York exhibited this courage; publishing in a science journal, they insisted that the solution to the problem was not to be found in the natural sciences. They cautiously qualified their statement with the phrase, 'It is our considered professional judgment. . . .' Whether they were right or not is not the concern of the present article. Rather, the concern here is with the important concept of a class of human problems which can be called 'no technical solution problems', and, more specifically, with the identification and discussion of one of these.

Extracts from an article in *Science*, Vol. 162, pp. 1243–8, 13 December 1968.

It is easy to show that the class is not a null class. Recall the game of tick-tack-toe (or noughts and crosses). Consider the problem, 'How can I win the game of tick-tack-toe?' It is well known that I cannot, if I assume (in keeping with the conventions of game theory) that my opponent understands the game perfectly. Put another way, there is no 'technical solution' to the problem. I can win only by giving a radical meaning to the word 'win'. I can hit my opponent over the head; or I can drug him; or I can falsify the records. Every way in which I 'win' involves, in some sense, an abandonment of the game, as we intuitively understand it. (I can also, of course, openly abandon the game – refuse to play it. This is what most adults do.)

The class of 'No technical solution problems' has members. My thesis is that the 'population problem', as conventionally conceived, is a member of this class. How it is conventionally conceived needs some comment. It is fair to say that most people who anguish over the population problem are trying to find a way to avoid the evils of over-population without relinquishing any of the privileges they now enjoy. They think that farming the seas or developing new strains of wheat will solve the problem – technologically. I try to show here that the solution they seek cannot be found. The population problem cannot be solved in a technical way, any more than can the problem of winning the game of tick-tack-toe.

What shall we maximize?

Population, as Malthus said, naturally tends to grow 'geometrically', or, as we would now say, exponentially. In a finite world this means that the *per capita* share of the world's goods must steadily decrease. Is ours a finite world?

A fair defense can be put forward for the view that the world is infinite; or that we do not know that it is not. But, in terms of the practical problems that we must face in the next few generations with the foreseeable technology, it is clear that we will greatly increase human misery if we do not, during the immediate future, assume that the world available to the terrestrial human population is finite. 'Space' is no escape.[2]

A finite world can support only a finite population; therefore, population growth must eventually equal zero. (The case of perpetual wide fluctuations above and below zero is a trivial variant that need not be discussed.) When this condition is met, what will be the situation of mankind? Specifically, can Bentham's goal of 'the greatest good for the greatest number' be realized?

No – for two reasons, each sufficient by itself. The first is a theoretical one. It is not mathematically possible to maximize for two (or more) variables at the same time. This was clearly stated by von Neumann and Morgenstern,[3] but the principle is implicit in the theory of partial differential equations, dating back at least to D'Alembert (1717–83).

The second reason springs directly from biological facts. To live, any organism must have a source of energy (for example, food). This energy is utilized for two purposes: mere maintenance and work. For man, maintenance of life requires about 1600 kilo-calories a day ('maintenance calories'). Anything that he does over and above merely staying alive will be defined as work, and is supported by 'work calories' which he takes in. Work calories are used not only for what we call work in common speech; they are also required for all forms of enjoyment, from swimming and automobile racing to playing music and writing poetry. If our goal is to maximize population it is obvious what we must do: we must make the work calories per person approach as close to zero as possible. No gourmet meals, no vacations, no sports, no music, no literature, no art. . . . I think that everyone will grant, without argument or proof, that maximizing population does not maximize goods. Bentham's goal is impossible.

In reaching this conclusion I have made the usual assumption that it is the acquisition of energy that is the problem. The appearance of atomic energy has led some to question this assumption. However, given an infinite source of energy, population growth still produces an inescapable problem. The problem of the acquisition of energy is replaced by the problem of its dissipation, as J. H. Fremlin has so wittily shown.[4] The arithmetic signs in the analysis are, as it were, reversed; but Bentham's goal is still unobtainable.

The optimum population is, then, less than the maximum. The difficulty of defining the optimum is enormous; so far as I know, no one has seriously tackled this problem. Reaching an acceptable and stable solution will surely require more than one generation of hard analytical work – and much persuasion.

We want the maximum good per person; but what is good? To one person it is wilderness, to another it is ski lodges for thousands. To one it is estuaries to nourish ducks for hunters to shoot; to another it is factory land. Comparing one good with another is, we usually say, impossible because goods are incommensurable. Incommensurables cannot be compared.

Theoretically this may be true; but in real life incommensurables *are* commensurable. Only a criterion of judgment and a system of weighting are needed. In nature the criterion is survival. Is it better for a species to be small and hideable, or large and powerful? Natural selection commensurates the incommensurables. The compromise achieved depends on a natural weighting of the values of the variables.

Man must imitate this process. There is no doubt that in fact he already does, but unconsciously. It is when the hidden decisions are made explicit that the arguments begin. The problem for the years ahead is to work out an acceptable theory of weighting. Synergistic effects, nonlinear variation, and difficulties in discounting the future make the intellectual problem difficult, but not (in principle) insoluble.

Has any cultural group solved this practical problem at the present time, even on an intuitive level? One simple fact proves that none has: there is no prosperous population in the world today that has, and has had for some time, a growth rate of zero. Any people that has intuitively identified its optimum point will soon reach it, after which its growth rate becomes and remains zero.

Of course, a positive growth rate might be taken as evidence that a population is below its optimum. However, by any reasonable standards, the most rapidly growing populations on earth today are (in general) the most miserable. This association (which need not be invariable) casts doubt on the optimistic assumption that the positive growth rate of a population is evidence that it has yet to reach its optimum.

We can make little progress in working toward optimum population size until we explicitly exorcize the spirit of Adam Smith in the field of practical demography. In economic affairs, *The Wealth of Nations* (1776) popularized the 'invisible hand', the idea that an individual who 'intends only his own gain' is, as it were, 'led by an invisible hand to promote . . . the public interest'.[5] Adam Smith did not assert that this was invariably true, and perhaps neither did any of his followers. But he contributed to a dominant tendency of thought that has ever since interfered with positive action based on rational analysis, namely, the tendency to assume that decisions reached individually will, in fact, be the best decisions for an entire society. If this assumption is correct it justifies the continuance of our present policy of *laissez-faire* in reproduction. If it is correct we can assume that men will control their individual fecundity so as to produce the optimum population. If the assumption is not correct, we need to re-examine our individual freedoms to see which ones are defensible.

Tragedy of freedom in a commons

The rebuttal to the invisible hand in population control is to be found in a scenario first sketched in a little-known pamphlet[6] in 1833 by a mathematical amateur named William Forster Lloyd (1794–1852). We may well call it 'the tragedy of the commons', using the word 'tragedy' as the philosopher Whitehead used it:[7] 'The essence of dramatic tragedy is not unhappiness. It resides in the solemnity of the remorseless working of things.' He then goes on to say, 'This inevitableness of destiny can only be illustrated in terms of human life by incidents which in fact involve unhappiness. For it is only by them that the futility of escape can be made evident in the drama.'

The tragedy of the commons develops in this way. Picture a pasture open to all. It is to be expected that each herdsman will try to keep as many cattle as possible on the commons. Such an arrangement may work reasonably satisfactorily for centuries because tribal wars, poaching, and disease keep the numbers of both man and beast well below the carrying capacity of the land. Finally, however, comes the day of reckoning, that is, the day when the long-desired goal of social stability becomes a reality. At this point, the inherent logic of the commons remorselessly generates tragedy.

As a rational being, each herdsman seeks to maximize his gain. Explicitly or implicitly, more or less consciously, he asks, 'What is the utility *to me* of adding one more animal to my herd?' This utility has one negative and one positive component:

1. The positive component is a function of the increment of one animal. Since the herdsman receives all the proceeds from the sale of the additional animal, the positive utility is nearly +1.

2. The negative component is a function of the additional overgrazing created by one more animal. Since, however, the effects of overgrazing are shared by all the herdsmen, the negative utility for any particular decision-making herdsman is only a fraction of −1.

Adding together the component partial utilities, the rational herdsman concludes that the only sensible course for him to pursue is to add another animal to his herd. And another; and another. . . . But this is the conclusion reached by each and every rational herdsman sharing a commons. Therein is the tragedy. Each man is locked into a system that compels him to increase his herd without limit – in a world that is limited. Ruin is the destination toward which all men rush, each pursuing his own best interest in a society that believes in the freedom of the commons. Freedom in a commons brings ruin to all.

Some would say that this is a platitude. Would that it were! In a sense, it was learned thousands of years ago, but natural selection favors the forces of psychological denial.[8] The individual benefits as an individual from his ability to deny the truth even though society as a whole, of which he is a part, suffers. Education can counteract the natural tendency to do the wrong thing, but the inexorable succession of generations requires that the basis for this knowledge be constantly refreshed.

A simple incident that occurred a few years ago in Leominster, Massachusetts, shows how perishable the knowledge is. During the Christmas shopping season the parking meters downtown were covered with plastic bags that bore tags reading: 'Do not open until after Christmas. Free parking courtesy of the mayor and city council.' In other words, facing the prospect of an increased demand for already scarce space, the city fathers reinstituted the system of the commons. (Cynically, we suspect that they gained more votes than they lost by this retrogressive act.)

In an approximate way, the logic of the commons has been understood for a long time, perhaps since the discovery of agriculture or the invention of private property in real estate. But it is understood mostly only in special cases which are not sufficiently generalized. Even at this late date, cattlemen leasing national land on the western ranges demonstrate no more than an ambivalent understanding, in constantly pressuring federal authorities to increase the head count to the point where overgrazing produces erosion and weed-dominance. Likewise, the oceans of the world continue to suffer from the survival of the philosophy of the commons. Maritime nations still respond automatically to the shibboleth of the 'freedom of the seas'. Professing to believe in the 'inexhaustible resources of the oceans', they bring species after species of fish and whales closer to extinction.[9]

Pollution

In a reverse way, the tragedy of the commons reappears in problems of pollution. Here it is not a question of taking something out of the commons, but of putting something in – sewage, or chemical, radioactive, and heat wastes into water; noxious and dangerous fumes into the air; and distracting and unpleasant advertising signs into the line of sight. The calculations of utility are much the same as before. The rational man finds that his share of the cost of the wastes he discharges into the commons is less than the cost of purifying his wastes before releasing them. Since this is true for everyone, we are locked into a system of 'fouling our own nest', so long as we behave only as independent, rational, free-enterprisers.

The tragedy of the commons as a food basket is averted by private property, or something formally like it. But the air and waters surrounding us cannot readily be fenced, and so the tragedy of the commons as a cesspool must be prevented by different means, by coercive laws or taxing devices that make it cheaper for the polluter to treat his pollutants than to discharge them untreated. We have not progressed as far with the solution of this problem as we have with the first. Indeed, our particular concept of private property, which deters us from exhausting the positive resources of the earth, favors pollution. The owner of a factory on the bank of a stream – whose property extends to the middle of the stream – often has difficulty seeing why it is not his natural right to muddy the waters flowing past his door. The law, always behind the times, requires elaborate stitching and fitting to adapt it to this newly perceived aspect of the commons.

The pollution problem is a consequence of population. It did not much matter how a lonely American frontiersman disposed of his waste. 'Flowing water purifies itself every ten miles', my grandfather used to say, and the myth was near enough to the truth when he was a boy, for there were not too many people. But as population became denser, the natural chemical and biological recycling processes became overloaded, calling for a redefinition of property rights.

How to legislate temperance?

Analysis of the pollution problem as a function of population density uncovers a not generally recognized principle of morality, namely: *the morality of an act is a function of the state of the system at the time it is performed.*[10] Using the commons as a cesspool does not harm the general public under frontier conditions, because there is no public; the same behavior in a metropolis is unbearable. A hundred and fifty years ago a plainsman could kill an American bison, cut out only the tongue for his dinner, and discard the rest of the animal. He was not in any important sense being wasteful. Today, with only a few thousand bison left, we would be appalled at such behavior.

That morality is system-sensitive escaped the attention of most codifiers of ethics in the past. 'Thou shalt not . . .' is the form of traditional ethical directives which make no allowance for particular circumstances. The laws of our society follow the pattern of ancient ethics, and therefore are poorly suited to governing a complex, crowded, changeable world. Our epicyclic solution is to augment statutory law with administrative law. Since it is practically impossible to spell out all the conditions under which it is safe to burn trash in the back yard or to run an automobile without smog-control, by law we delegate the details to bureaus. The result is administrative law, which is rightly feared for an ancient reason – *Quis custodiet ipsos custodes?* 'Who shall watch the watchers themselves?' John Adams said that we must have 'a government of laws and not men'. Bureau administrators, trying to evaluate the morality of acts in the total system, are singularly liable to corruption, producing a government by men, not laws.

Prohibition is easy to legislate (though not necessarily to enforce); but how do we legislate temperance? Experience indicates that it can be accomplished best through the mediation of administrative law. We limit possibilities unnecessarily if we suppose that the sentiment of *Quis custodiet* denies us the use of administrative law. We should rather retain the phrase as a perpetual reminder of fearful dangers we cannot avoid. The great challenge facing us now is to invent the corrective feedbacks that are needed to keep custodians honest. We must find ways to legitimate the needed authority of both the custodians and the corrective feedbacks.

Freedom to breed is intolerable

The tragedy of the commons is involved in population problems in another way. In a world governed solely by the principle of 'dog eat dog' – if indeed there ever was such a world – how many children a family had would not be a matter of public concern. Parents who bred too exuberantly would leave fewer descendants, not more, because they would be unable to care adequately for their children. David Lack and others have found that such a negative feedback demonstrably controls the fecundity of birds.[11] But men are not birds, and have not acted like them for millenniums, at least.

If each human family were dependent only on its own resources; *if* the children of improvident parents starved to death; *if*, thus, overbreeding brought its own 'punishment' to the germ line – *then* there would be no public interest in controlling the breeding of families. But our society is deeply committed to the welfare state,[12] and hence is confronted with another aspect of the tragedy of the commons.

In a welfare state, how shall we deal with the family, the religion, the race, or the class (or indeed any distinguishable and cohesive group) that adopts overbreeding as a policy to secure its own aggrandizement?[13] To couple the concept of freedom to breed with the belief that everyone born has an equal right to the commons is to lock the world into a tragic course of action.

Unfortunately this is just the course of action that is being pursued by the United Nations. In late 1967, some thirty nations agreed to the following:[14]

> The Universal Declaration of Human Rights describes the family as the natural and fundamental unit of society. It follows that any choice and decision with regard to the size of the family must irrevocably rest with the family itself, and cannot be made by anyone else.

It is painful to have to deny categorically the validity of this right; denying it, one feels as uncomfortable as a resident of Salem, Massachusetts, who denied the reality of witches in the seventeenth century. At the present time, in liberal quarters, something like a taboo acts to inhibit criticism of the United Nations. There is a feeling that the United Nations is 'our last and best hope', that we shouldn't find fault with it; we shouldn't play into the hands of the arch-conservatives. However, let us not forget what Robert Louis Stevenson said: 'The truth that is suppressed by friends is the readiest weapon of the enemy.' If we love the truth we must openly deny the validity of the Universal Declaration of Human Rights, even though it is promoted by the United Nations. We should also join with Kingsley Davis[15] in attempting to get Planned Parenthood–World Population to see the error of its ways in embracing the same tragic ideal.

Conscience is self-eliminating

It is a mistake to think that we can control the breeding of mankind in the long run by an appeal to conscience. Charles Galton Darwin made this point when he spoke on the centennial of the publication of his grandfather's great book. The argument is straightfoward and Darwinian.

People vary. Confronted with appeals to limit breeding, some people will undoubtedly respond to the plea more than others. Those who have more children will produce a larger fraction of the next generation than those with more susceptible consciences. The difference will be accentuated, generation by generation.

In C. G. Darwin's words: 'It may well be that it would take hundreds of generations for the progenitive instinct to develop in this way, but if it should do so, nature would have taken her revenge, and the variety *Homo contracipiens* would become extinct and would be replaced by the variety *Homo progenitivus.*'[16]

The argument assumes that conscience or the desire for children (no matter which) is hereditary – but hereditary only in the most general formal sense. The result will be the same whether the attitude is transmitted through germ cells, or exosomatically, to use A. J. Lotka's term. (If one denies the latter possibility as well as the former, then what's the point of education?) The argument has here been stated in the context of the population problem, but it applies equally well to any instance in which society appeals to an individual exploiting a commons to restrain himself for the general good – by means of his conscience. To make such an appeal is to set up a selective system that works toward the elimination of conscience from the race.

Pathogenic effects of conscience

The long-term disadvantage of an appeal to conscience should be enough to condemn it; but has serious short-term disadvantages as well. If we ask a man who is exploiting a commons to desist 'in the name of conscience', what are we saying to him? What does he hear? – not only at the moment but also in the wee small hours of the night when, half asleep, he remembers not merely the words we used but also the nonverbal communication cues we gave him unawares? Sooner or later, consciously or subconsciously, he senses that he has received two communications, and that they are contradictory: (i) (intended communication) 'If you don't do as we ask, we will openly condemn you for not acting like a responsible citizen'; (ii) (the unintended communication) 'If you *do* behave as we ask, we will secretly condemn you for a simpleton who can be shamed into standing aside while the rest of us exploit the commons.'

Everyman then is caught in what Bateson has called a 'double bind'. Bateson and his co-workers have made a plausible case for viewing the double bind as an important causative factor in the genesis of schizophrenia.[17] The double bind may not always be so damaging, but it always endangers the mental health of anyone to whom it is applied. 'A bad conscience', said Nietzsche, 'is a kind of illness.'

To conjure up a conscience in others is tempting to anyone who wishes to extend his control beyond the legal limits. Leaders at the highest level succumb to this temptation. Has any President during the past generation failed to call on labor unions to moderate voluntarily their demands for higher wages, or to steel companies to honor voluntary guidelines on prices? I can recall none. The rhetoric used on such occasions is designed to produce feelings of guilt in non-cooperators.

For centuries it was assumed without proof that guilt was a valuable, perhaps even an indispensable, ingredient of the civilized life. Now, in this post-Freudian world, we doubt it.

Paul Goodman speaks from the modern point of view when he says: 'No good has ever come from feeling guilty, neither intelligence, policy, nor compassion. The guilty do not pay attention to the object but only to themselves, and not even to their own interests, which might make sense, but to their anxieties.'[18]

One does not have to be a professional psychiatrist to see the consequences of anxiety. We in the Western world are just emerging from a dreadful two-centuries-long Dark Ages of Eros that was sustained partly by prohibition laws, but perhaps more effectively by the anxiety-generating mechanisms of education. Alex Comfort has told the story well in *The Anxiety Makers*;[19] it is not a pretty one.

Since proof is difficult, we may even concede that the results of anxiety may sometimes, from certain points of view, be desirable. The larger question we should ask is whether, as a matter of policy, we should ever encourage the use of a technique the tendency (if not the intention) of which is psychologically pathogenic. We hear much talk these days of responsible parenthood; the coupled words are incorporated into the titles of some organizations devoted to birth control. Some people have proposed massive propaganda campaigns to instill responsibility into the nation's (or the world's) breeders. But what is the meaning of the word 'responsibility' in this context? It is not merely a synonym for the word 'conscience'? When we use the word 'responsibility' in the absence of substantial sanctions are we not trying to browbeat a free man in a commons into acting against his own interest? 'Responsibility' is a verbal counterfeit for a substantial *quid pro quo*. It is an attempt to get something for nothing.

If the word 'responsibility' is to be used at all, I suggest that it be in the sense Charles Frankel uses it.[20] 'Responsibility', says this philosopher, 'is the product of definite social arrangements.' Notice that Frankel calls for social arrangements – not propaganda.

Mutual coercion mutually agreed upon

The social arrangements that produce responsibility are arrangements that create coercion, of some sort. Consider bank-robbing. The man who takes money from a bank acts as if the bank were a commons. How do we prevent such action? Certainly not by trying to control his behavior solely by a verbal appeal to his sense of responsibility. Rather than rely on propaganda we follow Frankel's lead and insist that a bank is not a commons; we seek the definite social arrangements that will keep it from becoming a commons. That we thereby infringe on the freedom of would-be robbers we neither deny nor regret.

The morality of bank-robbing is particularly easy to understand because we accept complete prohibition of this activity. We are willing to say 'Thou shalt not rob banks', without providing for exceptions. But temperance also can be created by coercion. Taxing is a good coercive device. To keep downtown shoppers temperate in their use of parking space we introduce parking meters for short periods, and traffic fines for longer ones. We need not actually forbid a citizen to park as long as he wants to; we need merely make it increasingly expensive for him to do so. Not prohibition, but carefully biased options are what we offer him. A Madison Avenue man might call this persuasion; I prefer the greater candor of the word 'coercion'.

Coercion is a dirty word to most liberals now, but it need not forever be so. As with the four-letter words, its dirtiness can be cleansed away by exposure to the light, by saying it over and over without apology or embarrassment. To many, the word 'coercion' implies arbitrary decisions of distant and irresponsible bureaucrats; but this is not a necessary part of its meaning. The only kind of coercion I recommend is mutual coercion, mutually agreed upon by the majority of the people affected.

To say that we mutually agree to coercion is not to say that we are required to enjoy it, or even to pretend we enjoy it. Who enjoys taxes? We all grumble about them. But we accept compulsory taxes because we recognize that voluntary taxes would favor the conscienceless. We institute and (grumblingly) support taxes and other coercive devices to escape the horror of the commons.

An alternative to the commons need not be perfectly just to be preferable. With real estate and other material goods, the alternative we have chosen is the institution of private property coupled with legal inheritance. Is this system perfectly just? As a genetically trained biologist I deny that it is. It seems to me that, if there are to be differences in individual inheritance, legal possession should be perfectly correlated with biological inheritance – that those who are biologically more fit to be the custodians of property and power should legally inherit more. But genetic recombination continually makes a mockery of the doctrine of 'like father, like son' implicit in our laws of legal inheritance. An idiot can inherit millions, and a trust fund can keep his estate intact. We must admit that our legal system of private property plus inheritance is unjust – but we put up with it because we are not convinced, at the moment, that anyone has invented a better system. The alternative of the commons is too horrifying to contemplate. Injustice is preferable to total ruin.

It is one of the peculiarities of the warfare between reform and the *status quo* that it is thoughtlessly governed by a double standard. Whenever a reform measure is proposed it is often defeated when its opponents triumphantly discover a flaw in it. As Kingsley Davis has pointed out,[21] worshippers of the *status quo* sometimes imply that no reform is possible without unanimous agreement, an implication contrary to historical fact. As nearly as I can make out, automatic rejection of proposed reforms is based on one of two unconscious assumptions: (i) that the *status quo* is perfect; or (ii) that the choice we face is between reform and no action; if the proposed reform is imperfect, we presumably should take no action at all, while we wait for a perfect proposal.

But we can never do nothing. That which we have done for thousands of years is also action. It also produces evils. Once we are aware that the *status quo* is action, we can then compare its discoverable advantages and disadvantages with the predicted advantages and disadvantages of the proposed reform, discounting as best we can for our lack of experience. On the basis of such a comparison, we can make a rational decision which will not involve the unworkable assumption that only perfect systems are tolerable.

Recognition of necessity

Perhaps the simplest summary of this analysis of man's population problems is this: the commons, if justifiable at all, is justifiable only under conditions of low population density. As the human population has increased, the commons has had to be abandoned in one aspect after another.

First we abandoned the commons in food gathering, enclosing farm land and restricting pastures and hunting and fishing areas. These restrictions are still not complete throughout the world.

Somewhat later we saw that the commons as a place for waste disposal would also have to be abandoned. Restrictions on the disposal of domestic sewage are widely accepted in the Western world; we are still struggling to close the commons to pollution by automobiles, factories, insecticide sprayers, fertilizing operations, and atomic energy installations.

In a still more embryonic state is our recognition of the evils of the commons in matters of pleasure. There is almost no restriction on the propagation of sound waves in the public medium. The shopping public is assaulted with mindless music, without its consent. Our government is paying out billions of dollars to create supersonic transport which will disturb 50,000 people for every one person who is whisked from coast to coast three hours faster. Advertisers muddy the airwaves of radio and television and pollute the view of travelers. We are a long way from outlawing the commons in matters of pleasure. Is this because our Puritan inheritance makes us view pleasure as something of a sin, and pain (that is, the pollution of advertising) as the sign of virtue?

Every new enclosure of the commons involves the infringement of somebody's personal liberty. Infringements made in the distant past are accepted because no contemporary complains of a loss. It is the newly proposed infringements that we vigorously oppose; cries of 'rights' and 'freedom' fill the air. But what does 'freedom' mean? When men mutually agreed to pass laws against robbing, mankind became more free, not less so. Individuals locked into the logic of the commons are free only to bring on universal ruin; once they see the necessity of mutual coercion, they become free to pursue other goals. I believe it was Hegel who said, 'Freedom is the recognition of necessity.'

The most important aspect of necessity that we must now recognize, is the necessity of abandoning the commons in breeding. No technical solution can rescue us from the misery of overpopulation. Freedom to breed will bring ruin to all. At the moment, to avoid hard decisions many of us are tempted to propagandize for conscience and responsible parenthood. The temptation must be resisted, because an appeal to independently acting consciences selects for the disappearance of all conscience in the long run, and an increase in anxiety in the short.

The only way we can preserve and nurture other and more precious freedoms is by relinquishing the freedom to breed, and that very soon. 'Freedom is the recognition of necessity' – and it is the role of education to reveal to all the necessity of abandoning the freedom to breed. Only so, can we put an end to this aspect of the tragedy of the commons.

REFERENCES

1 J. B. Wiesner and H. F. York, *Sci. Amer.* **211** (No. 4), 27 (1964).
2 G. Hardin, *J. Hered.* **50**, 68 (1959); S. von Hoernor, *Science* **137**, 18 (1962).
3 J. von Neumann and O. Morgenstern, *Theory of Games and Economic Behavior* (Princeton Univ. Press, Princeton, N.J., 1947), p. 11.
4 J. H. Fremlin, *New Sci.*, No. 415 (1964), p. 285.
5 A. Smith, *The Wealth of Nations* (Modern Library, New York, 1937), p. 423.
6 W. F. Lloyd, *Two Lectures on the Checks to Population* (Oxford Univ. Press, Oxford, England, 1833), reprinted (in part) in *Population, Evolution, and Birth Control*, G. Hardin, Ed. (Freeman, San Francisco, 1964), p. 37.
7 A. N. Whitehead, *Science and the Modern World* (Mentor, New York, 1948), p. 17.
8 G. Hardin, Ed., *Population, Evolution, and Birth Control* (Freeman, San Francisco, 1964), p. 56.
9 S. McVay, *Sci. Amer.* **216** (No. 8), 13 (1966).
10 J. Fletcher, *Situation Ethics* (Westminster, Philadelphia, 1966).
11 D. Lack, *The Natural Regulation of Animal Numbers* (Clarendon Press, Oxford, 1954).
12 H. Girvetz, *From Wealth to Welfare* (Stanford Univ. Press, Stanford, Calif., 1950).
13 G. Hardin, *Perspec. Biol. Med.* **6**, 366 (1963).
14 U Thant, *Int. Planned Parenthood News*, No. 168 (February 1968), p. 3.
15 K. Davis, *Science* **158**, 730 (1967).
16 S. Tax, Ed., *Evolution after Darwin* (Univ. of Chicago Press, Chicago, 1960), vol. 2, p. 469.

17 G. Bateson, D. D. Jackson, J. Haley, J. Weakland, *Behav. Sci.* **1**, 251 (1956).
18 P. Goodman, *New York Rev. Books* **10**(8), 22 (23 May 1968).
19 A. Comfort, *The Anxiety Makers* (Nelson, London, 1967).
20 C. Frankel, *The Case for Modern Man* (Harper, New York, 1955), p. 203.
21 J. D. Roslansky, *Genetics and the Future of Man* (Appleton-Century-Crofts, New York, 1966), p. 177.

The economics of permanence

E. F. SCHUMACHER

The dominant modern belief is that the soundest foundation of peace would be universal prosperity. One may look in vain for historical evidence that the rich have regularly been more peaceful than the poor, but then it can be argued that they have never felt secure against the poor; that their aggressiveness stemmed from fear; and that the situation would be quite different if everybody were rich. Why should a rich man go to war? He has nothing to gain. Are not the poor, the exploited, the oppressed most likely to do so, as they have nothing to lose but their chains? The road to peace, it is argued, is to follow the road to riches.

This dominant modern belief has an almost irresistible attraction as it suggests that the faster you get one desirable thing the more securely do you attain another. It is doubly attractive because it completely bypasses the whole question of ethics: there is no need for renunciation or sacrifice; on the contrary! We have science and technology to help us along the road to peace and plenty, and all that is needed is that we should not behave stupidly, irrationally, cutting into our own flesh. The message to the poor and discontented is that they must not impatiently upset or kill the goose that will assuredly, in due course, lay golden eggs also for them. And the message to the rich is that they must be intelligent enough from time to time to help the poor, because this is the way by which they will become richer still.

Gandhi used to talk disparagingly of 'dreaming of systems so perfect that no one will need to be good'. But is it not precisely this dream which we can now implement in reality with our marvellous powers of science and technology? Why ask for virtues, which man may never acquire, when scientific rationality and technical competence are all that is needed?

From *Resurgence, Journal of the Fourth World*, Vol. 3, No. 1, May/June 1970.

Instead of listening to Gandhi, are we not more inclined to listen to one of the most influential economists of our century, the great Lord Keynes? In 1930, during the world-wide economic depression, he felt moved to speculate on the 'economic possibilities for our grandchildren' and concluded that the day might not be all that far off when everybody would be rich. We shall then, he said, 'once more value ends above means and prefer the good to the useful.' 'But beware!' he continued. 'The time for all this is not yet. For at least another hundred years we must pretend to ourselves and to every one that fair is foul and foul is fair; for foul is useful and fair is not.'

This was written forty years ago and since then, of course, things have speeded up considerably. Maybe we do not even have to wait for another sixty years until universal plenty will be attained. In any case, the Keynesian message is clear enough: Beware! Ethical considerations are not merely irrelevant, they are an actual hindrance, 'for foul is useful and fair is not'. The time for fairness is not yet. The road to heaven is paved with bad intentions.

What is 'enough'?

I propose now to consider this proposition. It can be divided into three parts:

First, that universal prosperity is possible;

Second, that its attainment is possible on the basis of the materialist philosophy 'enrich yourselves';

Third, that this is the road to peace.

The question with which to start my investigation is obviously this: is there enough to go round? Immediately we encounter a serious difficulty: what is 'enough'? Who can tell us? Certainly not the economist who pursues 'economic growth' as the highest of all values, and therefore has no concept of 'enough'. There are poor societies which have too little; but where is the rich society that says: 'Halt! We have enough'? There is none.

Perhaps we can forget about 'enough' and content ourselves with exploring the growth of demand upon the world's resources which arises when everybody simply strives hard to have 'more'. As we cannot study all resources, I propose to focus attention on one type of resource which is in a somewhat central position – fuel. More prosperity means a greater use of fuel – there can be no doubt about that. At present, the prosperity gap between the poor of this world and the rich is very wide indeed, and this is clearly shown in their respective fuel consumption. Let us define as 'rich' all populations in countries with an average fuel consumption – in 1966 – of more than one metric ton of coal equivalent (abbreviated: c.e.) per head, and as 'poor' all those below this level.

On these definitions we can draw up the following table (using United Nations figures throughout):

TABLE 1 (*1966*)

	Rich	(%)	*Poor*	(%)	*World*	(%)
Population (millions)	1,060	(31)	2,284	(69)	3,344	(100)
Fuel Consumption (million tons c.e.)	4,788	(87)	721	(13)	5,509	(100)
Fuel Consumption per head (tons c.e.)	4.52		0.32		1.65	

The average fuel consumption per head of the 'poor' is only 0.32 tons, roughly one fourteenth of that of the 'rich', and there are very many 'poor' people in the world – on these definitions nearly seven-tenths of the world population. If the 'poor' suddenly used as much fuel as the 'rich', world fuel consumption would treble right away.

But this cannot happen as everything takes time. And in time both the 'rich' and the 'poor' are growing in desires and in numbers. So let us make an exploratory calculation. If the 'rich' populations grow at the rate of 1¼ per cent and the 'poor' at the rate of 2½ per cent a year, world population will grow to about 6,900 million by AD 2000 – a figure not very different from the most authoritative current forecasts. If at the same time the fuel consumption *per head* of the 'rich' population grows by 2¼ per cent, while that of the 'poor' grows by 4½ per cent a year, the following figures will emerge for the year 2000:

TABLE 2 (AD *2000*)

	Rich	(%)	*Poor*	(%)	*World*	(%)
Population (millions)	1,618	(23)	5,287	(77)	6,905	(100)
Fuel Consumption (million tons c.e.)	15,585	(67)	7,555	(33)	23,140	(100)
Fuel Consumption per head (tons c.e.)	9.63		1.43		3.35	

These exploratory calculations give rise to a number of comments: even after more than thirty years of rapid growth, the fuel consumption of the 'poor' would still be at poverty level.

Of the total *increase* of 17,630 million tons c.e. in world fuel consumption (an increase from 5,509 million tons in 1966 to 23,140 million tons in 2000), the 'rich' would take 10,800 million tons and the 'poor' only 6,800 million tons, although the 'poor' would be over three times as numerous as the rich.

The most important comment, however, is a question: is it plausible to assume that world fuel consumption *could* grow to anything like

23,000 million tons c.e. a year by the year 2000? If this growth took place during the thirty-four years in question about 400,000 million tons of c.e. would be used. In the light of our present knowledge of fossil fuel reserves this is an implausible figure, even if we assume that one-quarter or one-third of the world total would come from nuclear fission.

It is clear that the 'rich' are in the process of stripping the world of its once-for-all endowment of relatively cheap and simple fuels. It is their continuing economic growth which produces ever more exorbitant demands, with the result that the world's cheap and simple fuels could easily become dear and scarce long before the poor countries had acquired the wealth, education, industrial sophistication, and power of capital accumulation needed for the application of nuclear energy on any significant scale.

Exploratory calculations, of course, do not *prove* anything. A *proof* about the future is in any case impossible, and it has been sagely remarked that all predictions are unreliable, particularly those about the future. What is required is judgment, and exploratory calculations can at least help to inform our judgment. In any case, our calculations in a most important respect *understate* the magnitude of the problem. It is not realistic to treat the world as a unit. Fuel resources are very unevenly distributed, and any shortage of supplies, no matter how slight, would immediately divide the world into 'haves' and 'have-nots' along entirely novel lines. The specially favoured areas, such as the Middle East and North Africa, would attract envious attention on a scale scarcely imaginable today, while some high consumption areas, such as Western Europe and Japan, would move into the unenviable position of residual legatees. Here is a source of conflict if ever there was one.

Problem of pollution

As nothing can be *proved* about the future – not even about the relatively short-term future of the next thirty years – it is always possible to dismiss even the most threatening problems with the suggestion that something will turn up. There could be simply enormous and altogether unheard-of discoveries of new reserves of oil, natural gas, or even coal. And why should nuclear energy be confined to supplying one-quarter or one-third of total requirements? The problem can thus be shifted to another plane, but it refuses to go away. For the consumption of fuel on the indicated scale – assuming no insurmountable difficulties of fuel supply – would produce environmental hazards of an unprecedented kind.

Take nuclear energy. Some people say that the world's resources of relatively concentrated uranium are insufficient to sustain a really large nuclear programme – large enough to have a significant impact on the world fuel situation, where we have to reckon with thousands of millions, not simply with millions, of tons of coal equivalent. But assume that these people are wrong. Enough uranium will be found; it will be gathered together from the remotest corners of the earth, brought into the main centres of population, and made highly radio-active. It is hard to imagine a greater biological threat, not to mention the political danger that someone might use a tiny bit of this terrible substance for purposes not altogether peaceful.

On the other hand, if fantastic new discoveries of fossil fuels should make it unnecessary to force the pace of nuclear energy, there would be a problem of atmospheric pollution on quite a different scale from anything encountered hitherto.

Whatever the fuel, increases in fuel consumption by a factor of four and then five and then six . . . there is no plausible answer to the problem of pollution.

I have taken fuel merely as an example to illustrate a very simple thesis: that economic growth, which, viewed from the point of view of economics, physics, chemistry and technology, has no discernible limit, must necessarily run into decisive bottlenecks when viewed from the point of view of the environmental sciences. An attitude to life which seeks fulfilment in the single-minded pursuit of wealth – in short, materialism – does not fit into this world, because it contains within itself no limiting principle, while the environment in which it is placed is strictly limited. Already, the environment is trying to tell us that certain stresses are becoming excessive. As one problem is being 'solved', ten new problems arise as a result of the first 'solution'. As Professor Barry Commoner emphasizes, the new problems are not the consequences of incidental failure but of technological success.

Here again, however, many people will insist on discussing these matters solely in terms of optimism and pessimism, taking pride in their own optimism that 'science will find a way out'. They could be right only, I suggest, if there is a conscious and fundamental change in the *direction* of scientific effort. The developments of science and technology over the last hundred years have been such that the dangers have grown even faster than the opportunities. About this, I shall have more to say later.

Already, there is overwhelming evidence that the great self-balancing system of Nature is becoming increasingly unbalanced in particular respects and at specific points. It would take us too far if I attempted to assemble the evidence here. The condition of Lake Erie, to which Professor Barry Commoner, among others, has drawn attention, should serve as a sufficient warning. Another decade or two, and all the inland water systems of the United States may be in a similar condition. In other words, the condition of unbalance may then no longer apply to specific points but have become generalized. The further this process is allowed to go, the more difficult it will be to reverse it, if indeed the point of no return has not been passed already.

We find, therefore, that the idea of unlimited economic growth, more and more until everybody is saturated with wealth, needs to be seriously questioned on at least two counts: the availability of basic resources and, alternatively or additionally, the capacity of the environment to cope with the degree of interference implied. So much about the physical-material aspect of the matter. Let us now turn to certain non-material aspects.

There can be no doubt that the idea of personal enrichment has a very strong appeal to human nature. Keynes, in the essay from which I have quoted already, advised us that the time was not yet for a 'return to some of the most sure and certain principles of religion and traditional virtue – that avarice is a vice, that the exaction of usury is a misdemeanour, and the love of money is detestable.'

Economic progress, he counselled, is obtainable only if we employ those powerful human drives of selfishness, which religion and traditional wisdom universally call upon us to resist. The modern economy is propelled by a frenzy of greed and indulges in an orgy of envy, and these are not accidental features but the very causes of its expansionist success. The question is whether such causes can be effective for long or whether they carry within themselves the seeds of destruction. If Keynes says that 'foul is useful and fair is not', he propounds a statement of fact which may be true or false; or it may look true in the short run and turn out to be false in the longer run. Which is it?

I should think that there is now enough evidence to demonstrate that the statement is false in a very direct, practical sense. If human vices such as greed and envy are systematically cultivated, the inevitable result is nothing less than a collapse of intelligence. A man driven by greed or envy loses the power of seeing things as they really are, of seeing things in their roundness and wholeness, and his very successes become failures. If whole societies become infected by these vices, they may indeed achieve astonishing things but they become increasingly incapable of solving the most elementary problems of everyday existence. The Gross National Product may rise rapidly as measured by statisticians but not as experienced by actual people, who find themselves oppressed by increasing frustration, alienation, insecurity, and so forth. After a while, even the Gross National Product refuses to rise any further, not because of scientific or technological failure, but because of a creeping paralysis of non-co-operation, as expressed in various types of escapism, such as soaring crime, alcoholism, drug addiction, mental breakdown, and open rebellion on the part, not only of the oppressed and exploited, but even of highly privileged groups.

One can go on for a long time deploring the irrationality and stupidity of men and women in high positions or low, 'if only people would realize where their real interests lie!' But why do they not realize this? Either because their intelligence has been dimmed by greed and envy, or because in their heart of hearts they understand that their real interests lie somewhere quite different. There is a revolutionary saying that 'Man shall not live by bread alone but by every word of God'.

Here again, nothing can be 'proved'. But does it still look probable or plausible that the grave social diseases infecting many rich societies today are merely passing phenomena which an able government – if only we could get a really able government! – could eradicate by simply making a better use of science and technology or a more radical use of the penal system?

I suggest that the foundations of peace cannot be laid by universal prosperity, in the modern sense, because such prosperity, if attainable at all, is attainable only by cultivating such drives of human nature as greed and envy, which destroy intelligence, happiness, serenity, and thereby the peacefulness of man. It could well be that rich people treasure peace more highly than poor people, but only if they feel utterly secure – and this is a contradiction in terms. Their wealth depends on making inordinately large demands on limited world resources and thus puts them on an unavoidable collision course – not primarily with the poor (who are weak and defenceless) but with other rich people.

The economics of permanence

In short, we can say today that man is far too clever to be able to survive without Wisdom. No one is really working for peace unless he is working primarily for the restoration of Wisdom. The assertion that 'foul is useful and fair is not' is the antithesis of Wisdom. The hope that the pursuit of goodness and virtue can be postponed until we have attained universal prosperity and that by the single-minded pursuit of wealth, without bothering our heads about spiritual and moral questions, we could establish peace on earth, is an unrealistic, unscientific, and irrational hope. The exclusion of Wisdom from economics, science and technology was something which we could perhaps get away with for a little while, as long as we were relatively unsuccessful; but now that we have become very successful, the problem of spiritual and moral truth moves into the central position; in other words, we are far too clever to survive without Wisdom.

From an economic point of view, the central concept of Wisdom is Permanence. We must study the Economics of Permanence. Nothing makes economic sense unless its continuance for a long time can be projected without running into absurdities. There can be 'growth' towards a limited objective, but there cannot be unlimited, generalized growth. It is likely, as Gandhi said, that 'Earth provides enough to satisfy every man's need, but not for every man's greed'. Permanence is incompatible with a predatory attitude which rejoices in the fact that 'what were luxuries for our fathers have become necessities for us'.

The cultivation and expansion of needs is the antithesis of Wisdom. It is also the antithesis of freedom and peace. Every increase of needs tends to increase one's dependence on outside forces over which one cannot have control, and therefore increases existential fear. Only by a reduction of needs can one promote a genuine reduction in those tensions which are the ultimate causes of strife and war.

The Economics of Permanence implies a profound re-orientation of science and technology, which have to open their doors to Wisdom and, in fact, have to incorporate Wisdom into their very structure. Scientific or technological 'solutions' which poison the environment or degrade the social structure and man himself, are of no benefit, no matter how brilliantly conceived or how great their superficial attraction. Ever bigger machines, entailing ever bigger concentrations of economic power and exerting ever greater violence against the environment do not represent progress: they are a denial of Wisdom. Wisdom demands a new orientation of science and technology towards the organic, the gentle, the non-violent, the elegant and beautiful. Peace, as has often been said, is indivisible – how then could peace be built on a foundation of reckless science and violent technology? We must look for a revolution in technology to give us inventions and machines which reverse the destructive trends now threatening us all.

The virtues of cheapness

What is it that we really require from the scientists and technologists? I should answer: We need methods and equipment which are (*a*) cheap enough so that they are accessible to virtually everyone; (*b*) suitable for small-scale application; and (*c*) compatible with man's need for creativity.

Out of these three characteristics is born non-violence and a relationship of man to nature which guarantees permanence. If only one of these three is neglected, things are bound to go wrong. Let us look at them one by one.

Methods and machines cheap enough to be accessible to virtually everyone – why should we assume that our scientists and technologists are unable to develop them? This has been a primary concern of Gandhi's: 'I want the dumb millions of our land to be healthy and happy, and I want them to grow spiritually. As yet for this purpose we do not need the machine . . . If we feel the need of machines, we certainly will have them. Every machine that helps every individual has a place,' he said, 'but there should be no place for machines that concentrate power in a few hands and turn the masses into mere machine minders, if indeed they do not make them unemployed.'

Suppose it becomes the acknowledged purpose of inventors and engineers, observed Aldous Huxley, to provide ordinary people with the means of 'doing profitable and intrinsically significant work, of helping men and women to achieve independence from bosses, so that they may become their own employers, or members of a self-governing, co-operative group working for subsistence and a local market . . . this differently orientated technological progress (would result in) a progressive decentralization of population, of accessibility of land, of ownership of the means of production, of political and economic power.' Other advantages, said Huxley, would be 'a more humanly satisfying life for more people, a greater measure of genuine self-governing democracy and a blessed freedom from the silly or pernicious adult education provided by the mass producers of consumer goods through the medium of advertisements.'*

Self-help technology

If methods and machines are to be cheap enough to be generally accessible, this means that their cost must stand in some definable relationship to the level of incomes in the society in which they are to be used. I have myself come to the conclusion that the upper limit for the average amount of capital investment *per workplace* is probably given by the annual earnings of an able and ambitious industrial worker. That is to say, if such a man can normally earn, say, $3000 a year, the average cost of establishing one workplace should on no account be in excess of $3000. If the cost is significantly higher, the society in question is likely to run into serious troubles, such as an undue concentration of wealth and power among the privileged few; an increasing problem of 'drop-outs' who cannot be integrated into society and constitute an ever-growing threat; 'structural' unemployment; maldistribution of the population due to excessive urbanization, and general frustration and alienation, with soaring crime rates, etc.

To choose the appropriate level of technology is an absolutely vital matter for the (so-called) developing countries. It is in this connection that, some seven years ago, I began to talk of 'intermediate technology', and very energetic work has since been undertaken by the Intermediate Technology Development Group in London, and by others, to identify, develop and apply in developing countries a genuine self-help technology which involves the mass of the people, and not just the privileged few, which promotes the real independence of former colonial territories, and not just political independence nullified by economic subservience, and which thereby attempts to lay at least some of the essential foundations of freedom and peace.

The second requirement is suitability for small-scale application. On the problem of 'scale', Professor Leopold Kohr has written brilliantly and convincingly, and I do not propose to do more than emphasize its relevance to the Economics of Permanence. Small-scale operations, no matter how numerous, are always less likely to be harmful to the natural environment than large-scale ones, simply because their individual force is small in relation to the recuperative forces of nature. There is

* Quoted from *Towards New Horizons* by Pyarelal, a superbly excellent book.

Wisdom in smallness if only on account of the smallness and patchiness of human knowledge, which relies on experiment far more than on understanding. The greatest danger invariably arises from the ruthless application, on a vast scale, of partial knowledge, such as we are currently witnessing in the application of nuclear energy, of the new chemistry in agriculture, of transportation technology, and countless other things.

Although even small communities are sometimes guilty of causing serious erosion, generally as a result of ignorance, this is trifling in comparison with the devastations caused by large organizations motivated by greed, envy and the lust for power. It is moreover obvious that men organized in small units will take better care of *their* bit of land or other natural resources than anonymous companies or megalomanic governments which pretend to themselves that the whole universe is their legitimate quarry.

Creativity

The third requirement is perhaps the most important of all – that methods and equipment should be such as to leave ample room for human creativity. Over the last hundred years no one has spoken more insistently and warningly on this subject than have the Roman pontiffs. What becomes of man if the process of production 'takes away from work any hint of humanity, making of it a merely mechanical activity'? The worker himself is turned into a perversion of a free being.

> And so bodily labour [said Pius XI] which even after original sin was decreed by Providence for the good of man's body and soul, is in many instances changed into an instrument of perversion; for from the factory dead matter goes out improved, whereas men there are corrupted.

Again, the subject is so large that I cannot do more than touch upon it. Above anything else there is need for a proper philosophy of work which understands work not as that which it has indeed become, an inhuman chore as soon as possible to be abolished by automation, but as something 'decreed by Providence for the good of man's body and soul'. Next to the family, it is work and the relationships established by work that are the true foundations of society. If the foundations are unsound, how could society be sound? And if society is sick, how could it fail to be a danger to peace?

'War is a judgment that overtakes societies when they have been living upon ideas that conflict too violently with the laws governing the universe. . . . Never think that wars are irrational catastrophes: they happen when wrong ways of thinking and living bring about intolerable situations.' (Dorothy L. Sayers in *Creed or Chaos?*) Economically, our wrong living consists primarily in systematically cultivating greed and envy and thus building up a vast array of totally unwarrantable wants. It is the sin of Greed that has delivered us over into the power of the machine. If Greed were not the master of modern man – ably assisted by Envy – how could it be that the frenzy of economism does not abate as higher 'standards of living' are attained, and that it is precisely the richest societies which pursue their economic advantage with the greatest ruthlessness? How could we explain the almost universal refusal on the part of the rulers of the rich societies – whether organized along private enterprise or collectivist enterprise lines – to work towards the *humanization of work*? It is only necessary to assert that something would reduce the 'standard of living', and every debate is instantly closed. That soul-destroying, meaningless, mechanical, monotonous, moronic work is an insult to human nature which must necessarily and inevitably produce either escapism or aggression, and that no amount of 'bread and circuses' can compensate for the damage done – these are facts which are neither denied nor acknowledged but are met with an unbreakable conspiracy of silence, because to deny them would be too obviously absurd and to acknowledge them would condemn the central preoccupation of modern society as a crime against humanity.

The neglect, indeed, the rejection of Wisdom has gone so far that most of our intellectuals have not even the faintest idea what the term could mean. As a result, they always tend to try and cure a disease by intensifying its causes. The disease having been caused by allowing cleverness to displace Wisdom, no amount of clever research is likely to produce a cure. But what is Wisdom? Where can it be found? Here we come to the crux of the matter: it can be read about in numerous publications but it can be *found* only inside oneself. To be able to find it, one has first to liberate oneself interiorly from such masters as greed and envy. The stillness following liberation – even if only momentary – produces the insights of Wisdom which are obtainable in no other way.

They enable us to see the hollowness and fundamental unsatisfactoriness of a life devoted primarily to the pursuit of material ends, to the neglect of the spiritual. Such a life necessarily sets man against man and nation against nation, because man's needs are infinite and infinitude can be achieved only in the spiritual realm, never in the material. Man assuredly needs to rise above this humdrum 'world'; Wisdom shows him the way to do it; without Wisdom, he is driven to build up a monster economy, which destroys the world, and to seek fantastic satisfactions, like landing a man on the moon. Instead of overcoming the 'world' by moving towards saintliness, he tries to overcome it by gaining pre-eminence in wealth, power, science or indeed any imaginable 'sport'.

These are the real causes of war, and it is chimerical to try to lay the foundations of peace without removing them first. It is doubly chimerical to build peace on economic foundations which, in turn, rest on the systematic cultivation of greed and envy, the very forces which drive men into conflict.

How could we even begin to disarm greed and envy? Perhaps by being much less greedy and envious ourselves; perhaps by resisting the temptation of letting our luxuries become needs; and perhaps by even scrutinizing our needs to see if they cannot be simplified and reduced. If we do not have the strength to do any of this, could we perhaps stop applauding the type of economic 'progress' which palpably lacks the basis of permanence and give what modest support we can to those who, unafraid of being denounced as cranks, work for non-violence: as conservationists, ecologists, protectors of wild life, promoters of organic agriculture, distributists, cottage producers, and so forth? An ounce of practice is generally worth more than a ton of theory.

It will need many ounces, however, to lay the economic foundations of peace. Where can one find the strength to go on working against such obviously appalling odds? What is more: where can one find the strength to overcome the violence of greed, envy, hate and lust within oneself?

I think Gandhi has given the answer: 'There must be recognition of the existence of the soul apart from the body, and of its permanent nature, and this recognition must amount to a living faith; and, in the last resort, non-violence does not avail those who do not possess a living faith in the God of Love.'

The technological flaw

BARRY COMMONER

In the United States most of our serious pollution problems either began in the postwar years or have greatly worsened since then. While two factors frequently blamed for the environmental crisis, population and affluence, have intensified in that time, these increases are much too small to account for the 200 to 2000 per cent rise in pollution levels since 1946. The product of these two factors, which represents the total output of goods (total production equals population times production *per capita*), is also insufficient to account for the intensification of pollution. Total production – as measured by GNP – has increased by 126 per cent since 1946, while most pollution levels have risen by at least several times that rate. Something else besides growth in population and affluence must be deeply involved in the environmental crisis.

Not long ago, two of my colleagues and I went through the statistical tables* and selected from them the data for several hundred items, which together represent a major and representative part of over-all United States agricultural and industrial production. For each item, the average annual percentage change in production or consumption was computed for the years since 1946, or since the earliest date for which the statistics were available. Then we computed the over-all change for the entire twenty-five-year period – a twenty-five-year growth rate. When this list is rearranged in decreasing order of growth rate, a picture of *how* the United States economy has grown since World War II begins to emerge.

The winner of this economic sweepstake, with the highest postwar growth rate, is the production of non-returnable soda bottles, which has increased about 53,000 per cent in that time. The loser, ironically, is the horse; work animal horsepower has declined by 87 per cent of its original postwar value. The runners-up are an interesting but seemingly mixed bag. In second place is production of synthetic fibers, up 5980 per cent; third is mercury used for chlorine production, up 3930 per cent; succeeding places are held as follows: mercury used in mildew-resistant paint, up 3120 per cent; air conditioner compressor units, up 2850 per cent; plastics, up 1960 per cent; fertilizer nitrogen, up 1050 per cent; electric housewares (such as can-openers and corn-poppers), up 1040 per cent; synthetic organic chemicals, up 950 per cent; aluminum, up 680 per cent; chlorine gas, up 600 per cent; electric power, up 530 per cent; pesticides, up 390 per cent; wood pulp, up 313 per cent; truck freight, up 222 per cent; consumer electronics (TV sets, tape recorders), up 217 per cent; motor fuel consumption, up 190 per cent; cement, up 150 per cent.

Then there is a group of productive activities that, as indicated earlier, have grown at about the pace of the population (i.e., up about 42 per cent): food production and consumption, total production of textiles and clothes, household utilities, and steel, copper, and other basic metals.

Finally there are the losers, which increase more slowly than the population or actually shrink in total production: railroad freight, up 17 per cent; lumber, down 1 per cent; cotton fiber, down 7 per cent; returnable beer bottles, down 36 per cent; wool, down 42 per cent; soap, down 76 per cent; and, at the end of the line, work animal horsepower, down 87 per cent.

What emerges from all these data is striking evidence that while production for most basic needs – food, clothing, housing – has just about kept up with the 40 to 50 per cent or so increase in population (that is, production *per capita* has been essentially constant), the *kinds* of goods produced to meet these needs have changed drastically. New production technologies have displaced old ones. Soap powder has been displaced by synthetic detergents; natural fibers (cotton and wool) have been displaced by synthetic ones; steel and lumber have been displaced by aluminum, plastics, and concrete; railroad freight has been displaced by truck freight; returnable bottles have been displaced by non-returnable ones.

On the road, the low-powered automobile engines of the 1920s and 1930s have been displaced by high-powered ones. On the farm, while *per capita* production has remained about constant, the amount of harvested acreage has decreased; in effect, fertilizer has displaced land. Older methods of insect control have been displaced by synthetic insecticides, such as DDT, and for controlling weeds the cultivator has been displaced by the herbicide spray. Range-feeding of livestock has been displaced by feedlots.

In each of these cases, what has changed drastically is the technology of production rather than over-all output of the economic good. Of course, part of the economic growth in the United States since 1946 has been based on some newly introduced goods; air conditioners, television sets, tape recorders, and snowmobiles, all of which have increased absolutely without displacing an older product.

Distilled in this way, the mass of production statistics begins to form a meaningful pattern. In general, the growth of the United States economy since 1946 has had a surprisingly small effect on the degree to which individual needs for basic economic goods have been met. That statistical fiction, the 'average American', now consumes, each year, about as many calories, protein, and other foods (although somewhat less of vitamins); uses about the same amount of clothes and cleaners; occupies about the same amount of newly constructed housing; requires about as much freight; and drinks about the same amount of beer (twenty-six gallons *per capita*!) as he did in 1946. However, his food is now grown on less land with much more fertilizer and pesticides than before; his clothes are more likely to be made of synthetic fibers than of cotton or wool; he launders with synthetic detergents rather than soap; he lives and works in buildings that depend more heavily on aluminum, concrete, and plastic than on steel and lumber; the goods he uses are increasingly shipped by truck rather than rail; he drinks beer out of non-returnable bottles or cans rather than out of returnable bottles or at the tavern bar. He is more likely to live and work in air-conditioned surroundings than before. He also drives about twice as far as he did in 1946, in a heavier car, on synthetic rather than natural rubber tires, using more gasoline per mile, containing more tetraethyl lead, fed into an engine of increased horsepower and compression ratio.

These primary changes have led to others. To provide the raw materials needed for the new synthetic fibers, pesticides, detergents, plastics, and rubber, the production of synthetic organic chemicals has also grown very rapidly. The synthesis of organic chemicals uses a good deal of chlorine. Result: chlorine production has increased sharply. To make chlorine, an electric current is passed through a salt solution by way of a mercury electrode. Consequently, mercury consumption for this purpose has increased – by 3930 per cent in the twenty-five-year postwar period. Chemical products, along with cement for concrete and aluminum (also winners in the growth race), use rather large amounts of electric power. Not surprisingly, then, that item, too, has increased considerably since 1946.

All this reminds us of what we have already been told by advertising – which incidentally has *also* grown; for example, the use of newsprint for advertising has grown faster than its use for news – that we are blessed with an economy based on very modern technologies. What the advertisements do not tell us – as we are urged to buy synthetic shirts and detergents, aluminum furniture, beer in no-return bottles, and Detroit's latest creation – is that *all this 'progress' has greatly increased the impact on the environment.*

This pattern of economic growth is the major reason for the environmental crisis. A good deal of the mystery and confusion about the sudden emergence of the environmental crisis can be removed by pinpointing, pollutant by pollutant, how the postwar technological transformation of the United States economy has produced not only the much-heralded 126 per cent rise in GNP, but also, at a rate about ten times faster than the growth of GNP, the rising levels of environmental pollution.

Agriculture is perhaps the best example. To most people, the 'new technology' connotes computers, elaborate automation, nuclear power, and space exploration; these are the technologies that are often blamed for the discordant problems of our technological age. In comparison, the farm seems rather innocent. Yet, some of the most serious environmental failures can be traced to the technological transformation of the United States farm.

Among the many organized human activities, farming lies particularly close to nature. Before it was transformed by modern technology, the farm was no more than a place where, to serve the convenience of man, several quite natural biological activities were localized: the growth of plants in the soil and the nurture of animals on the crops. Plants and animals were nourished, grew, and reproduced by means long established in nature. Their interrelationships were equally natural; the crops withdrew nutrients, such as inorganic nitrogen, from the soil; the nutrients were derived by gradual bacterial action from the store of soil's organic matter; the organic store was maintained by the return of plant debris and animal wastes to the soil and by the fixation of nitrogen from the air into useful, organic form.

Here, the ecological cycles are nearly in balance, and with a little care, the natural fertility of soil can be maintained – as it has been, for example, in European countries and in many parts of the Orient – for centuries. Particularly important is the retention of animal manure in the soil and the similar utilization of every available scrap of vegetable matter –

including the return to the soil of the garbage generated in the cities by the food produced on the farm.

Almost every knowledgeable European observer who has visited the United States has been shocked by our carefree attitude toward soil husbandry. Not surprisingly, the American farmer has been in a constant struggle to survive economically. In the great Depression of the 1930s, some of the severest hardships were endured by farmers, as the soil was first degraded by poor husbandry and later literally lost to the winds and the rivers because of the resultant erosion. In the postwar period, new agricultural technology came to the rescue. This new technology has been so successful – as measured in the hard currency of the farmer's economic return – that it has become enshrined in a new kind of farm management so far removed from the ancient plan of farming as to merit a wholly new name – 'agribusiness'.

Agribusiness is founded on several technological developments, chiefly farm machinery, genetically controlled plant varieties, feedlots, inorganic fertilizers (especially nitrogen), and synthetic pesticides. But much of the new technology has been an ecological disaster; agribusiness is a main contributor to the environmental crisis.

Consider, for example, feedlots. Here cattle, removed from pasture, spend a considerable period of time being fattened in preparation for market. Since the animals are confined, their wastes become heavily deposited in a local area. The natural rate of conversion of organic waste to humus is limited, so that in a feedlot most of the nitrogenous waste is converted to soluble forms (ammonia and nitrate). This material is rapidly evaporated or leached into ground water beneath the soil or may run directly into surface waters during rainstorms. This is responsible, in part, for the appearance of high nitrate levels in some rural wells supplied by ground water, and for serious pollution problems due to algal overgrowths in a number of streams in the Midwest. Where untreated feedlot manure is allowed to reach surface water, it imposes a heavy oxygen demand on streams that may be already overloaded by municipal wastes.

A livestock animal produces much more waste than a human being. Much of this waste is now confined to feedlots. For example, in 1966 more than ten million cattle were maintained in feedlots before slaughter, an increase of 66 per cent over the preceding eight years. This represents about one-half of the total United States cattle population. Feedlots now produce more organic waste than the total sewage from all US municipalities. Our sewage disposal problem is, in effect, more than twice its usually estimated size.

The physical separation of livestock from the soil is related to an even more complex chain of events, which again leads to severe ecological problems. Animals confined in feedlots are supplied with grain rather than pasturage. When, as it has been in much of the Midwest, the soil is used for intensive grain production rather than pasturage, the humus content is depleted; farmers then resort to increasingly heavy applications of inorganic fertilizer, especially of nitrogen, setting off the ecologically disruptive sequence that has already been described.

At this point, a fertilizer salesman – and some agronomists – might counter with the argument that feedlots and intensive use of fertilizer have been essential to increase food production enough to keep up with the rising population of the United States and the world. The actual statistics on this matter are worth some attention, for they shed a new light not only on the role of new technologies in agricultural production, but also on the pollution problem.

Between 1949 and 1968 total United States agricultural production increased by about 45 per cent. Since the United States population grew by 34 per cent in that time, the over-all increase in production was just about enough to keep up with population; crop production *per capita* increased 6 per cent. In that period, the annual use of fertilizer nitrogen increased by 648 per cent, surprisingly larger than the increase in crop production. One reason for this disparity also turns up in the agricultural statistics: between 1949 and 1968 harvested acreage *declined* by 16 per cent. Clearly, more crop was being produced on less land (the yield per acre increased by 77 per cent). Intensive use of fertilizer nitrogen is the most important means of achieving this improvement in yield per acre. Thus, the intensive use of fertilizer nitrogen allowed 'agribusiness' to just about meet the population's need for food – and at the same time to reduce the acreage used for that purpose.

These same statistics also explain the resulting water pollution problem. In 1949, an average of about 11,000 tons of fertilizer nitrogen were used *per USDA unit of crop production*, while in 1968 about 57,000 tons of nitrogen were used for the *same* crop yield. This means that the efficiency with which nitrogen contributes to the growth of the crop declined fivefold. Obviously, a good deal of the fertilizer nitrogen did not enter the crop and must have ended up elsewhere in the ecosystem.

In Illinois, on the average, in 1949 about 20,000 tons of fertilizer nitrogen were used to produce a corn yield of about 50 bushels per acre. In 1968 the area used about 600,000 tons of nitrogen to produce an average of about 93 bushels of corn per acre. The reason for the disparity between the increase in fertilizer and in yield is a biological one: the corn plant, after all, does have a limited capacity for growth, so that more and more fertilizer must be used to force the plant to produce the last few bushels of increased yield. Therefore, in order to achieve such high yields the farmer *must* use more nitrogen than the plant can take up. Much of the leftover nitrogen leaches from the soil and pollutes the rivers; it is literally impossible to obtain such high fertilizer-induced yields without polluting the environment. And given the farmer's present economic situation, he cannot survive *unless* he pollutes. The economic break-even point in the area is in the range of 80 bushels of corn per acre; to get the last 20 bushels of corn that mean the difference between profit and loss, the farmer must nearly double his use of fertilizer nitrogen. But only part of the added nitrogen goes into the crop; the difference goes into the river and pollutes water supplies.

What the new fertilizer technology has accomplished for the farmer is clear: more crop can be produced on less acreage than before. Since the cost of fertilizer, relative to the resultant gain in crop sales, is lower than that of any other economic input, and since the Land Bank pays the farmer for acreage not in crops, the new technology pays him well. The cost – in environmental degradation – is borne by his neighbors in town who find their water polluted. The new technology is an economic success – but only because it is an ecological failure.

It is useful, at this point, to ask what are the relative effects of the three factors that might be expected to influence the intensity of environmental pollution – population size, degree of affluence, and the tendency of the productive technology to pollute? A rather simple mathematical relationship connects the amount of pollutant emitted into the environment to these factors: pollutant emitted is equal to the product of the three factors – population times the amount of a given economic good *per capita* times output of pollutant per unit of the economic good produced. In the United States all three factors have changed since 1946. By comparing these changes with the concurrent increase in total pollutant output, it is possible to assign to each of the three factors the fraction of the over-all increase in pollutant output for which it is responsible. When this computation is carried out for such economic goods as agricultural production (pollutant outputs: nitrogen fertilizer, pesticides), cleaners (pollutant output: phosphate), passenger car travel (pollutant outputs: lead and nitrogen oxides), and beer consumption (pollutant output: beer bottles) – a rather clear picture emerges.

The increase in population accounts for from 12 to 20 per cent of the various increases in total pollutant output since 1946. The affluence factor (i.e., amount of economic good *per capita*), accounts for from 1 to 5 per cent of the total increase in pollutant output, except in the case of passenger travel, where the contribution rises to about 40 per cent of the total. This reflects a considerable increase in vehicle miles traveled *per capita*. However, as already pointed out, a good deal of this increase does not reflect improved welfare, but rather the unfortunate need for increased travel incident upon the decay of the inner cities and the growth of suburbs. The technology factor – that is, the increased output of pollutants per unit production resulting from the introduction of new productive technologies since 1946 – accounts for 80 to 85 per cent of the total output of pollutants, except in the case of passenger travel, where it accounts for about 40 per cent of the total.

The foregoing conclusions are based on those instances in which quantitative data on pollution output of various productive activities are available. However, qualitative evidence on other pollution problems shows that they follow a similar pattern: most of the sharp increase in pollution levels is due not so much to population or affluence as to changes in productive technology.

The over-all evidence seems clear. The chief reason for the environmental crisis that has engulfed the United States in recent years is the sweeping transformation of productive technology since World War II. The economy has grown enough to give the United States population about the same amount of basic goods, *per capita*, as it did in 1946. However, productive technologies with intense impacts on the environment have displaced less destructive ones. The environmental crisis is the inevitable result of this counterecological pattern of growth.

We live in a time that is dominated by enormous technical power and extreme human need. The power is painfully self-evident in the megawattage of power plants, and in the megatonnage of nuclear bombs. The human need is evident in the sheer numbers of people now and soon to be living, in the deterioration of their habitat, the earth, and in the tragic world-wide epidemic of hunger and want. The gap between brute power and human need continues to grow, as the power fattens on the same faulty technology that intensifies the need.

Everywhere in the world there is evidence of a deep-seated failure in the effort to use the competence, the wealth, the power at human disposal for the maximum good of human beings. The environmental crisis is a major example of this failure. For we are in an environmental crisis because the means by which we use the ecosphere to produce wealth are destructive of the ecosphere itself. The present system of production is self-destructive; the present course of human civilization is suicidal.

The environmental crisis is somber evidence of an insidious fraud hidden in the vaunted productivity and wealth of modern, technology-based society. This wealth has been gained by rapid short-term exploitation of the environmental system, but it has blindly accumulated a debt to nature (in the form of environmental destruction in developed countries and of population pressure in developing ones) – a debt so large and so pervasive that in the next generation it may, if unpaid, wipe out most of the wealth it has gained us. In effect, the account books of modern society are drastically out of balance, so that, largely unconsciously, a huge fraud has been perpetrated on the people of the world. The rapidly worsening course of environmental pollution is a warning that the bubble is about to burst, that the demand to pay the global debt may find the world bankrupt.

This does *not* necessarily mean that to survive the environmental crisis, the people of industrialized nations will need to give up their 'affluent' way of life. For as shown earlier, this 'affluence', as judged by conventional measures – such as GNP, power consumption, and production of metals – is itself an illusion. To a considerable extent it reflects ecologically faulty, socially wasteful types of production rather than the actual welfare of individual human beings. Therefore, the needed productive reforms can be carried out without seriously reducing the present level of *useful* goods available to the individual; and, at the same time, by controlling pollution the quality of life can be improved significantly.

There are, however, certain luxuries which the environmental crisis, and the approaching bankruptcy that it signifies, will, I believe, force us to give up. These are the *political* luxuries which have so long been enjoyed by those who can benefit from them: the luxury of allowing the wealth of the nation to serve preferentially the interests of so few of its citizens; of failing fully to inform citizens of what they need to know in order to exercise their right of political governance; of condemning as anathema any suggestion which re-examines basic economic values; of burying the issues revealed by logic in a morass of self-serving propaganda.

To resolve the environmental crisis, we shall need to forego, at last, the luxury of tolerating poverty, racial discrimination, and war. In our unwitting march toward ecological suicide we have run out of options. Now that the bill for the environmental debt has been presented, our options have become reduced to two: either the rational, social organization of the use and distribution of the earth's resources, or a new barbarism.

This iron logic has recently been made explicit by one of the most insistent proponents of population control, Garrett Hardin. Over recent years he has expounded on the 'tragedy of the commons' – the view that the world ecosystem is like a common pasture where each individual, guided by a desire for personal gain, increases his herd until the pasture is ruined for all. Until recently, Hardin drew two rather general conclusions from this analogy: first, that 'freedom in a commons brings ruin to all', and second, that the freedom which must be constrained if ruin is to be avoided is not the derivation of private gain from a social good (the commons), but rather 'the freedom to breed'.

Hardin's logic is clear, and follows the course outlined earlier: if we accept as unchangeable the present governance of a social good (the commons, or the ecosphere) by private need, then survival requires the immediate, drastic limitation of population. Very recently, Hardin has carried this course of reasoning to its logical conclusion; in an editorial in *Science*, he asserts:

> Every day we [i.e., Americans] are a smaller minority. We are increasing at only one per cent a year; the rest of the world increases twice as fast. By the year 2000, one person in twenty-four will be an American; in one hundred years only one in forty-six. . . . If the world is one great commons,

> in which all food is shared equally, then we are lost. Those who breed faster will replace the rest. . . . In the absence of breeding control a policy of 'one mouth one meal' ultimately produces one totally miserable world. In a less than perfect world, the allocation of rights based on territory must be defended if a ruinous breeding race is to be avoided. It is unlikely that civilization and dignity can survive everywhere; but better in a few places than in none. Fortunate minorities must act as the trustees of a civilization that is threatened by uninformed good intentions.

Here, only faintly masked, is barbarism. It denies the equal right of all the human inhabitants of the earth to a humane life. It would condemn most of the people of the world to the material level of the barbarian, and the rest, the 'fortunate minorities', to the moral level of the barbarian. Neither within Hardin's tiny enclaves of 'civilization', nor in the larger world around them, would anything that we seek to preserve – the dignity and the humaneness of man, the grace of civilization – survive.

In the narrow options that are possible in a world gripped by environmental crisis, there is no apparent alternative between barbarism and the acceptance of the economic consequence of the ecological imperative – that the social, global nature of the ecosphere must determine a corresponding organization of the productive enterprises that depend on it.

One of the common responses to a recitation of the world's environmental ills is a deep pessimism, which is perhaps the natural aftermath to the shock of recognizing that the vaunted 'progress' of modern civilization is only a thin cloak for global catastrophe. I am convinced, however, that once we pass beyond the mere awareness of impending disaster and begin to understand *why* we have come to the present predicament, and where the alternative paths ahead can lead, there is reason to find in the very depths of the environmental crisis itself a source of optimism.

There is, for example, cause for optimism in the very complexity of the issues generated by the environmental crisis; once the links between the separate parts of the problem are perceived, it becomes possible to see new means of solving the whole. Thus, confronted separately, the need of developing nations for new productive enterprises, and the need of industrialized countries to reorganize theirs along ecologically sound lines, may seem hopelessly difficult. However, when the link between the two – the ecological significance of the introduction of synthetic substitutes for natural products – is recognized, ways of solving both can be seen. In the same way, we despair over releasing the grip of the United States on so much of the world's resources until it becomes clear how much of this 'affluence' stresses the environment rather than contributes to human welfare. Then the very magnitude of the present United States share of the world's resources is a source of hope – for its reduction through ecological reform can then have a large and favorable impact on the desperate needs of the developing nations.

I find another source of optimism in the very nature of the environmental crisis. It is not the product of man's *biological* capabilities, which could not change in time to save us, but of his *social* actions – which are subject to much more rapid change. Since the environmental crisis is the result of the social mismanagement of the world's resources, then it can be resolved and man can survive in a humane condition when the social organization of man is brought into harmony with the ecosphere.

Here we can learn a basic lesson from nature: that nothing can survive on the planet unless it is a cooperative part of a larger, global whole. Life itself learned that lesson on the primitive earth. For it will be recalled that the earth's first living things, like modern man, consumed their nutritive base as they grew, converting the geo-chemical store of organic matter into wastes which could no longer serve their needs. Life, as it first appeared on the earth, was embarked on a linear, self-destructive course.

What saved life from extinction was the invention, in the course of evolution, of a new life-form which reconverted the waste of the primitive organisms into fresh, organic matter. The first photosynthetic organisms transformed the rapacious, linear course of life into the earth's first great ecological cycle. By closing the circle, they achieved what no living organism, alone, can accomplish – survival.

Human beings have broken out of the circle of life, driven not by biological need, but by the social organization which they have devised to 'conquer' nature: means of gaining wealth that are governed by requirements conflicting with those which govern nature. The end result is the environmental crisis, a crisis of survival. Once more, to survive, we must close the circle. We must learn how to restore to nature the wealth that we borrow from it.

The historical roots of our ecologic crisis

LYNN WHITE, Jr

A conversation with Aldous Huxley not infrequently put one at the receiving end of an unforgettable monologue. About a year before his lamented death he was discoursing on a favorite topic: man's unnatural treatment of nature and its sad results. To illustrate his point he told how, during the previous summer, he had returned to a little valley in England where he had spent many happy months as a child. Once it had been composed of delightful grassy glades; now it was becoming overgrown with unsightly brush because the rabbits that formerly kept such growth under control had largely succumbed to a disease, myxomatosis, that was deliberately introduced by the local farmers to reduce the rabbits' destruction of crops. Being something of a Philistine, I could be silent no longer, even in the interest of great rhetoric. I interrupted to point out that the rabbit itself had been brought as a domestic animal to England in 1176, presumably to improve the protein diet of the peasantry.

All forms of life modify their contexts. The most spectacular and benign instance is doubtless the coral polyp. By serving its own ends, it has created a vast undersea world favorable to thousands of other kinds of animals and plants. Ever since man became a numerous species he has affected his environment notably. The hypothesis that his fire-drive method of hunting created the world's grasslands and helped to exterminate the monster mammals of the Pleistocene from much of the globe is plausible, if not proved. Quite unintentionally, changes in human ways often affect non-human nature. It has been noted, for example, that the advent of the automobile eliminated huge flocks of sparrows that once fed on the horse manure littering every street.

The history of ecologic change is still so rudimentary that we know little about what really happened, or what the results were. The extinction of the European aurochs as late as 1627 would seem to have been a simple case of overenthusiastic hunting. On more intricate matters it often is impossible to find solid information. For a thousand years or more the Frisians and Hollanders have been pushing back the North Sea,

Extracts from an article in *Science*, Vol. 155, pp. 1203–7, 10 March 1967.

and the process is culminating in our own time in the reclamation of the Zuider Zee. What, if any, species of animals, birds, fish, shore life, or plants have died out in the process? In their epic combat with Neptune have the Netherlanders overlooked ecological values in such a way that the quality of human life in the Netherlands has suffered? I cannot discover that the questions have ever been asked, much less answered.

People, then, have often been a dynamic element in their own environment, but in the present state of historical scholarship we usually do not know exactly when, where, or with what effects man-induced changes came. As we enter the last third of the twentieth century, however, concern for the problem of ecologic backlash is mounting feverishly. Natural science, conceived as the effort to understand the nature of things, had flourished in several eras and among several peoples. Similarly there had been an age-old accumulation of technological skills, sometimes growing rapidly, sometimes slowly. But it was not until about four generations ago that Western Europe and North America arranged a marriage between science and technology, a union of the theoretical and the empirical approaches to our natural environment. The emergence in widespread practice of the Baconian creed that scientific knowledge means technological power over nature can scarcely be dated before about 1850, save in the chemical industries, where it is anticipated in the eighteenth century. Its acceptance as a normal pattern of action may mark the greatest event in human history since the invention of agriculture, and perhaps in non-human terrestrial history as well.

Almost at once the new situation forced the crystallization of the novel concept of ecology; indeed, the word *ecology* first appeared in the English language in 1873. Today, less than a century later, the impact of our race upon the environment has so increased in force that it has changed in essence. When the first cannons were fired, in the early fourteenth century, they affected ecology by sending workers scrambling to the forests and mountains for more potash, sulfur, iron ore, and charcoal, with some resulting erosion and deforestation. Hydrogen bombs are of a different order: a war fought with them might alter the genetics of all life on this planet. By 1285 London had a smog problem arising from the burning of soft coal, but our present combustion of fossil fuels threatens to change the chemistry of the globe's atmosphere as a whole, with consequences which we are only beginning to guess. With the population explosion, the carcinoma of planless urbanism, the now geological deposits of sewage and garbage, surely no creature other than man has ever managed to foul its nest in such short order.

There are many calls to action, but specific proposals, however worthy as individual items, seem too partial, palliative, negative: ban the bomb, tear down the billboards, give the Hindus contraceptives and tell them to eat their sacred cows. The simplest solution to any suspect change is, of course, to stop it, or, better yet, to revert to a romanticized past: make those ugly gasoline stations look like Anne Hathaway's cottage or (in the Far West) like ghost-town saloons. The 'wilderness area' mentality invariably advocates deep-freezing an ecology, whether San Gimignano or the High Sierra, as it was before the first Kleenex was dropped. But neither atavism nor prettification will cope with the ecologic crisis of our time.

What shall we do? No one yet knows. Unless we think about fundamentals, our specific measures may produce new backlashes more serious than those they are designed to remedy.

Since both our technological and our scientific movements got their start, acquired their character, and achieved world dominance in the Middle Ages, it would seem that we cannot understand their nature or their present impact upon ecology without examining fundamental medieval assumptions and developments.

Medieval view of man and nature

Until recently, agriculture has been the chief occupation even in 'advanced' societies; hence, any change in methods of tillage has much importance. Early plows, drawn by two oxen, did not normally turn the sod but merely scratched it. Thus, cross-plowing was needed and fields tended to be squarish. In the fairly light soils and semiarid climates of the Near East and Mediterranean, this worked well. But such a plow was inappropriate to the wet climate and often sticky soils of northern Europe. By the latter part of the seventh century after Christ, however, following obscure beginnings, certain northern peasants were using an entirely new kind of plow, equipped with a vertical knife to cut the line of the furrow, a horizontal share to slice under the sod, and a moldboard to turn it over. The friction of this plow with the soil was so great that it normally required not two but eight oxen. It attacked the land with such violence that cross-plowing was not needed, and fields tended to be shaped in long strips.

In the days of the scratch-plow, fields were distributed generally in units capable of supporting a single family. Subsistence farming was the presupposition. But no peasant owned eight oxen: to use the new and more efficient plow, peasants pooled their oxen to form large plow-teams, originally receiving (it would appear) plowed strips in proportion to their contribution. Thus, distribution of land was based no longer on the needs of a family but, rather, on the capacity of a power machine to till the earth. Man's relation to the soil was profoundly changed. Formerly man had been part of nature; now he was the exploiter of nature. Nowhere else in the world did farmers develop any analogous agricultural implement. Is it coincidence that modern technology, with its ruthlessness toward nature, has so largely been produced by descendants of these peasants of northern Europe?

This same exploitive attitude appears slightly before AD 830 in Western illustrated calendars. In older calendars the months were shown as passive personifications. The new Frankish calendars, which set the style for the Middle Ages, are very different: they show men coercing the world around them – plowing, harvesting, chopping trees, butchering pigs. Man and nature are two things, and man is master.

These novelties seem to be in harmony with larger intellectual patterns. What people do about their ecology depends on what they think about themselves in relation to things around them. Human ecology is deeply conditioned by beliefs about our nature and destiny – that is, by religion. To Western eyes this is very evident in, say, India or Ceylon. It is equally true of ourselves and of our medieval ancestors.

The victory of Christianity over paganism was the greatest psychic revolution in the history of our culture. It has become fashionable today to say that, for better or worse, we live in 'the post-Christian age'. Certainly the forms of our thinking and language have largely ceased to be Christian, but to my eye the substance often remains amazingly akin to that of the past. Our daily habits of action, for example, are dominated by an implicit faith in perpetual progress which was unknown either to Greco–Roman antiquity or to the Orient. It is rooted in, and is indefensible apart from, Judeo–Christian teleology. The fact that Communists share it merely helps to show what can be demonstrated on many other grounds: that Marxism, like Islam, is a Judeo–Christian heresy. We continue today to live, as we have lived for about 1700 years, very largely in a context of Christian axioms.

What did Christianity tell people about their relations with the environment?

While many of the world's mythologies provide stories of creation, Greco–Roman mythology was singularly incoherent in this respect. Like Aristotle, the intellectuals of the ancient West denied that the visible world had had a beginning. Indeed, the idea of a beginning was impossible in the framework of their cyclical notion of time. In sharp contrast, Christianity inherited from Judaism not only a concept of time as nonrepetitive and linear but also a striking story of creation. By gradual stages a loving and all-powerful God had created light and darkness, the heavenly bodies, the earth and all its plants, animals, birds, and fishes. Finally, God had created Adam and, as an afterthought, Eve to keep man from being lonely. Man named all the animals, thus establishing his dominance over them. God planned all of this explicitly for man's benefit and rule: no item in the physical creation had any purpose save to serve man's purposes. And, although man's body is made of clay, he is not simply part of nature: he is made in God's image.

Especially in its Western form, Christianity is the most anthropocentric religion the world has seen. As early as the second century both Tertullian and Saint Irenaeus of Lyons were insisting that when God shaped Adam he was foreshadowing the image of the incarnate Christ, the Second Adam. Man shares, in great measure, God's transcendence of nature. Christianity, in absolute contrast to ancient paganism and Asia's religions (except, perhaps, Zoroastrianism), not only established a dualism of man and nature but also insisted that it is God's will that man exploit nature for his proper ends.

At the level of the common people this worked out in an interesting way. In antiquity every tree, every spring, every stream, every hill had its own *genius loci*, its guardian spirit. These spirits were accessible to men, but were very unlike men; centaurs, fauns and mermaids show their ambivalence. Before one cut a tree, mined a mountain, or dammed a brook, it was important to placate the spirit in charge of that particular situation, and to keep it placated. By destroying pagan animism, Christianity made it possible to exploit nature in a mood of indifference to the feelings of natural objects.

It is often said that for animism the Church substituted the cult of saints. True; but the cult of saints is functionally quite different from animism. The saint is not *in* natural objects; he may have special shrines, but his citizenship is in heaven. Moreover, a saint is entirely a man; he can be approached in human terms. In addition to saints, Christianity of course also had angels and demons inherited from Judaism and perhaps, at one remove, from Zoroastrianism. But these were all as mobile as the saints themselves. The spirits *in* natural objects, which formerly had protected nature from man, evaporated. Man's effective monopoly on spirit in this world was confirmed, and the old inhibitions to the exploitation of nature crumbled.

When one speaks in such sweeping terms, a note of caution is in order. Christianity is a complex faith, and its consequences differ in differing contexts. What I have said may well apply to the medieval West, where in fact technology made spectacular advances. But the Greek East, a highly civilized realm of equal Christian devotion, seems to have produced no marked technological innovation after the late seventh century, when Greek fire was invented. The key to the contrast may perhaps be found in a difference in the tonality of piety and thought which students of comparative theology find between the Greek and the Latin Churches. The Greeks believed that sin was intellectual blindness, and that salvation was found in illumination, orthodoxy – that is, clear thinking. The Latins, on the other hand, felt that sin was moral evil, and that salvation was to be found in right conduct. Eastern theology has been intellectualist. Western theology has been voluntarist. The Greek saint contemplates; the Western saint acts. The implications of Christianity for the conquest of nature would emerge more easily in the Western atmosphere.

The Christian dogma of creation, which is found in the first clause of all the Creeds, has another meaning for our comprehension of today's ecologic crisis. By revelation, God had given man the Bible, the Book of Scripture. But since God had made nature, nature also must reveal the divine mentality. The religious study of nature for the better understanding of God was known as natural theology. In the early Church, and always in the Greek East, nature was conceived primarily as a symbolic system through which God speaks to men: the ant is a sermon to sluggards; rising flames are the symbol of the soul's aspiration. This view of nature was essentially artistic rather than scientific. While Byzantium preserved and copied great numbers of ancient Greek scientific texts, science as we conceive it could scarcely flourish in such an ambience.

However, in the Latin West by the early thirteenth century natural theology was following a very different bent. It was ceasing to be the decoding of the physical symbols of God's communication with man and was becoming the effort to understand God's mind by discovering how his creation operates. The rainbow was no longer simply a symbol of hope first sent to Noah after the Deluge: Robert Grosseteste, Friar Roger Bacon, and Theodoric of Freiberg produced startlingly sophisticated work on the optics of the rainbow, but they did it as a venture in religious understanding. From the thirteenth century onward, up to and including Leibniz and Newton, every major scientist, in effect, explained his motivations in religious terms. Indeed, if Galileo had not been so expert an amateur theologian he would have got into far less trouble: the professionals resented his intrusion. And Newton seems to have regarded himself more as a theologian than as a scientist. It was not until the late eighteenth century that the hypothesis of God became unnecessary to many scientists.

It is often hard for the historian to judge, when men explain why they are doing what they want to do, whether they are offering real reasons or merely culturally acceptable reasons. The consistency with which scientists during the long formative centuries of Western science said that the task and the reward of the scientist was 'to think God's thoughts after him' leads one to believe that this was their real motivation. If so, then modern Western science was cast in a matrix of Christian theology. The dynamism of religious devotion, shaped by the Judeo–Christian dogma of creation, gave it impetus.

An alternative Christian view

We would seem to be headed toward conclusions unpalatable to many Christians. Since both *science* and *technology* are blessed words in our contemporary vocabulary, some may be happy at the notions, first, that, viewed historically, modern science is an extrapolation of natural theology and, second, that modern technology is at least partly to be explained as an Occidental, voluntarist realization of the Christian dogma of man's transcendence of, and rightful mastery over, nature. But, as we now recognize, somewhat over a century ago science and technology – hitherto quite separate activities – joined to give mankind powers which, to judge by many of the ecologic effects, are out of control. If so, Christianity bears a huge burden of guilt.

I personally doubt that disastrous ecologic backlash can be avoided simply by applying to our problems more science and more technology. Our science and technology have grown out of Christian attitudes toward man's relation to nature which are almost universally held not only by Christians and neo-Christians but also by those who fondly regard themselves as post-Christians. Despite Copernicus, all the cosmos rotates around our little globe. Despite Darwin, we are *not*, in our hearts, part of the natural process. We are superior to nature, contemptuous of it, willing to use it for our slightest whim. The newly elected Governor of California, like myself a churchman but less troubled than I, spoke for the Christian tradition when he said (as is alleged), 'when you've seen one redwood tree, you've seen them all'. To a Christian a tree can be no more than a physical fact. The whole concept of the sacred grove is alien to Christianity and to the ethos of the West. For nearly two millennia Christian missionaries have been chopping down sacred groves, which are idolatrous because they assume spirit in nature.

What we do about ecology depends on our ideas of the man–nature relationship. More science and more technology are not going to get us out of the present ecologic crisis until we find a new religion, or rethink our old one. The beatniks, who are the basic revolutionaries of our time, show a sound instinct in their affinity for Zen Buddhism, which conceives of the man–nature relationship as very nearly the mirror image of the Christian view. Zen, however, is as deeply conditioned by Asian history as Christianity is by the experience of the West, and I am dubious of its viability among us.

Possibly we should ponder the greatest radical in Christian history since Christ: Saint Francis of Assisi. The prime miracle of Saint Francis is the fact that he did not end at the stake, as many of his left-wing followers did. He was so clearly heretical that a General of the Franciscan Order, Saint Bonaventura, a great and perceptive Christian, tried to suppress the early accounts of Franciscanism. The key to an understanding of Francis is his belief in the virtue of humility – not merely for the individual but for man as a species. Francis tried to depose man from his monarchy over creation and set up a democracy of all God's creatures. With him the ant is no longer simply a homily for the lazy, flames a sign of the thrust of the soul toward union with God; now they are Brother Ant and Sister Fire, praising the Creator in their own ways as Brother Man does in his.

Later commentators have said that Francis preached to the birds as a rebuke to men who would not listen. The records do not read so: he urged the little birds to praise God, and in spiritual ecstasy they flapped their wings and chirped rejoicing. Legends of saints, especially the Irish saints, had long told of their dealings with animals but always, I believe, to show their human dominance over creatures. With Francis it is different. The land around Gubbio in the Apennines was being ravaged by a fierce wolf. Saint Francis, says the legend, talked to the wolf and persuaded him of the error of his ways. The wolf repented, died in the odor of sanctity, and was buried in consecrated ground.

I am not suggesting that many contemporary Americans who are concerned about our ecologic crisis will be either able or willing to counsel with wolves or exhort birds. However, the present increasing disruption of the global environment is the product of a dynamic technology and science which were originating in the Western medieval world against which Saint Francis was rebelling in so original a way. Their growth cannot be understood historically apart from distinctive attitudes toward nature which are deeply rooted in Christian dogma. The fact that most people do not think of these attitudes as Christian is irrelevant. No new set of basic values has been accepted in our society to displace those of Christianity. Hence we shall continue to have a worsening ecologic crisis until we reject the Christian axiom that nature has no reason for existence save to serve man.

The greatest spiritual revolutionary in Western history, Saint Francis, proposed what he thought was an alternative Christian view of nature and man's relation to it: he tried to substitute the idea of the equality of all creatures, including man, for the idea of man's limitless rule of creation. He failed. Both our present science and our present technology are so tinctured with orthodox Christian arrogance toward nature that no solution for our ecologic crisis can be expected from them alone. Since the roots of our trouble are so largely religious, the remedy must also be essentially religious, whether we call it that or not. We must rethink and refeel our nature and destiny. The profoundly religious, but heretical, sense of the primitive Franciscans for the spiritual autonomy of all parts of nature may point a direction. I propose Francis as a patron saint for ecologists.

The sacramental vision of nature

THEODORE ROSZAK

In my book *The Making of a Counter Culture* I tried to trace how deep youthful disaffiliation has gone in the United States and perhaps throughout much of the rest of the Western developed world. There are obviously many levels and nuances to this disaffiliation; it includes a lot of unfinished business in the United States like racial prejudice, and capitalist profiteering, and any number of other demands for social justice that have been on the radical political agenda for a very long time. But I think the most potentially important aspect of this disaffiliation arises where the counter culture begins to diverge markedly from something that has not been very seriously questioned in the mainstream of Western society for a few hundred years at least, and that is the scientific and technological tradition of our culture. This is the tradition we have long understood to represent 'Progress', 'Reason', and human dignity. The interest in drugs, oriental religions, mysticism, the occult, and in a great deal of what is now called in the United States 'affective education', or the 'human potentials movement' (stemming from growth centres like Esalen in California) represents a radical departure from scientific orthodoxy.

At the same time, this dissenting culture has also been marked by an intense interest in ecology, and there would seem to be a paradox. Ecology, after all, has all the appearances of being a scientific subject matter; and yet, I dare say there would not be any environmental politics in the United States if it had not been for the widespread interest of the counter cultural young in ecology. I have the feeling that ecology is perhaps the last rather tenuous link that the counter culture has with the scientific tradition. For what many young people see in ecology is a science that borders on mysticism. And in this fact there lies hidden a potential crisis for ecological thought and environmental politics. I want to discuss this crisis, which I suspect will surface within the next few years and which may very well split the ecological movement.

Perhaps I can illustrate the problem by quoting a few passages to you. Let me begin with two selections from American Indian literature.

This article, which is based on a recorded talk, originally appeared under the title 'Ecology and mysticism' in the *Humanist Magazine* (now *New Humanist*), May 1971. Published by the Pemberton Publishing Co. Ltd.

The first is from one of the great nineteenth-century visionaries: Smohala, who was a leader of the Columbia Basin Indian tribes. Smohala issued the following declaration in response to an attempt on the part of the American government to settle the Indians on the land and change their way of life from hunting and gathering to agriculture.

> You ask me to plough the ground; shall I take a knife and tear my mother's bosom? Then when I die she will not take me to her bosom to rest. You ask me to dig for stones; shall I dig under her skin for her bones? Then when I die I cannot enter her body to be born again. You ask me to cut grass and make hay and sell it and be rich like white men; but how dare I cut off my mother's hair?

The second text is from the Oglala Sioux shaman Black Elk. This is from a remarkable book called *Black Elk Speaks*, which is probably one of the most beautiful pieces of American literature ever written; it was dictated by Black Elk in the 1940s. This is one of Black Elk's prayers:

> Hear me four quarters of the world, a brother I am, give me the strength to walk the soft earth, a relative to all that is. Give me the eyes to see and the strength to understand that I may be like you. O, ancient rocks, you are now here with me, the great spirit has made the earth and has placed you next to her. Upon you the generations will walk and their steps shall not falter. O, rocks, you have neither eyes, nor mouth; you do not move; but by receiving your sacred breath, our people will be long-winded as they walk the path of life. Your breath is the very breath of life. And, O you people who are always standing, who pierce up through the earth, you tree-people are very many; you trees are the protectors of the winged people, for upon you they build their lodges and graze their families, and beneath you there are many people whom you shelter. May all these people and all their generations walk together as relatives.

These passages are examples of something our society has for several hundred years considered to be savage superstition. Before that they would have been called 'idolatry' by our Christian ancestors. In them you find the sense that the nature around us is a living presence that can be addressed and communicated with. And that is what idolatry means, and what superstition has meant to Western people. Let me offer what I think has been the prevailing opinion about this kind of world view. I will quote from an anthropologist, Alfred Kroeber, who, incidentally, made some of the most sensitive studies of the American Indians. Kroeber once set himself the problem of trying to find what he called a 'scientific and objective' standard of progress in human culture. He asked, how do we decide which cultures are backward and which are advanced? And the first criterion he turned up for distinguishing higher from backward cultures was what he called 'the criterion of magic and superstition'. He put it this way:

In proportion as the culture disengages itself from reliance on magic, it may be said to have registered and advanced. In proportion as it admits magic in its operation, it remains primitive or retarded. The backward cultures and their magic, shamanism, animistic ritual, recognize as objectively effective certain phenomena that the advanced cultures regard as objectively unreal and as subjectively psychotic or deranged. The limits of relation of personality and the world are differently drawn in the two series of culture. What higher cultures stigmatize as personal, non-real and non-social, abnormal and pathological, lower cultures treat as objective, conducive to ability and socially useful.

Now what Kroeber is talking about here is the sort of thinking that was reflected in the quotations I gave from Smohala and Black Elk. They represent a magical vision of nature, in the truest sense of the word 'magic'. Not magic as sleight-of-hand tricks, but magic as the conviction that the world can be prayed to, that there can be a transactionary relationship between people and their environment. When that same sensibility begins to appear within our civilized society, as it frequently does, it presents problems. What do we make of someone like the poet Shelley, who was no savage but who writes a poem that begins, 'Oh wild west wind, thou breath of Autumn's being'? What do we make of Wordsworth when he says 'the earth and common face of nature spake to me remarkable things'? What do we make of Dylan Thomas when he says 'the force that through the green fuse drives the flower drives my red blood'? Or what do we make of St Francis' Canticle of the Sun, when he addresses himself to 'Brother Water' and 'Brother Fire' and 'Brother Sun' and 'Sister Wind'? What does one make of Vincent van Gogh's *Starry Night* in which the very heavens seem shot through with a living presence, with a vitality that makes them seem to swirl and to move with a life of their own?

The usual attitude is to be very polite about these things, because after all everyone agrees that art is a necessary and important part of our lives, and to conclude that all this must be 'poetic licence'. One just doesn't take it seriously! Or perhaps one concludes that even madmen can produce decent paintings and write good poems. But one does not accept the work on the poet's or the artist's own terms. These must be *mere* metaphors; this is but a dramatic way of writing something. For Shelley surely could not have believed that the wind was a living person, a kind of vital breath. *Obviously* the wind is not that. In other words, one skims the aesthetic surface and leaves behind the vision. Perhaps one is not even aware that the vision is there.

Now the new ecological sensibility that's growing up in our society has come around to a very different evaluation of this magical vision of nature as it appears in art or as it appears in the primitive cultures. There is a much more sympathetic way of regarding the world view of primitive people. I'll give you one example. It's from Ian McHarg, a Scot living in America, who is an ecological city planner. McHarg is talking here about the Iroquois Indians and the way they handled their environment with great intelligence and success.

> Among the Iroquois, the bear was highly esteemed. When the hunted bear was confronted, the kill was preceded by a long monologue in which the needs of the hunter were fully explained and assurances were given that the killing was motivated by need, not the wish to dishonour. Now if you wish to develop an attitude to prey that would ensure stability in a hunting society, then such views are the guarantee. The hunter who believes that all matter and actions are sacramental and consequential will bring deference and understanding to his relations with the environment; he will achieve a steady state with his environment, he will live in harmony with nature and survive because of it.
>
> (From *Design With Nature*.)

There is currently a great deal of literature appearing by anthropologists, which attempts to salvage the wisdom within the eccentric, seemingly heretical world view of primitive people. For anthropologists have come to realize that primitive people usually do a very good job of creating what are called 'ritually regulated ecosystems'. Their rituals and their so-called superstitions seem to serve a useful purpose. They help to hold down population, preserve the supply of game, preserve the top soil, keep the water clean, and so on. Many people, caught by this new interest in ecology, are now trying to show the multitude of ways in which human beings have intelligently arranged their environment around them.

But the coming crisis in ecological thought arises precisely from this more sympathetic attitude toward what the primitives with their nature mysticism have accomplished. Look back at McHarg's remarks for a moment and you see at once that what he is offering us is a *purely functionalist analysis* of nature mysticism. His conclusion is that magic and ritual just *happen* to have worked in any number of cases; they just *happen* to be useful, presumably by dumb luck. And so McHarg goes on, as I think most other analysts of this kind do, to conclude that we must now draw off the ecological wisdom we find abiding in the magical vision of nature, and then integrate it into our scientific–technological tradition.

Will this do? Or is this functionalist approach that is growing up within ecological studies not an attempt to create still another, somewhat more sophisticated anthropocentric conception of nature? Does it not finally leave us with an essentially manipulative way of dealing with the environment, only now with kid gloves rather than with an iron fist?

I think that this is an attempt to *objectify* the magical vision of primitive people. For the magic of that world view is not being experienced; it is not personally and emotionally integrated into the person who does the analysis. Rather, its utility is recognized and drained off. But is there any justification in being so quick to dismiss that experience or to sidestep it?

This magical vision of nature is indeed heretical from the point of view of scientific respectability; but I think it deserves far more respect than even sympathetic people like Ian McHarg have given it. For it is, after all, part of the oldest tradition of the human race. It has been capable of producing prodigious religious insight and artistic expression. It is the vision people lived by, a thousand times longer than industrial society has any chance of surviving for.

Well, I think that the crisis I'm referring to in these rambling remarks will arise when people begin to wonder whether there is not a legitimacy, a truth, in the magical vision of nature which transcends its mere utility. I think the reason we shield ourselves from magic is for fear that we will lose power over our environment if we begin to regard it sacramentally. This sacramental vision of nature will not, we fear, give us control; it will interfere with 'progress'; it will cut back our standard of living. And we want power. Peculiarly in Western culture, we want power – and so badly that we are willing to call power 'truth', and will respect nothing as truth which does not yield power, control, prediction.

The chances are that the crisis I see emerging between these two approaches will split the ecological movement along the lines in which everything else has split in the United States in recent years. The more counter-cultural elements who have been drawn to ecology out of a perception of its inherent religious elements may find that their conception of ecology has no scientific respectability whatsoever. And so they will again become a radical fringe element. But I would hope that the study of ecology might become the midwife of what I would call 'visionary intellect'. That is: a science in which power is not the most important goal, and in which knowledge is not a kind of cold, alienated, prying, egotistical curiosity. Instead we would have a new science in which the object of knowledge will be rather like the poet's beloved: something to be contemplated but not analysed, something that is permitted to retain its mysteries. For mysteries are not always dirty secrets that have to be exposed. They can also be realities that beckon us toward other, inarticulate forms of awareness.

There is an interesting use of the word 'knowledge' in our Western tradition. We have the verb 'to know' as we find it in the book of Genesis: 'to know' as Adam knew Eve. And that was not a research project.

Part Four

THE TECHNOCRACY CHALLENGED

'Ravings of a fatigued, drunken, young ex-scientist', with which this section opens, is an extraordinary piece of writing – but one which captures perhaps more than any other the mood of the 1960s. First, the title itself seems deliberately chosen to put up the scientific back: who, in a scientific conference, would be expected to give much credence to 'ravings', particularly those compounded by tiredness and alcohol? Yet the text itself quickly dispels any attempt to dismiss it, for it is sharply analytical, scientific in tone, and mature beyond the bounds of what we normally mean by 'young' (time, the author notes, being the only known cure for the disease of being youthful).

As much is not actually surprising, for the author a few years previously gave up brain research to study full-time the crises which he describes here (all urgent, global, interconnected and concerned with growth). His paper is really a kind of dialogue with scientific orthodoxy, a challenge to the high priests of science to see that their work is not neutral, that Marxists though many of them may be, their attitudes are full of imperialisms which Marx never dreamt of (temporal and species imperialism), and that the 'good' which they so proudly claim for their scientific techniques may be at any time rendered meaningless by just one really big 'bad'. The lack of symmetry between the good and bad effects of science is superbly characterized by the game of American roulette, in which a revolver is pointed at the head, some chambers of which have been loaded with $20 bills but one of which contains a bullet. The bills are the 'goods' of science, all rendered irrelevant by the one bad bullet if it ever goes off.

All this may be heady stuff, but what does it really represent? Hasn't every age had its disenchanted young scientist with a chip on his shoulder? Of course – but not every age finds the same thing echoed up and down the land by young and old alike, scientific as well as non-scientific. At almost the same time, for instance, the distinguished Nobel laureate Sir Macfarlane Burnet was writing of all mission-oriented research: 'It is self-evidently true that the world would be the better for a prolonged moratorium on such activities while it learned to handle and make humanly satisfying use of established knowledge.' In the same *article,* he dealt with pure research with even greater pithiness: 'There cannot, surely, be much left to discover that matters,' he wrote.*

Yet 'Ravings' is the right place to start. To be sure, greater credence could be given the theme by reproducing the dissent of the establishment but we should not forget that it was the young that spearheaded the attack, and launched it with a generality and a lack of inhibition of which the Elders fought shy. This, if you like, was the full frontal of the period but we should not be so entranced by the novelty of the view as to forget the sideshows. And in the wings complementary visions were forming which interlocked nicely with the grand design. Malachi Martin, for instance, focused on an abuse of science. The 'abuse of science' is a term usually used by scientists to describe scientific activities of which they fear the public may not approve – defoliation, napalm, anti-personnel weapons, biological arms and such like. Whether these things actually deserve to be called abuses when, as Marcuse has pointed out, mathematics and physics so perfectly serve their development, is a deep philosophical point which Skolimowski raises later on. But Martin's abuse is of a different sort: his target is the way eminent scientists, using what he calls 'the great fudge', extrapolate on slim or non-existent grounds from their own special areas to pontificate on moral and ethical matters on which they have no special competence. He is after the Skinners, the Monods, and the Desmond Morrises. And with almost wicked delight he reduces them to pulp.

The fudge of which Martin complains starts with the sentence 'If it is true that . . .'. There usually follow thirty-odd pages of somewhat irrelevant and detailed science from the author's own speciality. And then, now that the 'if' has been forgotten, the scientian – as Martin calls him – goes on to summarize the human condition and list the conditions of the coming Utopia. Thus Monod: 'Man will live authentically protected by institutions which, seeing in him the subject of the kingdom and at the same time the creator, could be designed to serve him in his unique and precious essence.' What such drivel means is unclear (and why it should have such popular appeal totally mysterious). But as Martin says, 'Logically, all this is childish. Scientifically, it is bosh. Humanly, it is deceitful.'

But it is much more than an elaborate game for academics. What Martin is after is perhaps best called the great confusion of the twentieth century: the confusion of science with knowledge. It is true that the word 'science' comes from a Latin one meaning 'knowledge', but science now means something more specific. It is not the same as knowledge, and there are many categories of knowledge – in fact most of them in man's two-million-year history – which are not scientific. By claiming, as we do today, that the only legitimate form of

* Burnet, Sir Macfarlane, 'The implications of global homeostasis' in *Impact* (Unesco, Vol. XXII, No. 4, 1972).

knowledge is science, we deny man the most human aspects of human existence. Martin puts it better:

> *Scientians will outlaw the kinds of knowledge by which man loves and aspires and perseveres and trusts. They will reimpose on man the controls from without that man has laboriously worked to shed since he discovered fire. They will remove man from all the unplumbed areas of his mind, areas vital for the nourishment of man's wisdom beyond science and of man's actions beyond the dictates of blind nature. They will close man's mind to any possibility of ultimate mystery. This promises a boredom as great as the universe and an ennui as deathly as a row of gravestones.*

From Martin to Skolimowski is the step from the specific to the general. As a philosopher it is Skolimowski's aim to show how our conceptions of science have changed with time, and what are their implications. From the eighteenth century, he displays to us the three ideas of 'science as the embodiment of human dignity, science as glorious entertainment, and science as pure knowledge'. All of past relevance as far as today's scene is concerned, though to be sure there are plenty in the scientific establishment who try to re-create such ideas to justify their existence. And from today, Skolimowski singles out 'science as a civilization, science as a conceptual framework and science as technology'. For example, the public are often condemned for confusing science with technology (it wasn't science that dropped the bomb, says the learned professor, but technology and the politicians). No confusion, says Skolimowski; science and technology are now as inseparable as Siamese twins. It is scientists who confuse the issue by trying to define their work in terms of eighteenth-century ideals.

Skolimowski concludes that science is once again on trial, along with the civilization which it produced. And the last three pieces in this section have been chosen to represent the widely different viewpoints from which the scientific attack was mounted in the 1960s. Two are by very distinguished poets – W. H. Auden and Robert Graves. Note their superficial gentleness. There is an apparent softness to both these pieces which quite belies the fundamental onslaught they really make on our scientific fixations. Auden and Graves follow in a long line of poets who have sought to expose the monopoly of science, of which Blake, with his talk of 'single vision and Newton's sleep', was the first and best known.

But probably no one pulled out all the anti-scientific stops as far as did Dr Jerome Lettvin, Professor of Communications at MIT in the United States. I was at the rather pompous Unesco conference, on Science and Culture, at which Lettvin gave this address in 1971. Lettvin had been asked to speak first, had accepted, but had not sent an advance copy of his paper to the organizers. No one had any idea of what he was going to say. The effect of this bombshell, even after simultaneous translation into four languages, on the rather stuffy collection of academics gathered in Unesco's main conference hall, was explosive. If Professor Lettvin could be persuaded to open all such conferences in the future, they might at least have some chance of getting off on the right foot.

Ravings of a fatigued, drunken, young ex-scientist

at the World Federation of Scientific Workers Conference on Young Scientific Workers and Contemporary Society

I am writing this in the middle of the night, in the middle of the conference, in the middle of a bottle of Scotch. This confession will permit anyone who disagrees with me to dismiss my remarks as the ravings of a fatigued drunkard, so be thankful for that let-out. I am also doing most of the typing myself so if you find new words you don't recognize, the dictionary probably would not help you. I am sorry if this makes it harder to understand.

The case I have to make is too large and too complex for me to set it all down here, so I know I shall have to select heavily and caricature much of my intent, but what the hell. . . . In my present metabolic condition I have a diminished capacity for tact, so I may tread on a few toes. No offence meant; I love you all.

My first point concerns the Apocalypse. I believe we shall soon encounter a set of world-wide crises whose gravity and nature are unique in human history. These crises have in common the properties of being (*i*) *urgent* – they get worse if not solved, and are nearing the point of irreversibility; (*ii*) *global* – no country can be assured of safety, and no country can opt out of responsibility for facing these problems; (*iii*) *parallel* – it's no good simply solving *some* of the problems, because the others will get you anyway: they must *all* be solved; (*iv*) connected with *growth* against fixed limits. There are literally hundreds of important

Paper given at the World Federation of Scientific Workers conference on 'Young scientific workers and contemporary society', July 1971.

human problems, but I think those that satisfy the criteria listed can be subsumed under the following categories:

World order
Population
Environment
Resources

Dr Zaheer suggested poverty as an additional one, but I regard it as a corollary of population growth, and not intrinsically self-deteriorating. This is not to say that poverty is only caused by overpopulation (certain economic systems are of course a major factor) but that the problem of poverty cannot be solved without solving the population problem. Why are there more poor people in the world today than there ever were? Not because there is less wealth – there is more – nor because the distribution is less equitable, although the Northern Hemisphere nations are seizing much of the *potential* wealth of the Third World; but because there are *more people*.

I hope Frank Barnaby will forgive me if in the remaining discussion I neglect the question of catastrophic war and disarmament. That member of the apocalyptic list differs from the others in being a discontinuous risk situation rather than a steady cumulative one, and furthermore appears to require somewhat different political strategies than the others.

How is it best to think of the crisis situation? It can be visualized in various ways. One way is to observe that exponential growth cannot continue for ever: it always encounters limits sooner or later. What is puzzling to us is that the limits are often reached very suddenly after a period of restriction-free growth. There is an old French riddle which is apropos here. It concerns a vigorous lily plant in a pond, which doubles its size every day. It is known that the lily will fill the pond in thirty days, and then will choke out all the other creatures in the pond. Naturally you would like to save the life of these creatures, but the lily is an exceptionally pretty one, and you decide to postpone pruning until it has filled half of the pond. On which day should you prune the lily? The answer is, of course, the twenty-ninth day.

We are in the same situation with respect to the earth. We have been growing steadily for a long time, and on the whole with a tremendous excess of 'pond'. We always had plenty of land, water, air, metals, timber – at least, relative to our meagre needs, providing the distribution was equitable. Now it is no longer just a problem of distribution. It is the twenty-ninth day, and we cannot believe that our generation has been chosen to live at this strange point in history. It seems too much of a coincidence. Our problems are compounded by the fact that the 'lily' is growing so fast that we cannot prune it quickly enough: we are losing the battle. This makes it hard for us to face the harsh task of pruning. And there is an even worse factor. In the riddle, it is just a lily; in life, it is us, people, and our demands for higher productivity and higher consumption. Ethically, how can you cut people back? No wonder we spend so much effort dreaming of magic technological solutions that will make all our problems disappear.

It is enough, Professor Burhop would say, to allow science to find solutions to these problems, with a little help from our friends the politicians. Economic growth need not stop, science need not stop, technology need not stop. Science will allow us to have our growth cake and eat it too. I think we must be grateful to Professors Burhop and Kotovsky for their contributions to this symposium. They are the ground on which we all stand. They represent the technological orthodoxies of East and West. God bless their fundamental particles of faith.

But I disagree with them both on a number of points. This may be just a matter of age – maybe I will 'know better' when I 'grow up', time being the only known cure for the disease of being young. If this is the case, they should try to show very carefully and rigorously just where I have gone wrong, so that I may Repent and Believe.

I cannot do justice to the case in the time I have (my typing is awful slow), but let me give a few indications, kicking off from a typical statement in Professor Burhop's paper. 'In the great controversies of our age,' he says, 'science as a body of knowledge is neutral.' In some sense, this is true by definition, and therefore trivial. But practically, as certifying the innocence of the pure scientist, it is impossible to believe any longer. We know very well that 'knowledge is power', and that in every society that knowledge will be used in the interests of those in power. In the West, this means good old-fashioned imperialism and capitalist exploitation, so offensive and brutal that it is easy to identify and struggle against. In the socialist countries, as well as in the West, there are the more subtle phenomena of 'temporal imperialism' and 'species imperialism'. In a socialist state, power may indeed reside with the people, but this does not prevent them acting against the interests of groups outside the polity which are not considered important. 'Temporal imperialism' is the exploitation of one generation by another. The victims have no defence as they are not yet born. They are exploited by the removal of unrenewable resources such as oil, coal and minerals, and by the erosion of environmental integrity by urbanization and industrialization. We exploit them by consuming more, by producing more waste, and by producing many children – many more than can be supported *without* relying heavily on one-crop resources.

By 'species imperialism' I mean that, when there is a conflict of interest between another species and our own, we always opt for our own interest, no matter how trivial. Most of the troubles we are causing to other species are not, I suspect, the spectacular ones. They are private pains which we can only know about through the occasional accidental discovery. For instance, it is convenient for us to use oil for power, heating, transport etc. This often necessitates transport of oil across the oceans by tankers, and vast quantities of oil are inevitably spilled. We are just beginning to discover the terrible effects this oil is having on species which depend on a subtle sense of smell to catch food, to navigate, or to mate. To take another example, it has recently been discovered that humpback whales emit low sounds which can be heard by other whales thousands of miles away. Thus all the humpbacks in a given region would be part of a loose social system of whales covering, say, the entire Arctic Ocean. This is no longer true, since by the introduction of motor vessels, we have raised the background noise level of the oceans so that the distance over which the whales can communicate is drastically curtailed. Of course we have no way of estimating how important it was to the whales to have a social system of such vast geographical scope, but that is not the point. We should note that at the time we started motorizing our ships, we could never have known about such effects. Technology has continued growing exponentially since then. How many other such cases are there, which we could never know about, and perhaps never shall? Jacques Cousteau says that the vitality of the oceans has been halved since he started diving. Of course this is merely a subjective estimate, but I can well believe it. Due to overfishing, the humpback whale will probably not be worried about long-distance communication for very much longer, and will join the other 150 species extinguished in the past 300 years.

Is this just sentimentality? You may say that species have always lived, died and struggled against each other. Why not continue a natural pattern? I don't know why, but I find this attitude monstrously cynical. To me it is typical of a whole collection of thoughts, attitudes and feelings which scientists possess and lack in characteristic proportions. Their training has made them insensitive to such delicate moral questions as 'the rights of other species'. The feeling that the human race has a solemn responsibility not to interfere with the *arete* (fulfilment of destiny) of other species, is one which is incommunicable to those who do not understand it already, but is a strong element in the new philosophy of the uses of science which is emerging among many young scientists, at least in the West. Note that the traditional socialist concept of equity has been extended. In capitalist societies, there is only an equity of natural selection – 'liberty, and devil take the hindmost'; in socialist societies, men live for the good of other men; in truly equitable societies, men live for the good of all inhabitants of the planet Earth, now and for ever in the future. This goal we have yet to achieve.

Thus I disagree with Professor Burhop's characterization of Marcuse's remark as 'wrong, perverse and harmful'. Recall that Marcuse had said, 'When the most abstract achievements of mathematics and physics satisfy so adequately the needs of IBM and the Atomic Energy Commission, it is time to ask whether such applicability is not inherent in the concepts of science itself.'

I think for once Marcuse has got it right. The *applicability* is indeed inherent. There is a famous declaration of Einstein's that if he could have had his life over again, he would choose to be a plumber. The implications of this are dramatic: Einstein would therefore have 'dropped out' had he known that his research (in *pure physics*, Professor Burhop!) could lead to, or at least assist, the development of the greatest threat to mankind and the biosphere that, to our knowledge, has ever occurred. I think I know what Professors Burhop and Kotovsky would say to this, so let us ask, can we mollify this judgment of pure science by claiming that the good outcomes have outweighed the bad?

No, I think we cannot. Scientists used to picture science as a cornucopia, full of incorruptible blessings. The Luddites in Britain, and such thinkers as William Morris, already passed a dissenting verdict on the question; and Bernal himself pointed out that science was not in itself sufficient to bring about a golden age. The Bomb was a watershed. Science had produced its first undisputable Frankenstein's Monster. Suddenly, scientists had to ask themselves whether their work would be used for good or bad ends. The cornucopia model was replaced by a 'weighing balance' model. Science would produce some good effects, some bad. If the good outweighed the bad, one should go ahead; if the bad outweighed the good, one should refrain. This simple model assumed that 'good' and 'bad' could be calibrated equally and compared, and further, that the cumulative properties of each were the same.

I think these assumptions are mistaken. Bad effects seem to cumulate in a way that good effects do not. Consider a (rather weak, but the best I can think of at four o'clock in the morning) analogy. Imagine playing Russian roulette (perhaps in Russia it is called, with more justification, 'American roulette') with a very peculiar kind of gun that fires 20-dollar bills (usually) or bullets (sometimes). In repeated plays of Russian roulette with this gun, one would generally get rewarded handsomely. In fact, one may build up quite a little pile of dollars. One day, however, there will be a bullet in the chamber instead of a bill, and that will be your last game. The point of this eccentric analogy is that (*a*) the accumulated goodies do not protect you from the first bad outcome; (*b*) the first bad outcome completely destroys the value of the previously accumulated good ones.

Crudely applied, this is supposed to suggest that if science discovers ten, a hundred, or even a thousand good things to every single discovery in the Bomb category, even so, it is only a matter of time before a bad discovery of sufficient magnitude turns up and nullifies the previous benefits. Good and bad are not symmetrical. 'Bad' in this sense is ultimately superordinate to 'good'. Annoying isn't it?

Is this logic completely crazy? No, not completely, but almost. What is wrong with it? Our Russian colleagues would assure us perhaps that science is less likely to go wrong in a rationally planned society. I am sure this is correct, and that, for example, if the USA were not so aggressively militaristic, there would be no need for nuclear weapons, we would all be a great deal safer, and I would have a less persuasive example in the Bomb. Thus the risks of deleterious applications of science and technology can be reduced by *social control*.

Professor Burhop would add another caveat. In his opening remarks, he said that 'the problems science has created need not less science but more science for their solution. The problems of the pollution of our environment are surely capable of solution.' What he is suggesting is that, as science progresses, our model-building capacity improves, and our ability to conceptualize and to solve problems increases. Also, as we deal with existing problems, we learn more in general about remedial technologies. Each new problem is a stimulus for the general discovery of remedial techniques. Thus, in principle, we can deal with technological problems by *scientific and technological control*, as well as by social control.

Are these sufficient to ensure the proper use of science and technology? I wish they were, but am unconvinced. It seems that there are some problems which are intrinsically unpredictable, and cannot be controlled in advance by any means known. To control them retrospectively may be too late. The rate of production of these 'truly unpredictable' problems is, I conjecture, a direct function of the amount of scientific and technological activity. It may be possible to correct a given undesirable outcome after the event by remedial technology, but that remedial technology in itself presents risks. This second-order loop is not trivial. It may in fact represent a very large proportion of the entire technological effort. As Dennis Gabor, surely no Luddite, has pointed out,

> The most important and urgent problems of the technology of today are no longer the satisfaction of primary needs or of archetypal wishes, but the reparation of the evils and damage wrought by the technology of yesterday.

Professor Burhop emphasizes our increased capacity for dealing with problems. I emphasize our increased capacity for generating problems. The question is, which process has the greater growth coefficient? This question is certainly not answerable at the moment, and perhaps never will be. If there are no catastrophic accidents, Professor Burhop will consider his case proven, but I will say, 'It's just a matter of time; keep waiting.' If a catastrophic accident does occur, in the unlikely event that I would have the opportunity to speak to Professor Burhop about it, it would be small comfort to say, 'I told you so' (although I must admit, it would be *some* comfort).

I shall end this rambling with a word about the time-scales in which our apocalyptic problems are set. The main point I want to make is that the human race is a recent arrival on this planet, and that high science and technology is a quite extraordinarily novel experience for the Earth. Julian Huxley once suggested an apt comparison. If the history of life on Earth could be compared with the height of St Paul's Cathedral in

London, then the life-time of the human race up to now could be represented by a small block 3 cm high on top of the cathedral. The time since the beginning of agriculture could be represented by a postage stamp on top of the block. The ink on the postage stamp could represent the time since the rise of science, and the thin film of moisture on top of the ink represents that time – the twenty-ninth day – when the human race hit the limits of its little planet and brought a terrible crisis on itself, and wondered whether its recently acquired set of scientific tools would enable it to stave off disaster. Or whether, on the contrary, this coincidence of the arrival of the twenty-ninth day so soon after the advent of science constituted evidence for a causal relation, and that the only hope lay somehow, somewhere, in a less enthusiastic tinkering with the natural order.

Have you thought of this? Maybe the Stone Age is fun!

Shame! Heresy!

The scientist as shaman

MALACHI MARTIN

As far back in history as we can find traces of man's existence, there is evidence pointing to one perennial preoccupation of men's minds: the formulation of explanations to give meaning to the most puzzling and mysterious elements of life. Without ascribing Sartre's *angoisse du siècle* to Neanderthal man (his particular *nausée*, if he had any, was more probably due to an excess of bison flesh), and without supposing that the first maker of an axhead exclaimed in metaphysical delight with Jean-Paul Richter, 'I am an I' (although the primitive could well have stood, like Richter, on his father's dunghill and uttered a not-so-metaphysical but equivalently satisfied Paleolithic yowl), man seemingly always had questions about life, death, the future, light and darkness, his own thoughts and aspirations.

Once the merest details of man's history are filled in, we find that explanations were supplied by a variety of people: priests, witch doctors, shamans, wizards, soothsayers, oracles, clerical castes, and priestly orders; and that they used a variety of means to fulfill their purposes: red ocher,

Extracts from an article in *Harper's Magazine*, March 1972.

chicken entrails, the flight of birds, the sound of water and wind, incense, robes, gestures, sacrifices, amulets, incantations and formulas, sacred books, revelations, ethical systems, lists of commandments and prohibitions, sacred groups, and so on. Always it was fundamentally a question of explanation, of answering impossible questions.

Today the grip of the organized religions is failing, and their function as explanation-givers is either totally rejected or falling into desuetude. Nevertheless, man's questioning is still acutely felt. Neither modern technology nor such marvelous feats as walking on the moon, orbiting Mars, and transplanting organs have diminished the poignancy of the human condition. The desire for and expectation of sureties has, if anything, increased. It is hardly strange, then, that there should arise a new form of response, adapted to the specifically modern ache for answers yet marked by the three main characteristics of the more ancient responses: dogmatic absolutism, claimed omniscience, and mystic privilege. This modern response is offered by scientians, the practitioners of scientism.

There are three distinguishing marks of a scientian. First, he must be a scientist. He must have an impressive base in his own specialized field. And this field must be some recognized branch of science that strikes an immediate and general chord of understanding. A field such as astrology will simply not do, no matter how you dress it up with charts, maps, books, lectures, latinized terms, popular appeal, and mail-order doctorates. Of course, theology, philosophy, and the humanities are also out; they are no more scientific than astrology.

Scientism's most visible and influential practitioners and believers, the real scientians, are on the whole respected figures in the natural and social sciences: men such as Jacques Monod, geneticist and Nobel Laureate; B. F. Skinner, noted Harvard professor and behavioral psychologist; Konrad Lorenz, well-known ethologist; Lionel Tiger, Robin Fox, Desmond Morris, all respected names in the fields of paleontology, animal behavior, and anthropology. There are also some influential popularizers like Arthur Koestler, R. D. Laing, Jean-François Revel, Robert Ardrey, and Alvin Toffler, who do not have the credentials of the scientists but who seem to read a lot. They are not innovators so much as camp followers, formulators, and interpreters. Scientism in addition has an increasing vogue and influence with thinkers such as Zbigniew Brzezinski and Harvey Wheeler, and among ordinarily intelligent people amazed, as we all are, at the achievements and ever-fertile ingenuity of the scientific establishment.

While there are many scientists, only a few become scientians; few develop the second and third characteristics of the genuine scientian. Few get the 'call' – to borrow an older way of speaking. The *sine qua non* for the scientist who would become a scientian is that he use his background to extrapolate the currently known data of his field – and, if necessary, the data of other branches of science – in order to discourse on the *whole* of man, including, specifically, ethics, morality, religious instinct and practice (or what passes for these), humanism, and all the so-called values – the 'inner' things of man. The scientian, in other words, provides answers to those age-old questions of man. This is his second distinguishing mark.

The scientian performs this explanatory service by a great – and essentially ideological – leap, the scientian leap. Jacques Monod, for instance, on discovering the reign of chance in his own field, genetics (a science hardly complete in its own study), proceeds to a thesis in which he asserts that all philosophy, theology, and ethical systems of the past are forthwith invalid. B. F. Skinner, having established that some animal behavior can be modified by environmental controls, assumes a universality for his findings and asserts that human liberty, morality, and dignity are merely behavioral traits created by environment, that there is in fact no such thing as the 'inner' man. Lorenz, having catalogued the resemblances of behavior in animals and men, forthwith decides that aggression in men is the same as in animals, and that both men and animals are going about the same thing whenever resemblances occur in their behavior. He thus effectively wipes out all consideration of morality and ethics. Tiger and Fox, as an extension of their anthropological and paleontological ruminations, conclude that a 'biogrammer' (postulated by the authors to support still earlier assumptions) is built into man's genes and alone determines his behavior. All else, they declare on the basis of their pyramiding assumptions, is symbol and fantasy; 'nature' has programmed us to act.

Obviously, religious, ethical, or humanistic questions cannot be examined with the kinds of scientific tests by which Monod determined the regulatory modes assured by allosteric interactions, or by which Skinner trained a white rat to press bars. There are no empirical bridges to be crossed. How, then, do they proceed? Answer: by the scientian leap. The leap is to scientism what the syllogism was to Aristotle, the telescope to Galileo, the electric guitar to the Beatles. Without it, scientism would be impossible, for the scientist would be merely scientific.

While not many genuine scientists acquire this second characteristic, traces of it are abroad practically everywhere in our culture today. It is George Haber telling us that we can learn about ourselves and how we should behave by studying a pack of wolves; Kenneth Clarke admonishing us that the 'psychological and social sciences must enable us to control the animalistic, barbaric, and primitive propensities in man and subordinate these negatives to the uniquely human, moral, and ethical characteristics of love, kindness, and empathy'; Ernest Loebl stating that the social sciences must accept the task of creating a humane society.

Scientism lurks in the leitmotiv of novels such as Gilbert Rogin's *What Happens Next?* (the meaning of life lies not in its grand and heroic moments, he says, but in its velleities); in history writing such as Maxime Rodinson's *Mohammed* (where everything *but* religious experience is considered responsible for Mohammed's success); and in popularizations of science in *Life* and *Psychology Today* (where terms such as mind and brain lobe, knowledge and electric circuit, memory and brain fluids are completely interchangeable).

Scientians, deservedly well placed on the totem pole of excellence in their own fields, use the platform of their preeminence – and rely on the relatively new and very visible impact of science in the life of modern man – to catapult to the new absolutism of scientism. All true scientians are engaged in a gentleman's crusade to liberate man from the toils of superstition, animism, outmoded clerical domination, and all pre-scientific/unscientific/nonscientific moralities and systems.

The universal scope of interest leads directly to the third mark of the scientian: his extrapolations lead him to proclaim the existence of a force, an evil reality, in man's world. The scientian believes that he has, at last, pinpointed the unidentified fly in the cosmic ointment, the worm in Eden's apple. Oddly, the evil force seems to vary according to the branch of science from which the man springs, but its effect is nonetheless claimed to be not simply unique but universal. If man cannot be made aware of it, the argument goes, it will surely continue to lead him blindly on to ultimate disaster. Man must turn round and control the force that controls him.

Having identified man's nemesis at last, the scientian comes bearing his new salvation: a means of control that, fortunately for us, the scientian just happens to have, and that we are told will surely deliver a saving counterforce. For Monod, chance is the blind force, chance allied to 'animism'. Science is the means of control, and his 'ethic of knowledge' is the new counterforce. For Skinner, the cast-iron effect of environment on human behavior and the nefarious 'literatures of freedom and dignity' (by which he seems eventually to mean all literature and thought except the literature and thought of behaviorism) constitute the evil of man's condition. Control will be achieved by man's arrangement of his environment and by the exclusion of concepts such as the 'inner' man; his counterforce will be man's new behavioral patterns elicited by the new environment, itself 'freely' chosen in a state of total control beyond freedom, dignity, and morality.

The golden promise

One thing is clear from scientian proposals. We are not dealing with anything remotely on the order of the scientific achievements of the past. In fact, compared with scientian proposals, those achievements were little but venturesome stops and starts. Very well. Einstein did away with all our fixed horizons. Sigmund Freud unlocked the unconscious, ruining our belief in the possibility of sheer iniquity. And

Mickey Mouse henceforth has a phallus. One can live with and absorb these partial conclusions, justified or unjustified.

But scientism as the 'unconscious choice in the beginning', in Monod's cosmology, 'has launched the evolution of culture on a one-way path; onto a track that nineteenth-century scientism saw leading infallibly upward to an empyrean noon hour for mankind'. From scientism will come 'the defining of a new and unique source of truth, and the demand for a thorough revision of ethical premises, for a total break with the animist tradition, the definitive abandonment of the "old covenant", the necessity of forging a new one'.

Here probably is the greatest appeal of scientism. Men still dream the impossible dream, be their cities ever so dirty, their country's policies ever so immoral, their environment ever so polluted, and their traditional sources of religion and morality ever so effete and ridiculous. The golden promise of scientism is not merely an effective exorcism, but the total obliteration of whatever evils bedevil our twentieth-century world in the form of ignorance, aggression, poverty, mental and physical disease, and in general those distressing factors of the human condition that former religious and ethical systems failed to uproot. This will all come about, as Fox and Tiger state lyrically, if our swollen brains 'can contrive a method to harmonize all the massive schemes and affirm the absolute value of intimacies no more extensive than the reach of an unarmed arm'.

Details are, of course, hard to come by. But some things are clear. Certain basic flaws in human society would be automatically corrected. World leaders would be incapable of aggressive patterns of behavior; these traits, together with ordinary human criminality, would be eliminated by psychotechnology. No more Bangladeshes, Biafras, or Central Park muggings. Cerebral technology would shorten the work week, diversify the leisure of infants and elders alike, hasten learning processes, magnify pleasures, deepen inner peace, and enlarge the vision.

Even the spirit (better, the psychic life) of man would benefit. Telepathy, telekinesis, and various forms of ESP are distinct possibilities. Who knows, in addition, what space travel and interplanetary sojourns would introduce to men? Man could well exit from his age-old binary and discursive thinking molds, the 'yes–no' mentality, to develop a totally different mode of understanding.

Scientism, therefore, does not purport to be just fun-and-games. It is serious business, at least for scientians. Nor is it without tradition. Its principal historical origins lie back in the 'early days' when the *Beagle* carried Charles Darwin on his epoch-making voyage. It had a brief fling in late Victorian times and in the early twentieth century. But the timing was wrong: the atom was not fissioned; genetics was in its infancy; psychotechnology was unheard of; television, computers, lasers, quasars, organ transplants, jet engines – all were yet to come; and no man had walked in space while traveling at the speed of 18,000 miles per hour. Scientism is a solid claim, made by respected scientists in the name of science, and it bids fair to explain all of man to man himself.

Given the decline in humanistic values and of organized religion, it is no wonder that scientism, like any dog, is having the devil of a fine day. After all, science has a good record, and the most vociferous scientians are some of the best scientists – Nobel prizewinners to boot. Accountably, therefore, scientism produces a child-like hope, a certain trust and euphoria among intelligent people who want to hear some reassuring and confident voice speaking about the great issues of life at a time when all the signposts are twirling dizzily in the rush of high and uncharted winds.

In fact, at present, scientism is the headiest drink served in the bar-room at the intellectuals' saloon. But it is one thing to get high on Beaujolais. One can dream of great love and of endless heaven; even the hangover can be bittersweet. It is quite another thing to get sick on synthetic wine. Like the beer in the popular story, it may look, smell, pour, taste, and go down like wine, but when it is down 'it ain't got no authority'.

Scientism betrays man about whom it pontificates by threatening the integrity of his thought. It betrays science from which it springs by laying aside the *sine qua non* of any scientific process – conformity to objectively acquired data. It betrays the society of man that depends on science by offering a humanly inadequate panacea for society's ills. For scientians belie the very principle of scientific objectivity. They gloss over their illogic, presenting their own fantasies as fact, passing deceptively and self-forgivingly from a very conditional 'would be' or 'might have been' to a very dogmatic and assertive 'was', 'is', or 'will be'. If men were to accept as gospel the total scientian imbrication of hypothesis, prejudice, thoughtlessness, and wishful thinking, then into the heart of human society they would have accepted a time bomb that surely would reduce society to the status of amino acids. The scientian dream of total integration with nature would be an accomplished fact.

The great fudge

The primary characteristic of the scientian leap is its use of the great fudge, a *trompe-l'oeil* of logic. Always the great fudge is presented with the absolutism and authoritarianism of a scientian's *ipse dixit.* A few concrete examples might be helpful here.

In discussing the emergence of man, Lionel Tiger and Robin Fox argue that bipedalism started the trend toward man's *Homo sapiens* status. They write: 'Man made this change as he adapted to a hunting life on the hot savannas.' There then follows a description of how man's spine straightened, his buttocks expanded, and so on. The fudge appears in the phrase, 'man made this change as he adapted'. Somehow, man's mind development appears to be inextricably a by-product of spine lengthening and buttock expansion. They may well have been so connected; but we cannot presume it, much less present it as a fact, as the authors do. Scientifically, the phrase means nothing.

But Tiger and Fox go even further. To improve their lot, they continue, men '*had to improve* their brains in feedback with their improving skills . . . The improved brain was capable of *novel* symbolic processes . . . which enabled hominid hunters to create political structures. . . .' (Italics mine.) We find again the automotive power ascribed to man and the mysterious term 'novel' applied to symbolic processes. Of course, these terms and concepts contain no scientifically controlled and established conclusions. They are rank suppositions. As such, some of them are brilliant. But they are put forward as scientific fact.

Again the scientian admonishment is thrown in: 'Since there are no gods and no supernatural, the business of coping with these non-existent matters must relate to some real earthly human problems.' In fact, they are merely 'man's extensions of himself'. 'We create a god to whom *we* can be subordinate', they state in another place. And, lest there be any doubt about the ultimate meaning of whatever *Homo sapiens* does, they add: history is a 'web of symbols and reminiscences', and 'a beautiful woman who arouses a man's lust and a religious leader who inspires fanatical devotion are both playing the oldest game of all' (the blind, persistent struggle for dominance and reproductive advantage).

In the simple arrangement of a sequence of grammatical tenses we see a widely employed variant on the fudge. Monod gives us several fine examples. After a few pages of batting back and forth such awesome terms as neuromotor activity, sensory inputs, arthropoda, retinal images, and the cross-connecting *corpus callosum*, Monod summarizes: 'If we are correct in our surmise that thought reposes upon our underlying process of subjective stimulation . . .' And there then follows immediately, based on what began as an innocent 'if' clause, a nearly thirty-page exposition describing how men *actually* did and do develop and know. Every verb tense is in the indicative mood. The conditional 'if' has been lost in the wash of conviction. Monod, at the end of those thirty pages, is so convinced, and has left the underlying conditions so far behind, that all the subsequent statements of his general thesis depend on the actuality of that original supposition now made into arbitrary fact.

Desmond Morris provides the prize example of grammatical fudge in *The Naked Ape*. Morris has a problem about the female breasts in *Homo sapiens*. He actually holds that they are no more or less than fleshly copies of the buttocks. His final statement of this 'fact' is a model in scientian grammatical fudgery. He starts off quite modestly with two rhetorical questions: 'Could it be . . . ?' and 'Could our vertical . . . ?' These are followed by two 'if' clauses in the conditional mood, backed up by two clauses that begin with 'supposing', and rounded off with another 'if' clause. At the end of this delicate arrangement, Morris feels confident enough to state categorically that the protuberant hemispherical breasts of the female must surely be copies of the fleshy buttocks.

Such manipulative logic, of course, is not scientific. Monod, Skinner, Lorenz, Morris, Tiger, and Fox intend us to believe that their suppositions are true, to take them as fact, to assume they are sufficient because of the scientific reputation that buttresses them. Logically, all this is childish. Scientifically, it is bosh. Humanly, it is deceitful.

Apparent intimacy

Yet after we have listed all the illogicalities, it must be admitted that scientian thinking is overpowering for the unsuspecting mind. Take Konrad Lorenz, for instance. It is clear that this man knows his animals: mallard ducks, fallow deer, Greenland Eskimo dogs, *Corvidae*, songbirds, *Cichlosoma biocellatum*, ants, herons, fish of all kinds, hamsters, wolves, lizards, sloths, ganders, geese, foxes, rabbits, waterhens, and scores of others. Not only that, but he introduces readers to the intimacies of animal life; one has a certain feeling of privilege when reading about the drake's rab-rab palaver with its mate or the appeasement dance of cranes. He even tells us of his own favorite, 'my dear Greylag Goose, Ada, several times a widow', who 'was recognizable by the grief-marked expression of her eyes'.

The ordinary reader will not realize that what Lorenz has skilfully done is to describe the actions of animals using terms from the ethical and humanistic vocabulary. Some of Lorenz's fellow ethologists have taken samples from his pages and described the behavior of his animals in quite a different way. Lorenz, however, will succeed in impressing the layman with his knowledge of animals. 'He must know what he is talking about' is the almost inevitable reaction of the respectful non-specialist. When he has accomplished this, the rest is a foregone conclusion.

Lorenz proceeds to speak of man in the same way. If animals have a list of 'Thou Shalts', is it surprising that we men have the same? And he produces, as an explanation of moral considerations in men, what must rank as the prime scientian statement of all this vast literature. Moral considerations and behavior are due to ritualization, according to Lorenz, and this ritualization 'whose causation is so mysterious creates new instincts that dictate to the organisms their own "Thou Shalt"'.

Besides, who can resist the conclusions of men who can detail the little insignificant facts of personal and family life some 30,000 to 50,000 years ago? Not until Lorenz's study did we know that among our Paleolithic ancestors there was no greed or drunkenness, that gluttony and sloth were permitted, and that the 'only commandment at the time was: thou shalt not strike thy neighbor with a hand-ax, even if he angers thee'. From Desmond Morris come further personal touches. Paleolithic man was very like us; 'minute-by-minute snacks were out and big spaced meals were in'. Our earliest ancestors resembled us in love and marriage. 'Male and female apes had to fall in love and remain faithful to one another.' Lorenz has a further refinement of this particular phase of development. 'We know', he says, 'that in the evolution of vertebrates, the bond of personal love and friendship was the epoch-making invention created by the great constructors . . .' We never learn who these great constructors were. However, those early apes and men set the standards for modern man. How moral can we be today? asks Lorenz. His answer: 'Man can behave very decently in tight spots, provided they are of a kind that occurred often in the Paleolithic period.'

After the reader is dazzled with an apparent day-to-day knowledge of these far-off ancestors, is it any wonder that many are willing to bow to Morris's statements about the origin of man's specifically human activities? Your language? Do not deceive yourself: the 'grunts, moans, and screams [of our ape fathers] are the vocal foundation on which we build our verbal skyscraper'. Our painting, dancing, writing, money-making? They 'all emerge biologically as the extension of infantile play-patterns or play rules [he enumerates six of these] found equally in apes as in men'. Our artistic and scientific behavior? This is merely the product of 'a battle between the neophilic and neophobic urges' common to apes and men.

In any critical assessment of scientism, it is well to take an over-all look at the field that scientism claims. Obviously, scientians are intensely interested in what was hitherto the domain of ethics, religion, and humanism: the behavior of men within those particular relationships on which societal living has been built. How far has solid scientific analysis gone in this field, scientism apart? The answer must be: not very far. In fact, we are still grappling with basic issues and receiving rather truistic conclusions. Researchers are conducting limited experiments into such things as the Good Samaritan instinct, obedience, criminal behavior, the genius scale, environmental life, warring tendencies, and attitudes toward death. But all this is in its infancy.

One can only conclude that scientism is not scientific. Scientians proceed on the assumption that outside the realm of science there is nothing to discuss, and they tautologically presume that there is simply nothing beyond what can be observed by scientific means. This very assumption is unscientific, since by definition science cannot deal with any matter outside of scientific fact and scientific modes of knowing. Scientians then go even further and convert their basic assumptions into tenets rather than leaving them as hypotheses, and they draw vastly important conclusions without reference to the methods of the science whose data and dicta they invoke as witness. In drawing these conclusions, they abort the search for knowledge itself. The scientian's search becomes one for controls, and his writings come to resemble the proclamations of Dostoevsky's Grand Inquisitor.

Scientism's betrayal, however, goes beyond science. It betrays man himself. Cardinal to the scientian outlook is the belief that man, when he acts sensibly, has only one mode of knowing: the scientific. It was Loren Eiseley (who himself betrays scientian traits but occasionally rises above them) who best expressed the consequence of this view: 'When the human mind exists in the light of reason and no more than reason, we may say with absolute certainty that man and all that made him will be in that instant gone'.

The scientian program will expunge all knowledge of an intuitive kind, as well as all metaphysical knowledge, an aesthetic perception (which is also knowledge), and knowledge derived through religious experience. Knowledge becomes a knowing of facts and ceases to be a grasp of meaning. Meaning itself ceases to have significance, except insofar as it tells of material results and physical conditions. Thus scientians will outlaw the kinds of knowledge by which man loves and aspires and perseveres and trusts. They will reimpose on man the controls from without that man has laboriously worked to shed since he discovered fire. They will remove man from all the unplumbed areas of his mind, areas vital for the nourishment of man's wisdom beyond science and of man's actions beyond the diktats of blind nature. They will close man's mind to any possibility of ultimate mystery. This promises a boredom as great as the universe and an ennui as deathly as a row of gravestones.

Does science control people or do people control science?

HENRYK SKOLIMOWSKI

On 17 October 1780, the ship *Lincoln Galley* anchored in Williams's Cove on the east side of Isleboro, now in the state of Maine. On this ship there was a group of scientists and students from Harvard College led by the Reverend Professor Williams. Their purpose was to make observations of the total eclipse of the sun which was to take place in this part of the world on 28 October.

Unpublished paper, a shortened version of which was published in the *New Scientist*, 24 February 1972.

There is nothing remarkable about scientists making observations of the eclipse of the sun. What was remarkable about this expedition was the fact that it was in time of war and the part of the coast they were going to was held by the British. Earlier in October Professor Williams, representing the new American Academy of Arts and Sciences, wrote a letter to the British commander, Colonel Campbell, requesting permission for the expedition to enter British territory immediately. 'Our business', he wrote, 'is solely to promote the interest of Science which is the common interest of mankind.' Whereupon permission was granted. The gentlemen from Harvard directed their telescopes on the sun on the specified day and made their observations. These observations are now a part of our scientific library.

Science, as conceived by Professor Williams and his assistants, is the embodiment of human dignity and eternal truths. This kind of science, or rather science conceived in this manner, transcends the idea of who controls whom for, as we have said, science here is equivalent to the pursuit of eternal truths. Let us therefore note the first conception of *science as the embodiment of human dignity and eternal truths.*

The idea of the untouchability of science, of its entirely beneficial nature was so strongly embedded in the minds of the people at that time (the end of the eighteenth century) that the gentlemen from Harvard could not only devise the idea of crossing the enemy's lines in order to make some scientific observations, but could actually carry it out – war or no war.

Let us contrast this kind of untouchability of science with the disgraceful misuses of science in the twentieth century. It suffices to mention IG Farben in Hitler's Germany – the infamous chemical concern which provided chemicals for the gas chambers in concentration camps; lunatic asylums and special camps in the Soviet Union as described, for example, in Solzhenitsyn's *The First Circle*; or research on biological warfare conducted on our campuses, to see at once that in the twentieth century science can no longer be regarded as the embodiment of human dignity. Indeed it is often nowadays a disgrace to human dignity.

II

Before we engage in a more detailed analysis of contemporary science, let us review some other conceptions of science in the past. From the seventeenth century on we can distinguish another concept of science, *science as a glorious entertainment*. Molière beautifully satirizes this notion of science in his play, *The Learned Ladies*, where he shows science invading not only the fashionable boudoirs, but also the chambers of servant girls. Chrisalus complains to Belisa about his household.

> No science is too profound for 'em; and in my house, more than in any other place in the world, the most lofty secrets are conceived, and they

> understand everything but what they ought to understand. They know the motions of the moon, the Polar Star, Venus, Saturn, and Mars, which I have no business with; and with all this vain knowledge, which they go so far to look for, they don't know how my pot goes on, which I have occasion for.

In the French salons of the eighteenth century, particularly those attended by the French Encyclopedists, science as a glorious entertainment positively flourished. Voltaire's mistress, Madame du Châtelet, wrote a very learned and lucid account of Leibniz's philosophy (under the title *Institutions de physique*) of which La Mettrie said, 'Everybody understands monads since the Leibnizians made the brilliant acquisition of Madame du Châtelet'. In Madame du Châtelet's salon the charming Venetian fellow, Algarotti, presented and discussed his book, *Newtonianismo per le dame*. The learned duet, Voltaire and Madame du Châtelet, were slightly shocked by the frivolous tone of the narrative and by too many jokes in the text. However, *Newtonianismo per le dame* in a curious way epitomizes the conception of science as a glorious entertainment.

III

It might appear from these two conceptions of science that historically, that is before the twentieth century, science was an altogether benevolent entity, capable of causing no harm, ideologically indifferent, and exerting no significant influence on the destinies of societies and civilizations. Such a conclusion would be premature. For already, at the beginning of the seventeenth century, science can be seen in an altogether different role. The burning of Giordano Bruno in 1600 and the trial of Galileo in 1633 mark the appearance of science as an ideology, the ideology capable of swinging people's minds from the path of faith to the realm of doubt, from the truth as rendered by the Church to the inquiry of truth as rendered by human reason. The Holy Inquisition seems to have been perfectly aware of the potentials of science. Hence Galileo's trial.

When Galileo was on trial, science was on trial. But let us carefully observe the circumstances under which science was on trial. Science was at that time undercutting the foundations of a decaying civilization. The medieval civilization was coming to an end, unable to sustain itself through its own means. Science was helping man to evolve a new civilization. Science was at that time the torch of light, the agent of progress and liberation. It was put on trial by the agents of the dying epoch. These circumstances must be very clearly borne in mind. For the main point is that science was on trial at the beginning of the seventeenth century for attempting to extend man and his universe beyond the limits in which they were bound.

But one may imagine that science could be put on trial for quite a different reason and in quite different circumstances. Might it not be the case that in the course of time, science itself became a bondage, restraining and suffocating us as people, as society, as a civilization? I shall return to the 'second trial' of Galileo at the end of this essay.

IV

Nowadays we no longer believe that science is the embodiment of human dignity. And we do not believe that science is concerned with eternal truths either for we know that every theory established by science is tentative, subject to revision and replacement. Eternal truths are not replaceable. Replaceable truths are not eternal. Since every theory is replaceable, there are no eternal truths in science. However, the old idea of science as something beyond the sordid and immediate concerns of human beings still prevails in many quarters. Science is then equated with pure knowledge. Science handles ideas, as the argument goes. As such it is not responsible for the disastrous effects of the intrusions of technology into the fabric of society and into the sanctuaries of our private lives.

Science as pure knowledge is equated with the body of descriptions of nature, the sum total of ideas which illuminate for us the behavior of nature. In this context Russell's contention that 'equations do not explode' seems to be valid and relevant. Certain ideas may or may not be illuminating for the problem under consideration, but they do belong to the realm of intellectual contemplation and not to the realm which can control the destiny of society or people. Thus science, seen as pure knowledge, does not and cannot control people. It is simply a category mistake to ask in this context whether science *does* control people. For 'control', if it is to mean anything, must mean an influence on, and a determination of some courses of action of, many individuals and ultimately the determination of the course of the whole society. When we equate science with pure knowledge, the center of gravity remains within science. When we see science as *controlling* people, or people controlling science, we shift the center of gravity from science to society. It is only by broadening the concept of science to include its *social* implications that we can talk either about science controlling people or vice versa.

To say it once more, the conception of *science as pure knowledge* precludes the problem of science versus people because the theater of pure ideas is so hermetic that it does not include the social consequences of scientific ideas. The Pythagorean theorem, taken in its primary sense as expressing certain geometrical relationships, is a cognitive concept, not a social phenomenon.

Pope Urban VIII in Brecht's play *Galileo*, torn by indecision about what to do with Galileo, no doubt thought about science as pure knowledge when he said, 'I want no condemnation of physical facts, no battle-cries like "Here the Church, there Reason!"' But then, under the persuasive influence of the Inquisitor, he is made to *see* that science is much more than physical facts and pure ideas, that its reach extends to the sacred shrines of the Orthodoxy. And the Pope, concluding that 'That is certainly an impertinence', decides that the spirit that emanates from Galileo's mathematical tables must be destroyed. Galileo must be tried.

V

Now, science as an integral part of Western civilization is certainly much more than a collection of physical facts and a body of pure ideas. It is above all a social phenomenon. It is only with regard to science so conceived, as a social phenomenon, as a part of the fabric of society, that we can meaningfully ask: 'Does science control people, or do people control science?'

Paolo Soleri, the dreamer–architect–philosopher who conceived the idea of arcology, made a relevant comment on the subject when he said:

> If to collect litter may be the aim of the street sweeper, it is not the aim of sweeping institutions. The aim of the sweeping institutions is cleanliness. In a similar way, though the scientist may claim total indifference to what he calls the application of science, the institution of science is ultimately not the understanding of things but the power that man acquires through such understanding and, by this power, the ability to guide his destiny.

We have arrived at another conception of science: *science as a civilization*. The institution of science is the history of the development of science which includes its impact on and its interaction with society. The point is that our social institutions have been shaped by science, not only in their structure and organization, but in their goals and aspirations. Science has inspired us to set up such institutions that further foster the development of science. The most spectacular example illustrating this point is the United States space program which fired the imagination of the whole society but which drained a great deal of the resources from this society. If there is an insidious intent in science to self-perpetuate itself in a variety of disguises, the elephantine space program is a clear manifestation of this intent. Science is, as it were, a blind force which tends to multiply itself. Militarism, as an extension of contemporary science, is perhaps not so much an expression of the corruption of scientists' minds, but rather an expression of an inherent tendency of science to multiply itself in whatever form. Now, if it is true that science has pervaded the fabric of Western society, and if it is true that every established institution in society has a tendency to perpetuate itself, and if it is true that the American society is most saturated with science and technology, then it is quite natural that science will flourish here in a variety of forms of which militarism is one.

VI

An even more striking example of institutions inspired by science to further foster science are the institutions of learning. The course of a civilization is determined by the quality, quantity and character of learning pursued in the institutions of learning in that civilization. Since science has continually shaped the character of learning pursued in our schools and universities, its influence should be expected to be profound. And so it is. For we inherit from our schools not only knowledge about the world. We inherit also a particular conception of the world.

Now, our *Weltanschauung*, our world view, is acquired with and through our knowledge. It is the scientific *Weltanschauung* that we acquire in our schools and in our academia. The nature of knowledge determines the nature of the world around us. We perceive and understand what we are made to perceive and understand through the knowledge we acquire. The dominant position of science in our system of learning assures a further perpetuation of what is called the scientific outlook and what is tantamount to a vision of the world through the spectacles of science.

Seen in this context, science does control people; it does control people subtly and indirectly because it furnishes them with the categories of understanding; it acts as a series of filters through which we view reality.

To put the matter in more general terms: our thinking is to a large degree determined by our language. The conceptual framework is a matrix which enables us to express certain relationships and does not enable us to express other relationships. Every civilization is under the influence of these subtle yet all-encompassing conceptual determinants. The conceptual framework of Western man in modern times has been profoundly influenced by science; and so was his language and his thinking. Here again we see an indirect but an important influence of science on the thinking of man, thus on the thinking of society. According to proverbial wisdom our habits control our lives. Is it not also the case that the conceptual habits of a society control the destiny of the society?

We have thus analysed science in yet another context: *science as a conceptual framework* (determining our thinking). This conception of science may be regarded as a part of science as a civilization. Yet this context is distinctive enough to deserve separate treatment. There is one aspect of science so conceived (as a conceptual framework) which requires special attention. This aspect is related to the notion of rationality as developed by modern science. It is this notion which often determines whether our behavior, decision or action is deemed rational, thus acceptable or not. But it so happens that scientific rationality favors frameworks and situations which comply with the structure and scope of the universe as established by science. Our judgments (which are a subset of our conceptual habits) are without question under the influence of scientific rationality. There would be no room for conflict here if the universe of science encompassed everything there is, encompassed, in other words, all aspects of the human universe. However, since the universe of science does leave out certain aspects of the human universe, a conflict may arise between our human judgments and our scientific judgments. If the force of scientific rationality is such that we must obey it (for fear of being called unscientific quacks) even though we feel that some aspects of the human universe are violated, then the issue of science controlling us as people again arises.

VII

We are now ready to examine the last important conception of science: *science as technology*. A sharp distinction is often made, particularly by the priests of pure science, between science and technology; the rationale given is that science is innocent and that technology is responsible for the present crisis of society. This separation is, of course, artificial. Technology is a part of the rational *Weltanschauung* shaped by science. Technology is a part of the fabric of Western society which, for centuries, has been guided by the spirit of science. Technology, seen in the broad perspective of *science as a civilization*, is only an extension of science; and it is only within this broad perspective that we can meaningfully discuss the social consequences of either science or technology. One commits a category mistake, as we have argued, if one attempts to discuss the *social* function of science, when science is confined to the body of pure ideas.

Science is an integral part of the bloodstream of Western civilization. The new civilization was erected not only on the piles of Galileo's physics. Bacon's program, 'knowledge is power', was equally important in secularizing society, in seeking fulfilment for man here on earth rather than later on in heaven, and in realizing the idea of progress conceived in human rather than in theological terms. From the beginning of the new epoch science was designed to be a servant of human progress; thus science was designed to serve a social function. Technology is only a more ruthless embodiment of the tendency toward material progress as exemplified by Bacon's motto, 'knowledge is power'.

To repeat the main point: within the over-all structure of the rational *Weltanschauung* there is not much room for the distinction between science and technology; both serve the same function – that of perpetuating material progress. This is clearly realized by technocrats and militarists who insist, and they are quite correct in this, that they only extend the scope of the rational universe; and this is also clearly realized by many young people who want to escape this rational universe altogether by flights into lyricism and mysticism.

VIII

We are now ready to pose the question again: does science control people or do people control science? The most obvious but mutually exclusive answers are:

(1) Yes, people control science because individual people make contributions to science following their chosen line of inquiry;

(2) No, people do not control science because even scientists and the whole institution of science are manipulated by the power structures of society.

Neither of these answers is adequate. Science is an exceedingly complex affair and our loaded question can only be answered by reconstructing the various contexts of science.

Science as the pursuit of eternal truths, science as a glorious entertainment, science as pure knowledge does not control people. But it could hardly be said that people control science in these contexts. The idea of controls is somewhat irrelevant here. Science as a civilization, and especially science as a conceptual framework, as a form of the rational *Weltanschauung*, does control people; although its control is indirect, its consequences are far-reaching. Our mental habits, our thinking and perceiving have been pre-determined by the network of knowledge within which we grew up. And this network has been profoundly influenced by science.

We are even more obviously controlled by *science as technology*. There can be no question that our most grievous concerns are about technological change ruthlessly asserting itself over and above human controls. But technology is only an extension of our rational ideology.

Thus, when we question technology, we question our rational ideology, we question the whole enterprise of science. Our question at this point should be reformulated. What we are really asking is: do we control the course of our civilization? And the answer is: we do not. The crisis of scientific civilization is the crisis of scientific reason, is the crisis of science itself.

When an experiment does not come out right, we blame either the instruments or the scientist, but not science. Only on rare occasions do we blame science. On such occasions we know that our anomaly is not really an anomaly, but a manifestation of a crisis. We do not try to improve our instruments or our performance, but look for a different set of theories. We switch the whole idiom of science, we switch to another paradigm, we change science, so to speak.

Perhaps our predicament nowadays is similar with regard to science as a civilization. Perhaps we should not ask who controls whom – for obviously we as people, as scientists, as scholars, as citizens do not control science in the most profound sense as a scientific civilization – but ask ourselves, what kind of new science should we or must we develop to disentangle ourselves from the present crisis?

Perhaps what we witness nowadays is another trial of science and thereby another trial of Galileo. But science is being tried nowadays in new circumstances. It is not tried as a force which attempts to upset the *status quo*; but as a force which represents the *status quo*. It is not tried as an emerging civilization, but it is tried as a part of a dying civilization.

Science, technology and poetry

ROBERT GRAVES

Technology is now warring openly against the crafts, and science covertly against poetry. The original meaning of these terms has long been forgotten. Craft in Anglo-Saxon meant 'intelligence' with 'crafty' as its adjective, and applied mainly to manual dexterity in producing useful objects. But in the term 'arts and crafts' craft takes the less important position because art, its Norman–French equivalent, covered the production of a nobler range of objects, just as the Saxon word 'stool' (German *Stuhl*) came to mean a humbler chair without a back, whereas 'chair' (Greek *kathedra*) was what the Norman–French gentility used as a sign of their own importance – a stool with back, arms and footrest. This social distinction between stool and chair still survives; one is offered a stool of repentance or a dunce's stool, but a Chair of philosophy; and toads sit on toadstools not on toad chairs.

'Technology' is a Greek compound noun originally meaning 'the topic of craftsmanship', but now meaning 'the application of mechanics to manufacture', and 'manufacture', which originally meant a 'making by hand' and usually implied sweated labour, has come to cover the production of goods by almost wholly mechanical means; so that a home-knitted jersey can no longer be called a manufacture – it is a product of craftsmanship. As for the secret war between science and poetry, one must study their original meanings to make sense of it. Science, meaning the art of knowing, is the Latin equivalent of the Greek word philosophy meaning 'love of wisdom'. And poetry (it is strange how few scientists are aware of this) comes from the Greek verb *poiein* meaning 'to make or do', which explains 'maker' the early Anglo–Scottish word for 'poet' as in Dunbar's famous Lament for the Makers. True poetry makes things happen. Many ignorant young poets must

Published in the *New Scientist*, 2 December 1971.

have turned to Aristotle's Poetics in the hope of finding a poetic theory discussed there; but of course Plato, Aristotle's master, had banished all poets from his ideal republic and pretended that Greek poetic myth was mere nonsense, not tribal or civic history crystallized in dramatic form. Aristotle's Poetics therefore discusses how things are, or should be, made to happen – by any but poetic means. The power of true poetry, as opposed to academic versification, is of a sort that scientists cannot recognize: if only because at its most intense it works in the Fifth Dimension, independent of time. Several well-known mathematical discoveries, such as Rowan Hamilton's quarternion formula which came to him suddenly one day as he was walking across Phoenix Park, Dublin, plainly derive from fifth-dimensional thinking: they are not built up from similar theories but make a leap into the future. Yet scientists would dismiss a similar process in the writing of poems as 'illogical': meaning that the resultant poem does not make a prose sense precise enough to permit exact translation into another language.

Some years ago I was invited to give the Blashfield address in New York and took *Baraka* for my subject – *Baraka* is the Moslem sense of blessedness that attaches itself to buildings or objects after years of loving use by noble-hearted people. *Baraka* may seem a foolishly sentimental subject, but few practical people will deny that to break in a new guitar, typewriter or car and as it were humanize it, so that it never lets one down, takes a long time, even if one has used a predecessor of the same make for years previously. And a ship's engineer, especially if he is a Scot, often achieves so friendly a relationship with his engines that they somehow continue to work after apparently irremediable damage. The apprentice in the song 'Sally in our Alley' despises the alley and tells Sally that one day he will take her away from her rascally parents to a better place and there marry her. I wonder whether she lived happily ever after in a distant row of suburban residences all built on the same plan, with no neighbours whom she knew – her new house furnished throughout with machine-made fittings and furniture, everything ruled by straight lines with regular curves which tired her eyes. And whether she soon longed for the *baraka* of the cramped but homelike kitchen in the alley where she had been brought up, and learned as a child to make do with a bunch of rags for her doll and a shoe-box for its cradle. Briefly speaking, technology produces millions of identical and spiritually dead objects which as a rule take far longer to humanize than their expected length of service; whereas unmechanized crafts exercised by individuals or closely knit groups produce objects with the elements of life in them.

Science has come to imply a belief in so ordering our civilized life that every citizen will enjoy the same mechanical range of amenities as every other, and as much leisure as is needed: a leisure now usually occupied no longer by entertainment in pubs, cinemas and music-halls but by radio and television in the home.

The worst that one can say about modern science is that it lacks a unified conscience, or at least that it has been forced to accept the power of Mammon. Mammon – or at least the Talmudic Mammon of Unrighteousness, exploits the discoveries of science for the benefit of international financiers, enabling them to amass more and more money and, it is hoped, to control all markets and governments everywhere.

In ancient times the use of scientific discovery was closely guarded for social reasons – if not by the scientists themselves then by their rulers. Thus the steam engine invented in Ptolemaic Egypt for pumping water to the top of the famous lighthouse on the island of Pharos was soon abandoned, apparently because it encouraged laziness in slaves who had previously carried waterskins up the lighthouse stairs. The same with the early invention of the water-mill for grinding corn: it was left unexploited by the Romans for much the same reason as the Pharos pump – all corn had hitherto been ground in hand-querns by slave labour. Still more remarkable was the mediaeval invention of the electric battery by Baghdad Sufis and their abstention from putting it to commercial use for light, heat, and power lest it interfere with traditional arts and crafts. Then there is Suetonius's account of how an anonymous inventor came to the Emperor Tiberius, offering to show him a new sort of glass. He dropped a lump of this on the marble floor in front of Tiberius's throne as if by accident. When it bounced Tiberius asked him whether he had divulged the secret of its manufacture to anyone, and if so to whom. The man swore that it remained his own, so Tiberius sentenced him to death, remarking that glass of this nature would be found so valuable in the making of jewellery and table ware that it would depreciate the value of gold and upset the Imperial economy. Then again, the highly inventive Mexican Aztecs knew about wheels which they used in children's toys, but forbade their use on the roads, lest they should assist a surprise attack on the capital. And the mediaeval Pyramids, not far from Mexico City, have been cut so exactly that this can have been done only by the use of laser rays – but this secret was withheld from the Spanish conquerors and took five centuries to rediscover.

There need have been no war between Science and Poetry, nor between Technology and the Arts, had not the power of money forced too many poor, married scientists and technologists to break what should have been a Hippocratic oath to use their skills only for the benefit of mankind.

The second Dark Ages

JEROME Y. LETTVIN

The comprehensive involvement of man in science is now fatal. There are two distinct meanings to the word 'science'. The first meaning is what physicists and mathematicians do. The second meaning is a magical art, about which the general public has superstition. These views are related to each other as basic theology and priest-led religion in the Middle Ages. Politically it is the latter that is most useful. But just as one cannot divorce the deeds and policies of the Inquisition from the doctrines and propositions of the saints, so now one cannot really separate the tyrannies of government from the theories of scholars. This connection occurs now, as then, through the schools in which vulgar opinion entrains the disciplines and expediency reshapes the work.

This vulgar opinion, this second and now overriding view of science, deserves a brief description. To it science consists of facts and artefacts – actuarial tables on the one hand, lasers on the other. Theory is a kind of incantation that ensures the fact and makes the artefact work. Advertising agencies, when they want to show that some breakfast cereal, degraded from cardboard wastes, is scientifically designed, put $E = mc^2$ conspicuously in the picture. Equal nonsense occurs in other contexts in other countries. By itself such gimmickry is no more harm than a St Christopher medal. What is of harm is the blind faith in an imposed system that is implied. 'Science says' has replaced 'scripture tells us' but with no more critical reflection on the one than on the other. Scripture once told us through the voice of authority that we should not suffer witches to live, that slaves are legitimately taken, that to be poor is to be virtuous and, by this dreadful twisting, was the instrument of oppression through much of our history in Europe and America. Science now says that Vietnamese peasants do not have the proper infrastructure to maintain a progressive and democratic economy, that blacks cannot reason as well as whites and that to be selfish is to be sane.

Once formal religion held temporal authority on a promise of heaven, astonished the people with miracles long past, and sold them futures in remitted pain for today's bread. It is replaced by the new faith whose living figures ascend to the heavens, whose miracles are offered in the immediate, and which gives electric bread-knives as souvenirs. Most

Paper given to Unesco symposium on 'Culture and Science', held in Paris, 6–10 September 1971.

wonderful of all it is not prayer but reason that distributes this bounty. Man was God all the time. But reason is no more understandable this year than prayer a thousand years ago. Little Billy may become a scientist as earlier he might have turned priest, and know the sacred texts, making of his experiments prayers. The chromed apparatus is blessed by distant authority, the water thrice-filtered for purity, and he wears the white antiseptic gown we all know from TV commercials. But the masses still move by faith. And the cynical educators translate, like St Jerome, sacred works into the administrator's language, hold press conferences on the latest wonders, and display in picture magazines. Broadcast is important not because it explains but because daily life has been conditioned to depend on a faith that can move mountains.

Like the religion it supplants, this new one must have its messiah who cannot be the divine substance itself, the propositions of science, nor yet the mortal gadgets it creates. So now, conceived without error, got almost wholly at cost, delivered in a bedlam over new stars in the east, and amortized on Caesar's due, comes the son of man, taking our labors on his console. Neither human nor divine, neither suffering nor transcending – here he is, here at the telephone, a finger-tip away – not on a low hill elsewhere and long ago, but here to be touched, questioned, heard, here to reveal that disinterested justice no mortal man could ever attain. And he is promised to stay – world without end.

I have fear of what science says, not the science that is hard-won knowledge but that other science, the faith imposed on people by a self-elected administrating priesthood. The most vicious thing that this public science says, the supporting lie on which revolutionary and reactionary alike agree, is that truth is in number, numbers are in machines, machines are not human and therefore just. They are spared the original sin. In the hands of an unscrupulous and power-grasping priesthood, this efficient tool, just as earlier, the Final Man, has become an instrument of bondage.

In spite of great differences in economic and social structure, the Western World now resembles the Western World of the sixth century. A metaphysics that ushered in the first Dark Ages is again flourishing. I call it Antaeism after that unhappy giant that Hercules killed by keeping him from touching the earth. Antaeism is an overwhelming abandonment of the phenomenal world as the source of knowledge.

Without denying other kinds of analysis, let us look back to the middle of the first millennium with this syndrome in mind. The world then, as now, had become crowded, not for lack of land and resources, but for lack of ways to use them. Ethics and politics, the way men treat each other, had become a major preoccupation, and control of man insensibly became more important than control of nature. In the schools Greek was dropped as a dead language and mathematics decayed as a useless discipline. Natural sciences turned from description to a ruminative scholarship concerned with authority. An almost sensuous

Hippocratic immersion in observation of the patient gave way to the rationalist system of Galen whose style has reappeared in medical textbooks. Causes, broad enough in concept as to admit of no exceptions, gave a world of only accidentally modified effects. It did not matter, from the public and uninitiated view, that this system of reason was not truly productive, that mechanism was not truly explained by indwelling properties, that, indeed, an institution had grown powerful enough to fulfil its own prophecies. For the overwhelming daily problem that shadowed the sun by day and obscured the stars at night was how to live in a world more constrained by one's fellows than any of the forces offered by nature. Then as now, manipulators appeared and kept shop everywhere, then as priests, now as social scientists, arrogating control by an alleged divine order whose shibboleths are parodies of serious thought, but always such as hold men down. It mattered as little to organized and organizing religion then as to the social sciences now what the nature is of the single man, and the models of the 'good man' offered by heretic and patriarch alike are as astonishing and foolish as the 'economic man' of several decades ago or the interactive operator of today.

Nevertheless today seems, at first glance, very different. Control of nature has not been abandoned, rather is more violently and successfully pursued than ever in history. Indeed we seem almost at another extreme – allowing ethics and politics to lapse or be subverted to a progress manifest in consumer goods. But this first glance is superficial. When we penetrate the arts and sciences themselves we find a strange picture. With the sole exception of the physical sciences, including chemistry, a new style is ascendant, appearing in the arts as non-subjectivism, in the sciences as a mixture of positivism and operationalism. The foreseen accident of the computer, like the prophesied accident of Christ, has engendered a new mode of thought. Where Stoic and Talmudic rationalism shaped then fused with and finally disappeared into the figure of Jesus, so now technologic rationalism has constructed and is being embodied by the computer. Two metaphysical changes are already spreading rapidly: first, the denial of or indifference to generative law as distinct from convenient algorithm; second, the frank substitution of data for phenomena, an alteration in perception itself. These changes have appeared in engineering and biology and medicine, and almost overwhelmingly in social science. These changes are also central to the new religion.

In modelling the world one used to assume that laws are simple but hard to find. Parsimony and symmetry played the greatest part in setting up science as we know it. Had Newton's equations of motion been as long as the *Principia* itself, and proven, somehow, in an appendix to be necessarily that long, they would not have been so interesting even if they were true. Beauty lay in the economy, for the ideas were not only easy to grasp, but universally applicable – like quotations from Shakespeare. The laws found were necessary in the sense that the whole world, the very heavens, bore witness to them. But one can reasonably ask: is this aesthetic required to make working models of the world? Suppose instead of having a small set of lucid equations, one had an enormous set of measurements independently taken and covering most practical cases. Then suppose one had an immense machine of great storage capacity and high operating speed, and could show that for shooting cannon, computing freight costs and calculating orbits it was almost always a matter of practical indifference. whether he used Newton's system or the huge set of separate expressions. Would there be any practical reason for preferring Newton except by the superstition of taste?

What has just been given in travesty for physics can be taken as directly applicable in many other sciences. Computers have vastly increased our ability to work with data points. It is possible, for example, to patch together weather prediction, or the location of oil deposits, or putting a man on the moon, because the dogwork of patching data can be done easily and rapidly by machine. Where a clearly determined human goal can inform a human judge, to reorganize computation, patching becomes a fine art, the blending of apparently irrelevant procedures to produce wanted results. However, the patchwork is not usually a theory in any classical sense. It is prescriptive like a good recipe. But, when the same algorithms and programs, so successful in directed engineering, are used in cases where there is neither a theory to be checked nor a goal to be approached, the system turns bizarre, a thing out of Jonathan Swift. Then the output of the machine, whatever it is, can become the goal, the program become the theory, as you can actually see occurring in certain branches of biophysics. What first occasions the work disappears and the real objects of discourse are revealed as the workings of the machine.

It is more in technology than in science that the computing machines flourish. Not only in automatic book-keeping and traffic control of rolling stock but also in the design of special devices, useful circuits, optimal ways of constructing apparatus, these computers are without peer. One experiences almost a frisson of awe when watching an automated draughtsman lay out a set of complex plans, or an automated milling machine shape to perfection a piece of metal, or an automated editor justify the lines on a page and even proof-read. So much of what we formerly thought to be talents and crafts turn out to be a tedious exercise; so much labor, in retrospect, is slavery rather than work. And since the fruits of science are the gadgets and comforts now better made as well as better designed by machine, it is not unreasonable to imagine that science itself is of the same nature. From the popular view science becomes what computers handle – sets of numbers, preferably large, as in Isaac Asimov's explanations of cosmology. Thus the fusion of the science *qua* religion and science *qua* discipline is already occurring.

The universe, received as a large set of clever tricks, leads to a disengagement from it, makes it about as worthy of notice as a new car. This attitude is reinforced by a technology that has almost exclusive dominion over what we see. The ambient world now presented to the eyes of a city child is more the piling up of clever tricks than an orchestration of natural process. The stage is set for the flourishing of Antaeism. Taken without aesthetic, as a list of independent measures rather than chains of definite forms, correlated rather than caused, governed macroscopically by probability rather than necessity, the phenomenal world fades. What one perceives becomes not different in substance from confections that model it, and the models not different in principle one from the other.

Possibly our metaphysics could have withstood the strain if only the pressure of man on man were somewhat less. But along with the methodical devaluation of the world has come the pressure to learn how to deal with each other as men. That same expediency which destroyed the schools in the early Middle Ages, now drives us again. And attention turns from the whole nature (as somehow explicable, given money enough and time) to man himself. The accedia that palls the schools in the United States comes only partly from their conversion to an industry, or tissue culture for administrators. Most of my colleagues are also old prostitutes and we don't mind supporting ourselves that way. Indeed, we will continue to lie, cheat, embezzle, and pimp as is the custom, in order to keep our laboratories going and our students financed. Much more disheartening is to find now in the clear eyes of these students as in the bloodshot eyes of our administrators how the world has changed from a great chain of being to a jigsaw puzzle, the connections between the parts arbitrary or conventional, the nature of the parts accidental or contrived. Puzzles are, in the end, boring. So it is that many young physicists and chemists are turning to biology and biologists are turning to medicine and social science in one general compulsion to work with man himself. But the nature of man has also been compromised by the spirit of the age, the same Antaeism that governs whatever science has no central theory. From the nature of psychological tests, from the results of brain stimulation, from the discovery of 'centers' in the brain (e.g. those for 'pain' or 'pleasure'), from the attempts to make the blind see by inserting a primitive television set in the brain, from experiments on social interaction in small groups, from the studies of learning in children, in a word, from the whole of contemporary psychology and so-called brain sciences, the image of man is that of a determined mosaic of *stimulus–response* mechanisms, perhaps modified contingently, but still a clockwork that can be disassembled. Epistemology has become a dirty word. In this atmosphere the computerniks rightly call the brain 'merely a meat machine'.

From this over-riding materially determinist point of view, wherein mental causation is ultimately described in terms of a Cartesian mechanics, the social scientist proceeds to handle groups of men. The partitioning of work even tries to resemble what once happened in physics. It is left to the psychologist to say what are the eigen-characteristics of that social particle, man, but the social scientist writes the thermodynamics of the masses, defines social heat, social order, social equilibrium, etc. In his sphere man is a bundle of properties that can be abstracted only from the aggregate. As temperature has no meaning for the single particle, so do his group dynamics have no counterpart in the individual. Older theories like the tripartite soul of Plato, inverted by Freud, took society and the individual as mirrors of each other, but such an idealist bias corrupts the collection of data, and so is disappearing.

Here is our new priestling, despised by the theologian, the proper scientist, but heard in the parishes to which high learning never penetrates and it is from him that the new church emanates rather than from learned arguments. Already his asceticism is wondrous – a mortification of spirit in an air-conditioned desert where once the flesh wasted on the hot sands of Libya. For he has denied himself all those weaknesses that plague commoner and professor alike, mercy, empathy, understanding and, most important of all, that generative property of mind, taste itself. To test his powers he will even take compassion to discourse, as once the desert fathers took whores to bed, in order to show his faith unmoved. In his hands, through a ritual he need not understand, by instruments he need not know, a miracle occurs that transubstantiates flesh to number. So are the Vietnam peasants pacified by the six-fold connected society, plants shorn of their verdure when the threshold of hunger is calculated. How many men can we lose, by current opinion in the middle west? How many can they lose before the structure of their country submits to our will that is given precisely by models that even generals can grasp? And internally, how is dissent distributed, what connects and disconnects political action, how is credit distributed among the poor? How is intelligence related to class, how is class related to education, how is education related to profession, how is the hierarchy structured? What are the frames of reference from which the expendable ones hang as if on crosses? I do not need to give you specifics. You have read the newspapers, the Pentagon papers, Noam Chomsky's dissection of the arrogance in our social scientists turned to politics, the power behind the drone. But also you must read Professor Herrnstein's handling of the genetic inferiority of the lower classes, and Professor Jansen's discussion of the genetic inferiority of the black man, and the clever discovery of inherent inability to read in the American Indian, to realize the true power of endless number in the paper output, the interminable paper output that serves our Caesars. But do you think it is different in the Soviet Union, or France, or any other developed country? Of course, there are, possibly, some honest men in the field, as once there were honest monks, and they may even be in the majority for all I know or can read of what they issue, but I am not talking of them, rather their church, not of their beliefs, rather the public policies issued under their collective imprimatur. Yet, in fairness to them, as to the natural scientist, one must show the problems they face.

There are so damned many men, and so many diverse aspects to them, that sooner or later the social observer must interpose between himself and his material a data-gathering and data-arranging device – a kind of shaped filter or Procrustean bed to isolate features of moment. Gathering his data by questionnaire rather than by discussion, so as to exclude bias, counting noses and words rather than taking meanings, so as to define a set, converting people to symbols and then draining the symbols of reference, the social scientist is now, like a mathematician, almost completely abstract, and able to handle social relations with divine disinterest.

But the immense ease with which the data can be shuffled by machine has seduced him. Model after model springs to mind before the huge ink-blot of correlation matrices. He must test them, cautiously, carefully. Since he is studying an interactive and sensitive system that is willing, almost eager to accommodate itself to any imposed constraints, that, in fact, has been evolved like some transcendental Geisha girl to be all things to all customers, he can only enter into a *folie à deux*, a mutual delusion, with the society he studies. Whatever he does to it will have an effect, and the effect will always be significant, must be significant, for his model. It is a triumph, elsewhere in science, to find a technique that is useful in confirming or denying what one proposes. It would be a triumph to find a social experiment without consequences to the ideas of the experimenter. Not even economics, that almost decent discipline, is exempt.

What the epiphany of the computer has done in the social sciences is to remove any tendency to an aesthetic, to a judgment by taste, as it has done for all other sciences not yet possessed of a firm central theory. It has substituted for understanding a patchwork of rules of thumb, often neither tested nor intelligible. On the superstition that reduction to number is the same as abstraction, it permits any arbitrary assemblage of data to be mined for relations that can then be named and reified in the same way as Fritz Mauthner once imagined that myths arise. Nor can the differences between other science and this sort of science be exposed from the outside – since the programs, subroutines, software and hardware cannot be distinguished between a problem in cosmology and the calculation of probable incidence of sexual aberrations in radical students.

I have gone into these matters to a tedious extent in order to prepare you for a glimpse of the saviour himself, as noble in concept as any modern enterprise, possibly the noblest of them all, but also the most vicious in effect. This king, this bright star in the diadem of our paper universe is a project called Artificial Intelligence. You have heard vague rumors of his coming, and there will be a point at which you will be told that he came but you were looking elsewhere.

The venture is to change machine from being sorcerer's apprentice to being itself the sorcerer. Again, as always, there are two aspects to the science. On the one hand there is the serious attempt, first, to find what are the properties and limits of computers as they are now or can be shortly, and second, whether or not human perception and judgment have rules that can be formalized and so modelled on machines. These are complex and beautiful questions. On the other hand there is the public aspect that promises new hope for automatic baby-sitters, psychiatrists, and executives. Within any single project, whether at MIT or Stanford, Tokyo or Moscow, there are at the same time those who are concerned with theory and those who promise performance to the eagerly waiting government that waits on a new and powerful tool. From the government's point of view, I may add, it doesn't matter one bit whether or not the device can be used, for all that is required of it is proclaimed existence, the public belief in an inspired golem, for the government to let it be known it is in use. Wiener attributed too much integrity to our leaders in his warning on this subject – his book, *God and Golem*.

The aim of those who promise performance can be given by a recently occurred anecdote. You may have read that a Japanese consortium has convinced its government to invest many millions of dollars in an artificial intelligence. I suppose also that you know of recent Russian interest in the same topic. The leader of a major American computer project is trying to persuade the US government also to invest heavily. For, this leader points out, the first machine devised that can proceed by itself will be given the task of designing a yet cleverer machine, and so on, until the third or fourth generation should be able to take over the world, and which do we as Americans want to have, their machine taking us over, or our machine defending us? I assume, by now, that most of you understand our euphemisms.

This is the sort of language that Caesar understands, and if anything characterizes the administrative algebraist, it is an extended low cunning. But you will note the administrative aims and weigh them against the search for pure knowledge on the part of those few scientists left who are interested in the computer as an object of study. The same unscrupulousness that has taken social science into applied social engineering and poisoned enduringly the field, is now used to develop a complement to the social engineer that makes the new Church invincible. For it is that Church and not the rulers it will appear to support, that becomes our ruling class, but now with a cap of invisibility or impenetrability.

I, in common with many other teachers, have already conceded defeat. It is not apocalypse that we cry but a dull death-watch that we hold. The spirit has already become uniformly Antaeic, and the vision is of a moribund world plucking at the coverlet and babbling of clear waters and green fields. Distant trees, blue skies, lassitude and anger, my hand and your body are truly, truly no more than appropriately long sets in a set-theoretically definable cosmos. It is not, sadly, what a programmer would call a neat universe, and the only frames of reference in sight seem to be gallows.

Since I have come to fear the administrative use of any experiment, good or bad, in the social and behavioral sciences, I spend my time with those jolly friars that tend the computer. The world, to them, is a system of propositions about elements that have, through human muddle-headedness, been improperly defined. When the definitions can be made precise then the propositions can be handled. One remembers Confucius and the rectification of names. They have finally found the solution to the mind-body problem – there is no mind. The computernik leans over his drink in debate 'Well then, define the mind. I will not permit you to use undefined words'. Indeed, indeed. Why then let us define a man. There he is, a featherless biped with wide toenails to distinguish him from a plucked chicken. What in hell does he mean by defining, this jolly cleric? As if definition were applicable to phenomena at all, to a stone, a mote, a photon? But such is the gist of our foolish debates on thinking machines. And he has the advantage for he and I both know that physiology and psychology are dead issues, that it is probably easier to build a brain than analyse it. By the time he is ready, man will be evolved to act like his models.

One week he calls me up. There is a program devised by Professor Weizenbaum and it is an automatic non-directive psychiatrist. I type in, 'I feel lousy'. It types back, 'Why do you feel lousy?' I type in 'Because you are talking to me', and it types back 'Does it bother you that I am talking to you?' and so on and so on. I know Weizenbaum very well. I know he designed this program not for therapy but to show how little content there was in that therapeutic discipline. So I say this, and the computernik cries out 'But you can tell it from the real therapist? Operationally is there a difference?' There really is none. And this is the way it goes. Ingenious solutions of technical problems, and heaps and heaps of clever tricks, because to this new religion that is what evolution is, a concatenation of clever tricks.

In such hands our lives become trash. 'Love?' they say; 'come back week after next. We have a contract this week to translate Sir John Suckling into Icelandic.' But week after next a bug has shown up in the translating program. There is a regular museum of bugs by now – they are seeking a universal bug-killer, for all that stands between them and the final conquest of cognition are these few bugs.

Their attitude is infectious in spite of the barrenness of results. One wanders around like a patient after shock treatment. The stars, so what; the war, so what; my friends are dying, so what; I don't feel anything, so what. Precisely here comes my revelation. For the world, decomposed by the antipoetic act, can now be reassembled in a non-biodegradable way. Confronted by my own failure of nerve, by the senseless and brutal war in Vietnam, the starving of Pakistani people with American cooperation, the daily tally of planned, annotated and correlated disaster I feel as if almost any universe were preferable, that the metamorphosis of the vampire cannot come soon enough.

And that is, I imagine, how it will appear to others. Sooner or later the promised delivery of a guaranteed thinker to advise our elect representatives will be replaced by the noise that he exists, the rumour that he has just passed a street away, the certainty that he now rules.

Here, then, is the new saviour. And do not imagine that his retinue is different from what it was for Another after His rumour was inscribed. Attending the chrome-plated tradition are some of the sickest enthusiasts since St Simeon Stylites, faceless, empty-eyed, cooperating in their anonymity on programs inscribed like palimpsests on a poetry that no one understands any more anyway. To them is the truth revealed, and in their numbers as in the prayers of the African fathers, all our liberties and loves, our sex and our science will become as dust, independent sense-data points.

Science says, and the poor will be marked unto the *n*th generation. Science says, and not a sparrow falls but the machine slaps it down and takes the identification number. Culture will be preserved in this apostolic empire, and will be displayed weekends on the walls of an IBM musuem. Cultural imperialism? Nonsense. Our devices will bear the stamp of the country ordering them. Men will not be much changed in general. They will have achieved identity through indiscernibility as was foretold. Yet, as in Chicago, they will dance Ukrainian dances at least once a week to remind them of their heritage. Our sales representatives, trained in your tribal taboos, will call on you shortly. You have no choice but to buy. For this is the new rationalism, the new messiah, the new Church, and the new Dark Ages come upon us.

Ode to Terminus

W. H. AUDEN

The High Priests of telescopes and cyclotrons
keep making pronouncements about happenings
   on scales too gigantic or dwarfish
   to be noted by our native senses,

discoveries which, couched in the elegant
euphemisms of algebra, look innocent,
   harmless enough but, when translated
   into the vulgar anthropomorphic

tongue, will give no cause for hilarity
to gardeners or house-wives: if galaxies
   bolt like panicking mobs, if mesons
   riot like fish in a feeding-frenzy,

it sounds too like Political History
to boost civil morale, too symbolic of
   the crimes and strikes and demonstrations
   we are supposed to gloat on at breakfast.

How trite, though, our fears beside the miracle
that we're here to shiver, that a Thingummy
   so addicted to lethal violence
   should have somehow secreted a placid

tump with exactly the right ingredients
to start and to cocker Life, that heavenly
   freak for whose manage we shall have to
   give account at the Judgement, our Middle-

-Earth, where Sun-Father to all appearances
moves by day from orient to occident,
   and his light is felt as a friendly
   presence, not as a photonic bombardment,

where all visibles do have definite
outlines they stick to, and are undoubtedly
  at rest or in motion, where lovers
  recognise each other by their surface,

where to all species except the talkative
have been allotted the niche and diet that
  become them. This, whatever micro-
  -biology may think, is the world we

really live in and that saves our sanity,
who know all too well how the most erudite
  mind behaves in the dark without a
  surround it is called on to interpret,

how, discarding rhythm, punctuation, metaphor,
it sinks into a drivelling monologue,
  too liberal to see a joke or
  distinguish a penis from a pencil.

Venus and Mars are powers too natural
to temper our outlandish extravagance:
  You alone, Terminus, the Mentor,
  can teach us how to alter our gestures.

God of walls, doors and reticence, nemesis
overtakes the sacrilegious technocrat,
  but blessed is the City that thanks you
  for giving us games and grammar and metres.

By whose grace, also, every gathering
of two or three in confident amity
  repeats the pentecostal marvel,
  as each in each finds his right translator.

In this world our colossal immodesty
has plundered and poisoned, it is possible
  You still might save us, who by now have
  learned this: that scientists, to be truthful,

must remind us to take all they say as a
tall story, that abhorred in the Heav'ns are all
  self-proclaimed poets who, to wow an
  audience, utter some resonant lie.

Part Five

WAYS AHEAD

As introduction to this section I include a piece which I wrote in 1972, designed to chart an emerging landscape of which many people were beginning to get glimpses as the clouds of doom rolled away. Looking back, the tone though not the content of the article was perhaps somewhat over-optimistic. The work described here is still going ahead, and indeed more has been added to it, but the pace has been slower than seemed likely in 1972 – at least in one sense. The article is really about the alternative institutions that were set up to investigate and promote some of the new ideals to emerge from the doomsday debate. Those institutions have not made any substantial mark as yet. On the other hand, and this the article does fail to reflect, the number of men and women who have privately gone about the business of setting up their own solutions – even in as small a way as beginning once again to grow their own vegetables – has been enormous. There has been a substantial movement of people from the town and city towards the rural smallholding, in America, the UK and northern Europe. Little-used land is once more being intensively worked by people determined that life will be better for them with less money, more freedom and an acre or two plus odd jobs in the local community. If my own experiences in the Welsh borders are typical, this growing band of people is making a substantial impact, although it may not be one of which the media have become aware. But perhaps this too was the lesson of the 1960s: global change only makes sense when it is the sum of small individual changes, freely made and quietly taken.

All this would have delighted the anarchist prince, Peter Kropotkin. Writing in the 1890s, he summarizes exactly many of the reasons why this move back to the land has come about, even though it is eighty years since he foresaw its necessity.

But the anarchic implications of ecological action are too extraordinary to be left to history. Fortunately, in Murray Bookchin we have an able contemporary successor, one who bridges (his article was written and published in 1966) the gap between the essentially political Kropotkin and the much more sophisticated, scientific analysis by John Todd of the need for a humanized science which truly belongs to the people. The New Alchemy Institutes, which were John Todd's brain children as much as anyone else's, are perhaps the very real exceptions in terms of alternative institutions. As can be judged from his piece here, the NAI has not only found itself a job but appears to be getting on with it smartly.

John and Sally Seymour's piece I have included because I like it, I suppose, for its bluntness. Without having been near either a sociology department or a United Nations conference, they appear to have picked up the tune somewhere early in the 1950s, and they too have been getting on with it ever since. And what they feel, succinctly summarized in two or three paragraphs, about the post-industrial society is remarkably similar to what the much longer-winded academic ramblings in the same area would say if they could be boiled down half as well. All roads lead to . . . certainly not Rome, but at least towards a landscape suitable for human dwellings.

And finally, for humility, we have Derek Bryan on China. For humility, because it may well be that the West in its ardent new-found revolutionary zeal for novel solutions has missed the point: the solutions are not so novel, having been evolving for many centuries in a country which now boasts nearly a fifth of the world population. To be honest, I still don't know whether to believe or, if to believe it now, to believe that it could last. But there is at least a case for the willing suspension of disbelief. Maybe . . . and if so, the future is indeed an open book.

Technology for an alternative society

ROBIN CLARKE

The great doomsday debate of the past five years seems to be drawing to a close. The likelihood that the experiment of human evolution will shortly be brought to an abrupt close by any of several possible catastrophes – nuclear or biological warfare, ecological disaster, population collapse, the war of the southern poor against the northern rich or massive outbreaks of correlated disease and famine – seems to have become more distant in many people's minds. The 'facts', of course, have not changed, and I am talking here only of the psychological

From the *New Scientist*, 11 January 1973.

aspects of the paradigm debate between those who believe that the future will progress smoothly and improve, and those who believe that it will undergo a sharp discontinuity and suddenly worsen. Here it is not so much the facts which are important but the values and beliefs held by men who concern themselves with the future. To some of those, of course, real Doomsday would be reached were the world to continue smoothly on its present course of mass exploitation and pillage of the environment.

If then we now look round at the confusion left by half a decade of Earth days, Stockholm conferences and anti-Vietnam peace marches, what do we see? First, I believe, one lasting effect is that science and technology have taken a severe pounding from which they will not recover. The naïve analysis that even if most of our troubles stem from science and technology then only more science and technology will ever cure them has proved too frail a prop for any but the most thoughtless technocrats. On the other hand, and this is the point which now needs emphasis, the blanket rejection of all things scientific and technical – so notable a feature of, for example, the counter-culture's retreat to the woods and the fields of America and northern Europe – is also faltering. The new view that emerges is still that science and technology will not themselves find a way out of the present crisis – but that any real way out certainly will involve a science and a technology, even if those activities in the future bear little quantitative or qualitative resemblance to science and technology today. All this is evident from the concern now being shown for the invention of new forms of science. The literature includes suggestions for a compassionate science, a subjective science, a morphic science, radical science, democratic science, critical science, adversary science, science for the people and even a science for those experimenting with altered states of consciousness.

It is evident too from the attempts now being made to invent new technologies; words which three years ago were known to few indeed have begun to feature in sources as far apart as United Nations publications and the underground literature; they include intermediate technology, alternative technology, village technology, appropriate technology, people's technology, organic technology, ecological technology, biotechnics and 'soft' technology. Each of these sciences and technologies has its own exponents, and serious attempts are being made to outline their properties, and to assess their advantages.

What is interesting, then, is that the entirely negative stance of the professional doomsayers is transforming itself slowly into a faltering inquiry into possible new directions for new forms of 'progress'. At this stage it is perhaps more important to dwell on this general trend rather than to analyse in detail any one of the new sciences or technologies which is shaping up on the drawing boards of theory. And in broad terms they do all share common features which contrast harshly with those of existing science and technology. To generalize, they seek to put men before machines, people before governments, practice before theory, student before teacher, the country before the city, smallness before bigness, wholeness before reductionism, organic materials before synthetic ones, plants before animals, craftsmanship before expertise, and quality before quantity.

One could go on, and I do not pretend that any of these vague forms of words summarize succinctly any of the exact aims of the practitioners of the new science and technology. But I do think that a philosopher of set theory would find in these loose associations a cluster which may mark the beginning of a new scientific and technical paradigm. We see emerging a science and technology designed not to dominate nature but to mesh with it, and one whose objective will not be to push mankind ever faster into new follies but to help fulfil, along with other equally valuable forms of knowledge and technique, an ethical and social function within the norms of a new society.

'Safe' levels and 'permissible' doses

One of the most attractive features of the new paradigm is the way it deals with 'side-effects'. In the old paradigm, for example, the crucial question of any technical development was how to evaluate the negative effects of the advance and how to arrive at a conclusion that they were either smaller or bigger than the positive ones. Thus arose such bizarre concepts as 'safe' levels of radiation, pollution or environmental destruction. Economists would calculate 'permissible' levels of domestic saving in theory attainable by a grindingly poor people to achieve a level of economic growth which in the end benefited only the already rich. In the process men became counted as statistics and a development which produced a mortality of say, only 0.005 per cent could be heralded as 'completely safe'. In fact 0·005 per cent of the world population is more than 150,000 people, and if you were one of them you could surely be excused for a refusal to partake in any such elaborate calculus.

Take the question of thermal pollution from power stations, a problem which seems to worsen all the way along the technocratic line from fossil fuel plants to conventional nuclear ones, to breeder reactors to fusion factories. The old paradigm makes a theoretical calculation about the amount of heat that must be lost for every kilowatt generated, discounts for heat exchangers and cooling towers, plays around with the idea of transferring the thermal waste from one area to another (and thus neatly losing it from the calculations), estimates that even if 20 billion people used 20 kilowatts each the black body radiation temperature of the Earth would rise only a degree or so, and declares the matter closed.

The new paradigm says, quite rightly, that if you put that power plant on my doorstep I will certainly feel the effect and the matter is far from closed. Instead, it says, it will use solar power or wind power, sources which add precisely nothing to the Earth's thermal load and hence make meaningless the whole question of 'safe thermal loads'. And if those sources do not provide enough power, then two things are needed: more research, and cultural and social adaptation, the two factors to be considered carefully in conjunction with one another. 'How safe is safe' thus becomes a meaningless question (and in any case we always knew it was unanswerable): the meaningful exercise is to find the new technology which blends so well with the natural systems on which we depend that the question never arises. In this context, it should be noted that a new technology is far from the easy way out and certainly requires fiendish scientific ingenuity. The old cliché that any future lapse from current forms of science and technology will in some curious way leave man's brain in an addled condition is thus disposed of, without recourse to arguments about what it was that went on in the minds of Beethoven, Bach, Plato and Abelard.

Nothing, of course, is ever really new and the 'new' directions into which science and technology soon seem bound to venture have an important political, if not technical, history. Going no farther back than the nineteenth century, one can cite first the Russian prince Kropotkin and the American writer Thoreau as examples of people who were already searching for new meanings to the Victorian ideal of progress, in the form of constructive anarchy. In the United States the movement flowered briefly in the 1930s under the gentle patronage of men like Ralph Borsodi, Scott Nearing and Peter van Dresser. In 1938 the last-named wrote for *Harper's Magazine* an article entitled 'New tools for democracy'* which described how the liberating force of science and technology could be used to spell out a non-technocratic future on a human scale. With the date changed by thirty-four years, that article would still pass as a perfect critique of our present ills, and it provides a vivid comparison to van Dresser's 1972 publication *A Landscape for Humans* which describes a detailed plan for a gentle and ecological development of a part of New Mexico. More recently, the philosophy of Gandhi and the efforts of Schumacher in England in setting up the Intermediate Technology Development Group in the 1960s are classic examples of dissident attempts to reunite human beings with human tasks.

And now that the ecological input has been added, the contemporary writings of Murray Bookchin take on huge significance. Bookchin was one of the first to try to unite an anarchist libertarian philosophy with the revolutionary implications of science and technology. The flowering of local culture, individual expression and human diversity which has always been a hallmark of constructive anarchy seems almost too perfect a fit with the 'new' discovery that nature abhors not only the vacuum but also monoculture: diversity, as a key word both in global political

* Reprinted in the present volume, p. 14.

development and in the management and orchestration of natural systems, is certainly in the ascendancy in this Age of Aquarius.

Constructive new thought

New Scientist readers have already been well cared for in the general area of the existing critiques of scientific progress in the form of the writings of men like Roszak, Mishan, Galbraith, Skolimowski and Ravetz. But they have not, I think, yet been exposed to much of the constructive thought that is now beginning to find expression in many parts of the world, and this may be a good opportunity to light a candle for some bold new experiments. In Ethiopia John Morgan, with the help of the University of Addis Ababa, is working at the level of village technology, producing a heady blend of primitive technology and counter-culture inventions such as the solar heating device developed at Drop-out City in the United States. In Cape Cod, California, New Mexico, Costa Rica and soon Nova Scotia, the New Alchemy Institute ('to restore the land, protect the seas, and inform the Earth's stewards') continues its programme to promote social and biological transformations. Its director, John Todd, who believes that we should turn people into scientists as it may be too late to make humanitarians out of scientists, is the only man I know who has actually set in operation a science performed by the people for the people. Through the pages of *Organic Gardening and Farming* he has persuaded Americans from all over the country to join with his institute in making their own experiments with highly productive, small-scale food-producing systems. The most notable is that in which the experimenters construct small geodesic domes in their back yards, which act as hot houses for the breeding of protein-rich Tilapia fish in water seeded with algae and fertilized with grass clippings contained in a child's paddling pool – a development which promises to make the protein yields of the protagonists of the green revolution look frankly silly.

In India a weekly newspaper on village development and technology is soon to appear and several model village developments are under way or being planned. From Salzburg Robert Jungk is spreading the message of soft technology to the fifty or sixty people he appears to meet on his average working day. In the Ardèche in southern France Phillippe Arreteau began last summer his three-month courses on intermediate and soft technologies, designed equally for students from the Third World and from the French communes. In London the Intermediate Technology Development Group continues to gather strength, and a company called Low Impact Technologies has been set up. In Normandy and Wales, Biotechnic Research and Development is about to begin research operations in its two centres which are designed to become models of how small groups of people might want to live in the not-so-distant future.

The motives behind it all

I have left to last the most important question: what, exactly, is it that these and many other people are driving at? First, they would like to see the appalling global flight from the country to the city halted and reversed, in the name of sanity, ecology and the population explosion (which in most countries of the world is evident only in cities; thanks to capital intensive, mechanized, large-scale farming techniques, the countryside has in many places been reduced to a desolate, food-producing factory). Second, they would like to see real development for the Third World as fast as possible – but a development that benefited the people, was compatible with existing social norms and cultures, and made maximum use of local resources. Third, they would like to see the ecological crisis resolved in what is the only possible way – by a reintegration of man with the natural systems of which he is and must always remain a part. And fourth, they would like to see science and technology reduced to a proper perspective from their present monopolistic position in relation to all other forms of disciplined inquiry, craft technique and creative activity.

One might imagine the landscape of this new Utopia looking something like this: a countryside dotted with windmills and solar houses, studded with intensively but organically worked plots of land; food production systems dependent on the integration of many different species, with timber, fish, animals and plants playing mutually dependent roles, with wilderness areas plentifully available where perhaps even our vicious distinction between hunting and domestication was partially broken down; a life style for men and women which involved hard physical work but not over excessively long hours or in a tediously repetitive way; an architecture which sought to free men from external services and which brought them into contact with one another, rather than separated them into cubicles where the goggle box and bed were the only possible diversions; a political system so decentralized and small that individuals – all individuals – could play more than a formal, once-every-five-years role; a philosophy of change that viewed the micro-system as the operative unit; and a city-scape conceived on a human scale and as a centre for recreation. Whoever conceived the idea that the country was best suited to become a human dormitory, and the city best suited to provide space for people to sit at desks, has much to answer for.

If there is hope that a future of this kind might one day be realized, it is not because men who are clever enough to go to the Moon can fix anything. But it may be because once having been there, and seen what it's like, men could once again learn to rejoice in the greenness of their planet and, to use Ivan Illich's words, 'celebrate their diversity'.

Fields, factories and workshops tomorrow

PETER KROPOTKIN

I once took a knapsack and went on foot out of London, through Sussex. I had read Léonce de Lavergne's work and expected to find a soil busily cultivated; but neither round London nor still less farther south did I see men in the fields. In the Weald I could walk for twenty miles without crossing anything but heath or woodlands, rented as pheasant-shooting grounds to 'London gentlemen', as the labourers said. 'Ungrateful soil' was my first thought; but then I would occasionally come to a farm at the crossing of two roads and see the same soil bearing a rich crop; and my next thought was *tel seigneur, telle terre*, as the French peasants say. Later on I saw the rich fields of the midland counties; but even there I was struck by not perceiving the same busy human labour which I was accustomed to admire on the Belgian and French fields. But I ceased to wonder when I learnt that only 1,383,000 men and women in England and Wales work in the fields, while more than 16,000,000 belong to the 'professional, domestic, indefinite, and unproductive class', as these pitiless statisticians say. One million human beings cannot productively cultivate an area of 33,000,000 acres, unless they can resort to the Bonanza farms methods of culture.

Again, taking Harrow as the centre of my excursions, I could walk five miles towards London, or turning my back upon it, and I could see nothing east or west but meadow land on which they hardly cropped 2 tons of hay per acre – scarcely enough to keep alive one milch cow on each 2 acres. Man is conspicuous by his absence from those meadows; he rolls them with a heavy roller in the spring; he spreads some manure every two or three years; then he disappears until the time has come to make hay. And that – within ten miles from Charing Cross, close to a city with 5,000,000 inhabitants, supplied with Flemish and Jersey potatoes, French salads and Canadian apples. In the hands of the Paris gardeners, each 1000 acres situated within the same distance from the city would be cultivated by at least 2000 human beings, who would get vegetables to the value of from £50 to £300 per acre. But here the

From *Fields, Factories and Workshops Tomorrow*, ed. Colin Ward (Allen & Unwin, and Harper & Row, 1974). The book was first published in 1899.

acres which only need human hands to become an inexhaustible source of golden crops lie idle, and they say to us, 'Heavy clay!' without even knowing that in the hands of man there are no unfertile soils; that the most fertile soils are not in the prairies of America, nor in the Russian steppes; that they are in the peat-bogs of Ireland, on the sand downs of the northern sea-coast of France, on the craggy mountains of the Rhine, where they have been made by man's hands.

The most striking fact is, however, that in some undoubtedly fertile parts of the country things are even in a worse condition. My heart simply ached when I saw the state in which land is kept in South Devon, and when I learned to know what 'permanent pasture' means. Field after field is covered with nothing but grass, 3 inches high, and thistles in profusion. Twenty, thirty such fields can be seen at one glance from the top of every hill; and thousands of acres are in that state, notwithstanding that the grandfathers of the present generation have devoted a formidable amount of labour to the clearing of that land from the stones, to fencing it, roughly draining it, and the like. In every direction I could see abandoned cottages and orchards going to ruin. A whole population has disappeared, and even its last vestiges must disappear if things continue to go on as they have gone. And this takes place in a part of the country endowed with a most fertile soil and possessed of a climate which is certainly more congenial than the climate of Jersey in spring and early summer – a land upon which even the poorest cottages occasionally raise potatoes as early as the first half of May. But how can that land be cultivated when there is nobody to cultivate it? 'We have fields; men go by, but never go in', an old labourer said to me; and so it is in reality.

Such were my impressions of British agriculture twenty years ago. Unfortunately, both the official statistical data and the mass of private evidence published since tend to show that but little improvement took place in the general conditions of agriculture in this country within the last twenty years. Some successful attempts in various new directions have been made in different parts of the country, and I will have the pleasure to mention them farther on, the more so as they show what a quite average soil in these islands can give when it is properly treated. But over large areas, especially in the southern counties, the general conditions are even worse than they were twenty years ago.

Many causes have combined to produce that undesirable result. The concentration of land-ownership in the hands of big land-owners; the high profits obtained previously; the development of a class of both landlords and farmers who rely chiefly upon other incomes than those they draw from the land, and for whom farming has thus become a sort of pleasant by-occupation or sport; the rapid development of game reserves for sportsmen, both British and foreign; the absence of men of initiative who would have shown to the nation the necessity of a new departure; the absence of a desire to win the necessary knowledge, and the absence of institutions which could widely spread practical agricultural knowledge and introduce improved seeds and seedlings, as the Experimental Farms of the United States and Canada are doing; the dislike of that spirit of agricultural co-operation to which the Danish farmers owe their successes, and so on – all these stand in the way of the unavoidable change in the methods of farming, and produce the results of which the British writers on agriculture are complaining.

It may be said, of course, that this opinion strangely contrasts with the well-known superiority of British agriculture. Do we not know, indeed, that British crops average 28 to 30 bushels of wheat per acre, while in France they reach only from 17 to 20 bushels? Does it not stand in all almanacs that Britain gets every year £200,000,000 sterling worth of animal produce – milk, cheese, meat and wool – from her fields? All that is true, and there is no doubt that in many respects British agriculture is superior to that of many other nations. But a closer acquaintance with British agriculture as a whole discloses many features of inferiority.

However splendid, a meadow remains a meadow, much inferior in productivity to a cornfield; and the fine breeds of cattle appear to be poor creatures as long as each ox requires 3 acres of land to be fed upon. As regards the crops, certainly one may indulge in some admiration at the average 28 or 30 bushels grown in this country; but when we learn that only 1,600,000 to 1,900,000 acres out of the cultivable 33,000,000 bear such crops, we are quite disappointed. Anyone could obtain like results if he were to put all his manure into one-twentieth part of the area which he possesses. Again, the 28 to 30 bushels no longer appear to us so satisfactory when we learn that without any manuring, merely by means of a good culture, they have obtained at Rothamstead an average of 14 bushels per acre from the same plot of land for forty consecutive years.

If we intend to have a correct appreciation of British agriculture, we must not base it upon what is obtained on a few selected and well-manured plots; we must inquire what is done with the territory, taken as a whole. Now, out of each 1000 acres of the aggregate territory of England, Wales and Scotland, 435 acres are left under wood, coppice, heath, buildings, and so on. We need not find fault with that division, because it depends very much upon natural causes. In France and Belgium one-third of the territory is in like manner also treated as uncultivable, although portions of it are continually reclaimed and brought under culture. But, leaving aside the 'uncultivable' portion, let us see what is done with the 565 acres out of 1000 of the 'cultivable' part (32,145,930 acres in Great Britain in 1910). First of all, it is divided into two parts, and one of them, the largest – 308 acres out of 1000 – is left under 'permanent pasture', that is, in most cases it is entirely uncultivated. Very little hay is obtained from it, and some cattle are grazed upon it. More than one-half of the cultivable area is thus left without cultivation, and only 257 acres out of each 1000 acres are under culture. Out of these last, 124 acres are under corn crops, 21 acres under potatoes, 53 acres under green crops, and 73 acres under clover fields and grasses under rotation. And finally, out of the 124 acres given to corn crops, the best 33, and some years only 25 acres (one-fortieth part of the territory, one-twenty-third of the cultivable area), are picked out and sown with wheat. They are well cultivated, well manured, and upon them an average of from 28 to 30 bushels to the acre is obtained; and upon these 25 or 30 acres out of 1000 the world superiority of British agriculture is based.

The net result of all that is, that on nearly 33,000,000 acres of cultivable land the food is grown for one-third part only of the population (more than two-thirds of the food it consumes is imported), and we may say accordingly that, although nearly two-thirds of the territory is cultivable, British agriculture provides home-grown food for each 125 or 135 inhabitants only per square mile (out of 466). In other words, nearly 3 acres of the *cultivable area* are required to grow the food for each person. Let us then see what is done with the land in France and Belgium.

Now, if we simply compare the average 30 bushels per acre of wheat in Great Britain with the average 19 to 20 bushels grown in France within the last ten years, the comparison is all in favour of these islands; but such averages are of little value because the two systems of agriculture are totally different in the two countries. The Frenchman also has his picked and heavily manured '25 to 30 acres' in the north of France and in Ile-de-France, and from these picked areas he obtains average crops ranging from 30 to 33 bushels. However, he sows with wheat, not only the best picked out areas, but also such fields on the Central Plateau and in Southern France as hardly yield 10, 8 and even 6 bushels to the acre, without irrigation; and these low crops reduce the average for the whole country.

The Frenchman cultivates much that is left here under permanent pasture – and this is what is described as his 'inferiority' in agriculture. In fact, although the proportion between what we have named the 'cultivable area' and the total territory is very much the same in France as it is in Great Britain (624 acres out of each 1000 acres of the territory), the area under wheat crops is nearly *six times* as great, in proportion, as what it is in Great Britain (182 acres instead of 25 or 30, out of each 1000 acres): the corn crops altogether cover nearly two-fifths of the cultivable area (375 acres out of 1000), and large areas are given besides to green crops, industrial crops, vine, fruit and vegetables.

Taking everything into consideration, although the Frenchman keeps less cattle, and especially grazes less sheep than the Briton, he nevertheless obtains from his soil nearly all the food that he and his cattle consume. He imports, in an average year, but one-tenth only of what the nation consumes, and he exports to this country considerable quantities of food produce (£10,000,000 worth), not only from the south, but also, and especially, from the shores of the Channel (Brittany butter and vegetables; fruit and vegetables from the suburbs of Paris, and so on).

The net result is that, although one-third part of the territory is also treated as 'uncultivable', the soil of France yields the food for 170 inhabitants per square mile (out of 188), that is, for 40 persons more, per square mile, than this country.

The above will be enough to caution the reader against hasty conclusions as to the impossibility of feeding 46,000,000 people from 78,000,000 acres. They also will enable me to draw the following conclusions: (1) If the soil of the United Kingdom were cultivated only as it *was* forty-five years ago, 24,000,000 people, instead of 17,000,000, could live on home-grown food; and this culture, while giving occupation to an additional 750,000 men, would give nearly 3,000,000 wealthy home customers to the British manufactures. (2) If the cultivable area of the United Kingdom were cultivated as the soil is cultivated *on the average* in Belgium, the United Kingdom would have food for at least 37,000,000 inhabitants; and it might export agricultural produce without ceasing to manufacture, so as freely to supply all the needs of a wealthy population. And finally (3) if the population of this country came to be doubled, all that would be required for producing the food for 90,000,000 inhabitants would be to cultivate the soil as it is cultivated in the best farms of this country, in Lombardy, and in Flanders, and to utilize some meadows, which at present lie almost unproductive, in the same way as the neighbourhoods of the big cities in France are utilized for market-gardening. All these are not fancy dreams, but mere realities; nothing but the modest conclusions from what we see round about us, without any allusion to the agriculture of the future.

If we want, however, to know what agriculture *can be*, and what can be grown on a given amount of soil, we must apply for information to such regions as the district of Saffelare in East Flanders, the island of Jersey, or the irrigated meadows of Lombardy. Or else we may apply to the market-gardeners in this country, or in the neighbourhoods of Paris, or in Holland, or to the 'truck farms' in America, and so on.

While science devotes its chief attention to industrial pursuits, a limited number of lovers of nature and a legion of workers whose very names will remain unknown to posterity have created of late a quite new agriculture, as superior to modern farming as modern farming is superior to the old three-field system of our ancestors. Science seldom guided them, and sometimes misguided – as was the case with Liebig's theories, developed to the extreme by his followers, who induced us to treat plants as glass recipients of chemical drugs, and who forgot that the only science capable of dealing with life and growth is physiology, not chemistry. Science seldom has guided them: they proceeded in the empirical way; but, like the cattle-growers who opened new horizons to biology, they have opened a new field of experimental research for the physiology of plants. They have created a totally new agriculture. They smile when we boast about the rotation system, having permitted us to take from the field one crop every year, or four crops each three years, because their ambition is to have 6 and 9 crops from the very same plot of land during the twelve months. They do not understand our talk about good and bad soils, because they make the soil themselves, and make it in such quantities as to be compelled yearly to sell some of it: otherwise it would raise up the level of their gardens by half an inch every year. They aim at cropping, not 5 or 6 tons of grass on the acre, as we do, but from 50 to 100 tons of various vegetables on the same space; not £5 worth of hay but £100 worth of vegetables, of the plainest description, cabbage and carrots, and more than £200 worth under intensive horicultural treatments. This is where agriculture is going now.

We know that the dearest of all varieties of our staple food is meat; and those who are not vegetarians, either by persuasion, or by necessity, consume on the average 225 pounds of meat – that is, roughly speaking, a little less than the third part of an ox – every year. And we have seen that, even in this country and Belgium, 2 to 3 acres are wanted for keeping one head of horned cattle; so that a community of, say, 1,000,000 inhabitants would have to reserve somewhere about 1,000,000 acres of land for supplying it with meat. But if we go to the farm of M. Goppart – one of the promoters of *ensilage* in France – we shall see him growing, on a drained and well-manured field, no less than an average of 120,000 pounds of corngrass to the acre, which gives 30,000 pounds of dry hay – that is, the food of 1 horned beast per acre. The produce is thus trebled.

The above examples are striking enough, and yet those afforded by the market-gardening culture are still more striking. I mean the culture carried on in the neighbourhood of big cities, and more especially the *culture maraîchère* round Paris. In this culture each plant is treated according to its age. The seeds germinate and the seedlings develop their first four leaflets in especially favourable conditions of soil and temperature; then the best seedlings are picked out and transplanted into a bed of fine loam, under a frame or in the open air, where they freely develop their rootlets, and, gathered on a limited space, receive more than the usual care. Only after this preliminary training are they bedded in the open ground, where they grow till ripe. In such a culture the primitive condition of the soil is of little account, because loam is made out of the old forcing beds. The seeds are carefully tried, the seedlings receive proper attention, and there is no fear of drought, because of the variety of crops, the liberal watering with the help of a steam engine, and the stock of plants always kept ready to replace the weakest individuals. Almost each plant is treated individually.

There prevails, however, with regard to market-gardening, a misunderstanding which it would be well to remove. It is generally supposed that what chiefly attracts market-gardening to the great centres of population is the market. It must have been so; and so it may be still, but to some extent only. A great number of the Paris *maraîchers*, even of those who have their gardens within the walls of the city and whose main crop consists of vegetables in season, export the whole of their produce to England. What chiefly attracts the gardener to the great cities is stable manure; and this is not wanted so much for increasing the richness of the soil – one-tenth part of the manure used by the French gardeners would do for that purpose – but for keeping the soil at a certain temperature. Early vegetables pay best, and in order to obtain early produce not only the air but the soil as well must be warmed; and this is done by putting great quantities of properly mixed manure into the soil; its fermentation heats it. But it is evident that with the present development of industrial skill, the heating of the soil could be obtained more economically and more easily by hot-water pipes. Consequently, the French gardeners begin more and more to make use of portable pipes, or *thermosiphons*, provisionally established in the cool frames. This new improvement becomes of general use, and we have the authority of Barral's *Dictionnaire d'Agriculture* to affirm that it gives excellent results. Under this system, stable manure is used mainly for producing loam.

As to the different degrees of fertility of the soil – always the stumbling-block of those who write about agriculture – the fact is that in market-gardening the soil is always *made*, whatever it originally may have been. Consequently, it is now a usual stipulation of the renting contracts of the Paris *maraîchers* that the gardener may carry away his soil, down to a certain depth, when he quits his tenancy. He himself makes it, and when he moves to another plot he carts his soil away, together with his frames, his water-pipes, and his other belongings.

Let us take, for instance, the orchard – the *marais* – of M. Ponce, the author of a well-known work on the *culture maraîchère*. His orchard covered only two and seven-tenths acres. The outlay for the establishment, including a steam engine for watering purposes, reached £1136. Eight persons, M. Ponce included, cultivated the orchard and carried the vegetables to the market, for which purpose 1 horse was kept; when returning from Paris they brought in manure, for which £100 was spent every year. Another £100 was spent in rent and taxes. But how to enumerate all that was gathered every year on this plot of less than 3 acres, without filling two pages or more with the most wonderful figures? One must read them in M. Ponce's work, but here are the chief items: More than 20,000 pounds of carrots; more than 20,000 pounds of onions, radishes and other vegetables sold by weight; 6000 heads of cabbage; 3000 of cauliflower; 5000 baskets of tomatoes; 5000 dozen of choice fruit; and 154,000 heads of salad; in short, a total of 250,000 pounds of vegetables. The soil was made to such an amount out of forcing beds that every year 250 cubic yards of loam had to be sold. Similar examples could be given by the dozen, and the best evidence against any possible exaggeration of the results is the very high rent paid by the gardeners, which reaches in the suburbs of London from £10 to £15 per acre, and in the suburbs of Paris attains as much as £32 per acre.

No less than 2125 acres are cultivated round Paris in that way by 5000 persons, and thus not only the 2,000,000 Parisians are supplied with vegetables, but the surplus is also sent to London.

The above results are obtained with the help of warm frames, thousands of glass bells, and so on. But even without such costly things, with only 36 yards of frames for seedlings, vegetables are grown *in the open air* to the value of £200 per acre. It is obvious, however, that in such cases the high selling prices of the crops are not due to the high prices fetched by early vegetables in winter; they are entirely due to the high crops of the plainest ones.

Let me add also that all this wonderful culture has entirely developed in the second half of the nineteenth century. Before that, it was quite primitive. But now the Paris gardener not only defies the soil – he would grow the same crops on an ashphalt pavement – he defies climate. His walls, which are built to reflect light and to protect the wall-trees from the northern winds, his wall-tree shades and glass protectors, his frames and *pépinières* have made a real garden, a rich Southern garden, out of the suburbs of Paris. He has given to Paris the 'two degrees less of latitude' after which a French scientific writer was longing; he supplies his city with mountains of grapes and fruit at any season; and in the early spring he inundates and perfumes it with flowers. But he does not only grow articles of luxury. The culture of plain vegetables on a large scale is spreading every year; and the results are so good that there are now practical *maraîchers* who venture to maintain that if all the food, animal and vegetable, necessary for 4,500,000 inhabitants of the departments of Seine and Seine-et-Oise had to be grown on their own territory (3250 square miles), it could be grown without resorting to any other methods of culture than those already in use – methods already tested on a large scale and proved to be successful.

And yet the Paris gardener is not our ideal of an agriculturist. In the painful work of civilization he has shown us the way to follow; but the ideal of modern civilization is elsewhere. He toils, with but a short interruption, from 3 in the morning till late in the night. He knows no leisure; he has no time to live the life of a human being; the commonwealth does not exist for him, his world is his garden, more than his family. He cannot be our ideal; neither he nor his system of agriculture. Our ambition is, that he should produce even *more* than he does with *less* labour, and should enjoy all the joys of human life. And this is fully possible.

If we take all into consideration; if we realize the progress made of late in the gardening culture, and the tendency towards spreading its methods to the open field; if we watch the cultural experiments which are being made now – experiments today and realities tomorrow – and ponder over the resources kept in store by science, we are bound to say that *it is utterly impossible to foresee at the present moment the limits as to the* maximum *number of human beings who could draw their means of subsistence from a given area of land*, or as to what a variety of produce they could advantageously grow in any latitude. Each day widens former limits, and opens new and wide horizons. All we can say now is, that, *even now*, 600 persons could easily live on a square mile; and that, with cultural methods already used on a large scale, 1000 human beings – not idlers – living on 1000 acres could easily, without any kind of overwork, obtain from that area a luxurious vegetable and animal food, as well as the flax, wool, silk and hides necessary for their clothing. As to what may be obtained under still more perfect methods – also known but not yet tested on a large scale – it is better to abstain from any forecast: so unexpected are the recent achievements of intensive culture.

We thus see that the over-population fallacy does not stand the very first attempt at submitting it to a closer examination. Those only can be horror-stricken at seeing the population of this country increase by one individual every 1000 seconds who think of a human being as a mere claimant upon the stock of material wealth of mankind, without being at the same time a contributor to that stock. But we, who see in each newborn babe a future *worker* capable of producing much more than his own share of the common stock – we greet his appearance.

Ecology and revolutionary thought

MURRAY BOOKCHIN

Until recently, attempts to resolve the contradictions created by urbanization, centralization, bureaucratic growth, and statification were viewed as a vain counterdrift to 'progress' – a counterdrift that, at best, could be dismissed as chimerical and, at worst, reactionary. The anarchist was regarded as a forlorn visionary, a social outcast, filled with nostalgia for the peasant village or the medieval commune. His yearnings for a decentralized society, for a humanistic community at one with nature and the needs of the individual – spontaneous and unfettered by authority – were viewed as the reactions of a romantic, of a declassed craftsman or an intellectual 'misfit'. His protest against centralization and statification seemed all the less persuasive because it was supported

From *Post-Scarcity Anarchism* (Times Change Press, and Wildwood House, 1970).

primarily by ethical considerations, by utopian, ostensibly 'unrealistic' notions of what man could be, not what he was. To this protest, opponents of anarchist thought – liberals, rightists, and authoritarian 'leftists' – argued that they were the voices of historic reality, that their statist, centralist, and political notions were rooted in the objective, practical world.

Time is not very kind to the conflict of ideas. Whatever may have been the validity of libertarian and non-libertarian views a few generations ago, historical development has rendered virtually all objections to anarchist thought meaningless today. The modern city and state, the massive coal-steel technology of the Industrial Revolution, the later, more rationalized systems of mass production and assembly-line systems of labor organization, the centralized nation, the state and its bureaucratic apparatus – all have reached their limits. Whatever progressive or liberatory role they may have possessed has clearly become entirely regressive and oppressive. They are regressive not only because they erode the human spirit and drain the community of all its cohesive solidarity and ethico-cultural standards; they are regressive from an objective standpoint, from an ecological standpoint. For they undermine not only the human spirit and the human community but also the viability of the planet and all living things on it.

What I am trying to say – and it cannot be emphasized too strongly – is that the anarchist concept of a balanced community, a face-to-face democracy, a humanistic technology, and a decentralized society – these rich libertarian concepts are not only desirable but they are also necessary. They belong not only to the great visions of man's future but they now constitute the preconditions for human survival. The process of social development has carried them from an ethical, subjective dimension into a practical, objective dimension. What was once regarded as impractical and visionary has now become eminently practical. And what was once regarded as practical and objective has become eminently impractical and irrelevant in terms of man's development towards a fuller, unfettered existence. If community, face-to-face democracy, a humanistic, liberatory technology, and decentralization are conceived of merely as reactions to the prevailing state of affairs – a vigorous 'nay' to the 'yea' of what exists today – a compelling, objective case can now be made for the practicality of an anarchist society.

This reflex-like reaction, this rejection of the prevailing state of affairs accounts, I think, for the explosive growth of intuitive anarchism among young people today. Their love of nature is a reaction against the highly synthetic qualities of our urban environment and its shabby products. Their informality of dress and manners is a reaction against the formalized, standardized nature of modern institutionalized living. Their predisposition for direct action is a reaction against the bureaucratization and centralization of society. Their tendency to drop out, to avoid toil and the rat-race reflects a growing anger towards the mindless industrial routine bred by modern mass manufacture, be it in the factory, office, or university. Their intense individualism is, in its own elemental way, a *de facto* decentralization of social life – a personal abdication from the demands of a mass society.

What is most significant about ecology is its ability to convert this rejection of the *status quo*, often nihilistic in character, into an emphatic affirmation of life – indeed, into a reconstructive credo for a humanistic society. The essence of ecology's reconstructive message can be summed up in the word 'diversity'. From an ecological viewpoint, balance and harmony in nature, in society, and by inference, in behavior, is achieved not by mechanical standardization, but precisely by its opposite, organic differentiation. This message can be understood clearly only by examining its practical meaning on several levels of experience.

Let us consider the ecological principle of diversity – what Charles Elton calls the 'conservation of variety' – as it applies to biology, specifically to agriculture. A number of studies – Lotka's and Volterra's mathematical models, Gause's experiments with protozoa and mites in controlled environments, and extensive field research – clearly demonstrate that fluctuations in populations, ranging from mild to pest-like proportions, depend heavily upon the number of species in an ecosystem and the degree of variety in the environment. The greater the variety of prey and predators, the more stable the population; the more diversified the environment in terms of flora and fauna, the less likely is there to be ecological instability. Complexity, variety, and diversity – choose whatever term you will – are a function of stability. If the environment is simplified and the variety of animal and plant species is reduced, fluctuations in population become marked and tend to get out of control. They tend to reach pest proportions.

In the case of pest control, many ecologists now conclude that we can avoid the repetitive use of toxic chemicals such as insecticides and herbicides by allowing for a greater interplay between living things. We must accord more room for natural spontaneity, for the diverse biological forces that make up an ecological situation. 'European entomologists now speak of managing the entire plant–insect community', observes Robert L. Rudd. 'It is called manipulation of the biocenose. The biocenotic environment is varied, complex and dynamic. Although numbers of individuals will constantly change, no one species will normally reach pest proportions. The special conditions which allow high populations of a single species in a complex ecosystem are rare events. Management of the biocenose or ecosystem should become our goal, challenging as it is.'

To 'manipulate' the biocenose in a meaningful way, however, presupposes a far-reaching decentralization of agriculture. Wherever feasible, industrial agriculture must give way to soil and agricultural husbandry; the factory floor must yield to gardening and horticulture. I do not wish to imply that we must surrender the gains acquired by large-scale agriculture and mechanization. What I *do* contend, however, is that the land must be cultivated as though it were a garden – its flora diversified and carefully tended, balanced by a fauna and tree shelter appropriate to the region. Decentralization is important, moreover, not only for the development of the agricultural situation, but also for the development of the agriculturist. Food cultivation, practised in a truly ecological sense, presupposes that the agriculturist is familiar with all the features and subtleties of the terrain on which the crops are grown. By this I mean that he must have a thorough knowledge of the physiography of the land, its variegated soils – crop land, forest land, pasture land; mineral and organic content – its micro-climate, and he must be engaged in a continuing study of the effects produced by new flora and fauna. He must acquire a sensitivity to its possibilities and needs to a point where he becomes an organic part of the agricultural situation. We can hardly hope to achieve this high degree of sensitivity and integration in the food cultivator without reducing agriculture to a human scale, without bringing agriculture within the scope of the individual. To meet the demands of an ecological approach to food cultivation, agriculture must be rescaled from huge industrial farms to moderate-sized units.

The same reasoning applies to a rational development of energy resources. The Industrial Revolution increased the *quantity* of energy available to industry, but it diminished the *variety* of energy resources used by man. Although it is certainly true that pre-industrial societies relied primarily on animal power and human muscles, complex energy patterns developed in many regions of Europe, involving a subtle integration of resources such as wind and water power, and a variety of fuels (wood, peat, coal, vegetable starches, and animal fats).

The Industrial Revolution overwhelmed and largely destroyed these regional energy patterns, initially replacing them by a single energy system (coal) and later by a dual system (coal and petroleum). Regions disappeared as models of integrated energy patterns – indeed, the very concept of *integration through diversity* was obliterated. As I indicated earlier, many regions became predominantly mining areas, devoted to the extraction of a single resource, while others were turned into immense industrial areas, often devoted to the production of a few commodities. We need not review the role this breakdown in true regionalism has played in producing air and water pollution, the damage it has inflicted on large areas of the countryside, and the prospect we face in the depletion of our precious hydrocarbon fuels.

We can, of course, turn to nuclear fuels. Conceived as a single energy-resource, it is chilling to think of the lethal radioactive wastes that would require disposal as power reactors replace conventional fuel systems. Eventually, an energy system based on radioactive materials would lead to the widespread contamination of the environment – at first, in a subtle form, but later on a massive and palpably destructive scale.

Or we could apply ecological principles to the solution of our energy problems. We could try to re-establish earlier regional energy patterns – a combined system of energy provided by wind, water, and solar power. But today we would be aided by more sophisticated devices than any known in the past. We have now designed wind turbines that could supply electricity in a number of mountainous areas to meet the electric-power needs of a community of 50,000 people. We have perfected solar-energy devices that yield temperatures high enough in our warmer latitudes to deal with most metallurgical problems. Used in conjunction with heat pumps, many solar devices could provide as much as three-quarters – if not all – of the heat required to comfortably maintain a small family house. And at this writing the French are completing a tidal dam at the mouth of the Rance River in Brittany that is expected to produce more than 500 million kilowatt-hours of electricity a year. In time, the Rance River project will meet most of the electric needs of northern France.

Solar devices, wind turbines, and hydro-electric resources – each, taken singly, does not provide a solution for our energy problems and the ecological disruption created by conventional fuels. Pieced together as a mosaic, more precisely, as an organic energy pattern *developed from the potentialities of a region*, they could amply meet the needs of a decentralized society. In warm, sunny latitudes, we could rely more heavily on solar energy than on combustible fuels. In areas marked by atmospheric turbulence, we could rely more heavily on wind devices, and in suitable coastal areas or inland regions with a good network of rivers, the greater part of our energy would come from hydro-electric installations. In all cases, we would use a *mosaic* of non-combustible energy resources, filling whatever gaps develop by combustible and nuclear fuels. The point I wish to make is that by diversifying our use of energy resources, by organizing them into an ecologically balanced pattern, we could combine wind, solar, and water power in a given region to meet all the industrial and domestic needs of a community with only a minimal use of hazardous fuels. And eventually, we would sophisticate all our non-combustion energy devices to a point where all harmful sources of energy could be eliminated from the pattern.

As in the case of agriculture, however, the application of ecological principles to energy resources presupposes a far-reaching decentralization of society and a truly regional concept of social organization. To maintain a large city requires immense packages of fuel – mountains of coal and veritable oceans of petroleum. By contrast, solar, wind, and tidal energy can reach us mainly in small packets; except for spectacular tidal dams, the new devices seldom provide more than a few thousand kilowatt-hours of electricity. It is difficult to believe that we will ever be able to design solar collectors that can furnish us with immense blocks of electric power produced by a giant steam plant; it is equally difficult to conceive of a battery of wind turbines that will provide us with enough electricity to illuminate Manhattan Island. If homes and factories are heavily concentrated, devices for using clean sources of energy will probably remain mere playthings, but if urban communities are reduced in size and widely dispersed over the land, there is no reason why these devices cannot be combined to provide us with all the amenities of an industrialized civilization. To use solar, wind and tidal power effectively, the megalopolis must be decentralized. A new type of community, carefully tailored to the characteristics and resources of a region, must replace the sprawling belts that are emerging today.

An objective case for decentralization, to be sure, does not end with a discussion of agriculture and the problems created by combustible energy resources. The validity of the decentralist case can be demonstrated for nearly all the 'logistical' problems of our time. At the risk of being cursory, let me cite an example from a problematical area such as transportation. A great deal has been written quite recently about the harmful effects of petrol-driven motor vehicles – their wastefulness, their role in urban air pollution, the noise they contribute to the city environment, the enormous death toll they claim annually in the large cities of the world and on highways. In a highly urbanized civilization, it would be meaningless to replace those noxious vehicles by clean, efficient, virtually noiseless, and certainly safer battery-powered vehicles. The best of our electric cars must be recharged about every hundred miles – a feature which limits their usefulness for transportation in large cities. In a small, decentralized community, however, it becomes eminently feasible to use these electric vehicles for intra-urban or regional transportation and establish monorail networks for long-distance transportation.

It is fairly well known, today, that petrol-powered vehicles contribute enormously to urban air pollution, and there is a strong sentiment to 'engineer' the more noxious features of the automobile into oblivion. Our age characteristically tries to solve all its irrationalities with a gimmick – blow-by devices and after-burners for toxic petrol fumes, antibiotics for ill-health, tranquillizers for psychic disturbances. The problem of urban air pollution is more intractable than we care to believe. Basically, air pollution is caused by high population densities, by an excessive concentration of people in a small area. The fact is that millions of people, densely concentrated in a large city, necessarily produce serious *local* air pollution merely by their day-to-day activities. They must burn fuels for domestic and industrial reasons; they must construct or tear down buildings (the aerial debris produced by these activities is a major source of urban air pollution); they must dispose of immense quantities of rubbish; they must travel on roads with rubber tires (again, the particles produced by the erosion of tires and roadway materials adds significantly to air pollution). Quite aside from the pollution-control devices we add to automobiles and power plants, it should be fairly clear that whatever improvements these devices will produce in the quality of urban air will be more than cancelled out by future megalopolitan growth.

The social possibilities opened by decentralization could be discussed indefinitely and, in any case, there is more to anarchism than decentralized communities. If I have examined these possibilities in some detail, it has been to demonstrate that an anarchist society, far from being a remote ideal, has become a pre-condition for the practice of ecological principles. To sum up the critical message of ecology: if we diminish variety in the natural world, we debase its unity and wholeness. We destroy the forces making for natural harmony and stability, for a lasting equilibrium, and what is even more significant, we introduce an absolute retrogression in the development of the natural world, eventually rendering the environment unfit for advanced forms of life. To sum up the reconstructive message of ecology: if we wish to advance the unity and stability of the natural world, if we wish to harmonize it on ever higher levels of development, we must conserve and promote variety. To be sure, mere variety for its own sake is a vacuous goal. In nature, variety emerges spontaneously. The capacities of a new species are tested by the rigors of climate, by its ability to deal with predators, by its capacity to establish and enlarge its niche. *Yet the species that succeeds in enlarging its niche in the environment also enlarges the ecological situation as a whole*. To borrow E. A. Gutkind's phrase, it 'expands the environment', both for itself and for the species with which it enters into a balanced relationship.

How do these concepts apply to social theory? To many, I suppose, it should suffice to say that, inasmuch as man is part of nature, an expanding natural environment enlarges the basis for social development. But the answer to the question, I think, goes much deeper than many ecologists and libertarians suspect. Again, allow me to return to the ecological principle of wholeness and balance as a product of diversity. Keeping this principle in mind, the first step towards an answer is provided by a passage in Herbert Read's *The Philosophy of Anarchism*. In presenting his 'measure of progress', Read observes: 'Progress is measured by the degree of differentiation within a society. If the individual is a unit in a corporate mass, his life will be limited, dull, and mechanical. If the individual is a unit on his own, with space and potentiality for separate action, then he may be more subject to accident or chance, but at least he can expand and express himself. He can develop – develop in the only real meaning of the word – develop in consciousness of strength, vitality, and joy.'

Read's thought, unfortunately, is not fully developed, but it provides an interesting point of departure for our discussion. Leaving the quotation aside, for the moment, what first strikes us is that both the ecologist and the anarchist place a strong emphasis on spontaneity. The ecologist, in so far as he is more than a technician, tends to reject the notion of 'power' over nature. He speaks instead of 'steering' his way through an ecological situation, of *managing* rather than *re-creating* an ecosystem. The anarchist, in turn, speaks in terms of social spontaneity, of releasing the potentialities of society and humanity, of giving free and unfettered rein to the creativity of people. Both, in their own ways, regard authority as inhibitory, as a weight limiting the creative potential of a natural and social situation. Their object is not to *rule* a domain, but to *release* it. They regard insight, reason and knowledge as means for fulfilling the potentialities of a situation, as facilitating the working out of the logic of a situation, not of replacing these potentialities with preconceived notions or distorting their development with dogmas.

Turning, now, to Read's words, the next thing that strikes us is that both the ecologist and the anarchist view differentiation as a measure of progress. The ecologist uses the term 'biotic pyramid' in speaking of biological advances; the anarchist, the word 'individuation' to denote social advances. If we go beyond Read, we will observe that to both the ecologist and the anarchist, an ever-enlarging unity is achieved by growing differentiation. *An expanding whole is created by the diversification and enrichment of the parts.*

Just as the ecologist seeks to elaborate the range of an ecosystem and promote a freer interplay between species, so the anarchist seeks to elaborate the range of social experience and remove all fetters to its development. To state my point more concretely: anarchism is not only a stateless society but also a harmonized society which exposes man to the stimuli provided by both agrarian and urban life, physical activity and mental activity, unrepressed sensuality and self-directed spirituality, communal solidarity and individual development, regional uniqueness and world-wide brotherhood, spontaneity and self-discipline, the elimination of toil and the promotion of craftsmanship. In our schizoid society, these goals are regarded as mutually exclusive dualities, sharply opposed to each other. To a large extent, they appear as dualities because of the very logistics of present-day society – the separation of town and country, the specialization of labor, the atomization of man – and it would be preposterous, I think, to believe that these dualities could be resolved without a general idea of the *physical* structure of an anarchist society. We can gain some idea of what such a society would be like by reading William Morris's *News From Nowhere* and the writings of Peter Kropotkin. But these are mere glimpses. They do not take into account the post-war developments of technology and the contributions made by the development of ecology. This is not the place to embark on 'utopian writing', but certain guide lines can be presented even in a general discussion. And in presenting these guide lines, I am eager to emphasize not only the more obvious ecological premises that support them, but also the humanistic ones.

An anarchist society should be a decentralized society not only to establish a lasting basis for the harmonization of man and nature, *but also to add new dimensions to the harmonization of man and man*. The Greeks, we are often reminded, would have been horrified by a city whose size and population precluded a personal, often familiar, relationship between citizens. However true this precept may have been in practice two thousand years ago it is singularly applicable today. There is plainly a need to reduce the dimensions of the human community – partly to solve our pollution and transportation problems, partly also to create *real* communities. In a sense, we must *humanize* humanity. There should be a minimum of electronic devices – telephones, telegraphs, radios, television receivers and computers – to mediate the relations between people. In making collective decisions – and the ancient Athenian ecclesia was, in some ways, a model for making social decisions during the classical period – all members of the community should have an opportunity to acquire in full the measure of anyone who addresses the assembly. They should be in a position to absorb his attitudes, study his expressions, weigh his motives as well as his ideas in a direct personal encounter and through full debate, face-to-face discussion and inquiry.

Our small communities should be economically balanced and well rounded, partly so that they can make full use of local raw materials and energy resources, partly also to enlarge the agricultural and industrial stimuli to which individuals are exposed. The member of a community who has a predilection for engineering, for instance, should be encouraged to steep his hands in humus; the man of ideas should be encouraged to employ his musculature; the 'inborn' farmer should gain a familiarity with the workings of a rolling mill. To separate the engineer from the soil, the thinker from the spade, and the farmer from the industrial plant may well promote a degree of vocational over-specialization that would lead to a dangerous measure of social control by specialists. What is equally important, professional and vocational specialization would prevent society from achieving a vital goal: the humanization of nature by the technician and the naturalization of society by the biologist.

I submit that an anarchist community, in effect, would approximate a clearly definable ecosystem – diversified, balanced, and harmonious. It is arguable whether such an ecosystem would acquire the configuration of an urban entity with a distinct center, such as we find in the Greek *polis* or the medieval commune, or whether, as Gutkind proposes, society would consist of widely dispersed communities without a distinct center. In either case, the ecological scale for any of these communities would be the smallest biome capable of supporting a moderate-sized population.

A relatively self-sufficient community, visibly dependent on its environment for the means of life, would gain a new respect for the organic inter-relationships that sustain it. In the long run, the attempt to approximate self-sufficiency would, I think, prove more efficient than the prevailing system of a national division of labor. Although there would doubtless be many duplications of small industrial facilities from community to community, the familiarity of each group with its local environment and its rootedness in the area would make for a more intelligent and more loving use of its environment. I submit that far from producing provincialism, relative self-sufficiency would create a new matrix for individual and communal development – a oneness with the surroundings that would vitalize the community.

The rotation of civic, vocational, and professional responsibilities would awaken all the senses in the being of the individual, stimulating and rounding out new dimensions in self-development. In a complete society we could hope again to create complete men; in a rounded community, rounded men. In the Western world, the Athenians, for all their shortcomings and limitations, were the first to give us a notion of this completeness. 'The *polis* was made for the amateur', Kitto tells us. 'Its ideal was that every citizen (more or less, according as the *polis* was democratic or oligarchic) should play his part in all of its many activities – an ideal that is recognizably descended from the generous Homeric conception of *arete* as an all-round excellence and an all-round activity. It implies a respect for the wholeness or the oneness of life, and a consequent dislike of specialization. It implies a contempt for efficiency – or rather a much higher ideal of efficiency; an efficiency which exists not in one department of life, but in life itself.' An anarchist society, although it would surely aspire for more, could hardly hope to achieve less than this state of mind.

If the foregoing attempts to mesh ecological with anarchist principles is ever achieved in practice, social life would yield a sensitive development of human and natural diversity, falling together into a well-balanced, harmonious unity. Ranging from community, through region, to entire continents, we would see a colorful differentiation of human groups and ecosystems, each developing its unique potentialities and exposing members of the community to a wide spectrum of economic, cultural, and behavioral stimuli. Falling within our purview would be an exciting, often dramatic, variety of communal forms – here, marked by architectural and industrial adaptations to semi-arid biomes, there to grasslands, elsewhere to forest lands. We would witness a dynamic interplay between individual and group, community and environment, man and nature. Freed from an oppressive routine, from paralysing repressions and insecurities, from the burdens of toil and false needs, from the trammel of authority and irrational compulsion, the individual would finally be in a position, for the first time in history, to fully realize his potentialities as a member of the human community and the natural world.

A modest proposal: science for the people

JOHN TODD

> I HAVE been assured by a very knowing *American* of my Acquaintance in *London*; that a young healthy Child, well nursed, is, at a Year old, a most delicious, nourishing, and wholesome Food. . . .
> I GRANT this Food will be somewhat dear, and therefore very *proper for landlords*; who, as they have already devoured most of the Parents, seem to have the best Title to the Children.
>
> *A Modest Proposal*, Jonathan Swift, 1729

A few years ago a group of scientists and humanists began a search for ways in which science and the individual could come to the aid of people and the stressed planet. We all shared the uneasy feeling that modern science and technology have created a false confidence in our techniques and abilities to solve problems. We were also disturbed that most futurology seemed to jeopardize the continued survival of man by displaying a real ignorance of biology. It was clear from the outset that social and biological diversity needed to be protected and if at all possible extended.

We felt that a plan for the future should create alternatives and help counter the trend towards uniformity. It should provide immediately applicable solutions for small farmers, homesteaders, native peoples everywhere and those seeking ecologically sane lives, enabling them to extend their uniqueness and vitality. Our ideas could also have a beneficial impact on a wider scale if some of the concepts were incorporated into society-at-large. Perhaps they could save millions of lives during crisis periods in the highly developed states. This modest and very tentative proposal suggests a direction which society might well consider.

At the foundation of the proposal is the creation of a biotechnology which by its very nature would:

(*a*) function most effectively at the lowest levels of society,
(*b*) be comprehensible and utilizable by the poorest of peoples,

From *Newsletter No. 1* of the New Alchemy Institute, 1970.

(*c*) be based upon ecological as well as economic realities, leading to development of local economies,
(*d*) permit the evolution of small decentralized communities which in turn might act as beacons for a wiser future for many of the world's population,
(*e*) be created at local levels and require relatively small amounts of financial support. This would enable poorer regions or nations to embark upon the creation of indigenous biotechnologies.

It is necessary, before describing a way of reviving diversity at all levels, to evaluate how its loss threatens the future of man. If an extremely wise ecologist–philosopher from another planet were commissioned to investigate the earth he would be dismayed at the outset by our nuclear weaponry and our inability to reach a genuine arms agreement. In fact, he might drop the assignment and leave immediately for fear of his life. If he were daring enough to remain, his confidence in our future would be further shattered by the tendency of the dominant societies, whether 'communist' or 'capitalist', to be constantly selecting the most efficient or profitable ways of doing things. Our ecologist would ascertain clearly that our narrow approaches are reducing our options. The problem is compounded further by the tendency to condition people to the options which remain. To him it would represent an evolutionary trap and after his survey of energy use and agriculture was completed, he would confidently predict a major catastrophe. There would be no need to go on to industry, the university, or government, despite the fact that much ecological insanity resides in them also.

Examples of unnatural selection are everywhere.

For hundreds of years prior to the industrial revolution a wide variety of energy resources were used by man. Besides animal power and human toil there was a subtle integration of resources such as the wind and water power and a variety of fuels including peat, wood, coal, dung, vegetable starches and animal fats.[1] This approach of integration through diversity in providing the energy for society has been replaced by an almost exclusive reliance on fossil fuels and nuclear power. Energy sources are often linked together into huge transmission grids which provide electric power over large sections of the country. The industrial revolution took place only where there was a large-scale shift to fossil fuels as an energy source. The costs resulting may yet overshadow its benefits, The production of air pollutants and highly dangerous radioactive wastes continues to increase rapidly, and no downward trend is immediately in sight, despite an increased environmental awareness. Modern society, by reducing the variety of its basic energy sources while increasing its *per capita* energy needs, is now vulnerable to disruption on an unprecedented scale. It would be foolhardy to disregard the very real possibility of a small group of people destroying our power transmission systems. Tragically there are no widely disseminated backup sources of power available to help the majority of people in a nation hooked on massive amounts of electricity. Society was not as precariously based as this in 1776, or even 1929.

On the country's farmlands changes have taken place over the past fifty years which have not yet had their full impact. The majority of the population has been displaced from relatively self-sufficient farms by large monoculture farm industries. That many of the displaced farm people are on welfare or adding to the ghetto's problems is not usually considered by agricultural planners. Unfortunately, the trend is world-wide as former colonial regimes and present economic involvement by the powerful industrial nations have created a climate of uncontrolled urbanization in third-world countries. There is a contemporary theory which contends that the industrial powers have contributed directly to the conditions that led to their dangerously high population levels.[2]

Proselytizers on behalf of modern agribusiness rarely consider the key role of numerous small farms as a social buffer during periods of emergency or social breakdown. This oversight could well be the result of a lack of civilian research into the needs of a major industrial nation under the stress of severe crises, despite the fact that a disaster could occur.[3] A depression like that of 1929 could well take place; but if one should happen in the 1970s the social consequences would be much more severe. In 1929, many people had friends or relatives on farms which could operate on a self-sufficient basis during lean periods. Today the situation is alarmingly different as the rural buffer is largely gone and far fewer people have access to the land. The problem is compounded by the fact that today's farms have little resemblance to those of forty years ago; the modern farm is in no way independent and, like other businesses, requires large amounts of capital, machinery and chemicals to maintain its operations.

The replacement of rural populations and cultures by agribusiness, operated primarily on the basis of short-term incentives rather than as legacies for future generations, is resulting in a tremendous loss of biological and social diversity in the countryside. When the land and landscapes become just another commodity, society as a whole suffers. It might not be too serious if the loss of a viable countryside were all that was threatened by modern agriculture, but a close look at present agricultural methods suggests that many of them are causing a severe loss of biological variability, so vital to any sound and lasting agriculture.

The green revolution: unnatural selection

Over the past several decades the agricultural sciences have created a number of major advances in food raising, and the widely acclaimed green revolution has come to symbolize the power of applied science and technology working on behalf of all people. Our confidence has been renewed that the mushrooming populations can be fed if only Western agriculture can be spread rapidly enough throughout the world.[4, 5] But the green revolution has not been shaped by an ecological ethic, and its keenest enthusiasts are usually manufacturers of chemicals and agricultural implements backed by government officials, rather than farmers and agricultural researchers who are generally aware of the immense complexity of stable agricultural systems.

A number of biologists and agricultural authorities are cautious about the future, as they foresee environmental decimation which will offset the agricultural gains before the turn of the century.[6–8] Among some of them, there is a disquieting feeling that we are witnessing the agricultural equivalent of the maiden voyage of the *Titanic*, only this time there are several billion passengers.

The modernization of agriculture has resulted in the large-scale use of chemical fertilizers upon which many of the new high-yielding strains of grains depend. Coupled with this is a basic emphasis on single cash crops which are grown on increasingly larger tracts of land. The dependency on fertilizers for successful crops has created depressed soil faunas and an alarming increase in nitrates in the ground waters in some areas. The nitrate levels are often above the safety limits set by the US Public Health Service for infants' drinking water.[6]

With the widespread use of chemical fertilizers has been the rapid increase of biocides to control pests and weeds. These substances, particularly the chlorinated hydrocarbons and the shorter-lived organophosphates, are altering ecosystems and have the potential to threaten their stability. The use of weedkillers and pesticides has reduced the number of species of soil animals in many farm fields, with subsequent reductions in the quality of humus which is essential to the sustained health of soils.[9] Unfortunately, these changes are occurring just as we are beginning to discover how much the soil fauna, particularly the earthworms, contribute to plant growth and health.[10] The use of biocides has triggered a vicious cycle; soils decline in quality, which in turn makes crops more vulnerable to attack by pests or disease organisms. This creates a need for increasingly large amounts of pesticides and fungicides for agricultural production to be sustained.

The full impact of biocides has yet to come. It is as if ecology and agriculture represent a modern Janus in their antithetic stances. While a team of ecologists has recently announced that the full impact of DDT often does not show up in long-lived birds, predatory animals and humans for twenty-five years after application,[11] agricultural planners confidently predict a 600 per cent increase in the use of pesticides in third-world countries over the next few years.[7, 12] By the year 2000 the developing nations, as the benefactors of an uncontrolled experiment, will have reason to resent the blessings of modern technology.

The most notable achievement of the green revolution has been the creation of new, high-yield strains of rice, wheat and maize.[13] World agriculture has in the space of a few years been made more efficient, and in the short run, more productive because of these super grains, particularly the Mexican semi-dwarf varieties of wheat. They represent a triumph of the modern plant breeder's art, but they are in no way a panacea to the world food shortage. The grain revolution has an Achilles' heel; the new varieties, grown on increasingly vast acreages, are causing the rapid extinction of older varieties and a decline in diversity of the germ plasm in nature. The genetic variability which initially enabled the new types to be created is threatened, and the very foundation of the new agriculture is being eroded. In Turkey and Ethiopia thousands of local wheats have become extinct over the last several decades and the phenomenon is widespread.[14] It is possible that the genetic variability of wheats could be irreplaceably lost. Some of the most influential agricultural experts are deeply aware of the problem and are attempting to create the necessary 'gene banks' before it is too late. It has been suggested that the race to save our genetic resources may be hampered by another biological fact of life, namely that seed storage may not be enough since 'reserves' of the original microclimates and ecosystems may also be required if the viability of the local strains is to be maintained.[15]

The trend away from cultivating local varieties to a few higher-yielding forms is placing much of the world's population out on a limb. If the new varieties are attacked by pathogens the consequences could be world-wide rather than local, and plant breeders may not be able to create new strains before it is too late. Such events are not without precedent. An earlier counterpart of the green revolution occurred in Ireland in the eighteenth century, with the introduction of the Irish potato from the western hemisphere.[12] Production of food dramatically increased and by 1835 a population explosion had taken place as a result of the land's increased carrying capacity. During the 1840s a new fungal plant disease appeared, destroying several potato crops and one-quarter of the Irish people died of starvation.[16] The recent devastation of coffee plants in Brazil is partly the result of their narrow genetic base and their consequent vulnerability to leaf rust disease.[14] The 1970 corn leaf blight in the US was caused by a fungus which attacks plants that carry the *T* gene for male sterility and 70–90 per cent of the corn hybrids carry this gene.[17] Despite heavy applications of fungicides, corn blight spread with heavy crop losses.

Clearly, a modern agriculture, frantically struggling to right the wrongs of its single vision, is not ecologically sane, no matter how productive, efficient or economically sound it may seem.

There are other hidden perils associated with the modernization of agriculture,[18] but the loss of genetic diversity is perhaps the most obvious example of general changes taking place at every level of society. Since a scientific or technological advance on one level (e.g. the super grains) may be pushing us closer to disaster on another, it is time to look carefully at the alternatives before these avenues have disappeared behind us.

Psychic diversity and the human experience: a narrowing path?

The environmental dilemma is mirrored by comparable changes in people themselves. Unnatural selection is causing a loss of diversity in the human sphere, and this loss may lead towards social instability. Unlike the biosphere, society as a whole may either have remained fairly constant or increased in complexity and diversity. However, the roles of most individuals are becoming ever more reduced as they relinquish the various tasks of living and governing to myriads of machines and specialists. Unlike our ancestors we have little direct control over the creation of our power and energy, food, clothing or shelter, and this loss may be harmful to the human psyche. Levi-Strauss[19] has shown how far this narrowing of roles has progressed, particularly with regard to our direct experience of the world around us. People fly faster, travel farther and partake of more of the world, and yet in doing so the world, sampled widely but without depth, becomes more elusive and farther from their grasp.

It is highly probable, although difficult to prove, that the simplification and impoverishment of the lives of most of us lies close to the roots of much of the chaos, violence and disintegration threatening modern society. Erich Fromm[20] has suggested that violence particularly is related to boredom: it seems highly likely that boredom is one result of impoverishment or retreat from function.

Function, in the twentieth century, is being replaced by social dither. The immense popularity of snowmobiles, garden 'tractors', motorboats, hunting and contact sports indicates that we have a strong need to recapture the roles of explorer, farmer, navigator, hunter–provider and warrior. These are in part displacement activities and attempts to regain equilibrium with the progressive specialization of most people's lives.

Retreat from function is a negative trend since it removes the individual from the totality of his world. Restoring and extending genuine interaction with the life processes is the only lasting way to reverse this course and this should begin at the basic functional levels of society, within the lifespaces of the individual or the small group. Fraser Darling, in his perceptive studies of remote Scottish people,[21] showed how self-sufficiency was a positive force in their lives. The most independent communities were far more diverse and socially vital than single-industry towns heavily dependent on a lifeline to the outside. He also came to realize that they coped far better in their dealings with the world at large. Equally important, the independent communities cared for their environment and were less prone to despoil it for short-term monetary gain.

Little is understood about the adaptiveness of human social behavior. Modern science and its technologies have shaped industrially based societies which dominate the world today. These societies have an almost unlimited capacity to manipulate and destroy nature and men. In the long run they will not prove adaptive: as our options narrow, the spectre of a future which is inhumane and in violation of nature looms larger. To reverse this trend, a moral, intellectual and scientific renaissance will be required. Fortunately the basis for an adaptive view of society in nature is beginning to emerge, and an attendant science and philosophy exists in embryonic form today.

New alchemy and a reconstructive science: an alternative future

The direction of contemporary science is powerfully influenced by its patrons, the military and large corporations with their governmental cohorts. If a major scientific project or discipline does not hold out some promise of profit or military supremacy, it is not usually supported. The driving wheel of science in industrial societies is not a dispassionate seeking of knowledge. Science rarely addresses itself to the needs of human beings at the level of the individual or small group. With a sprinkling of notable exceptions, particularly in medicine, modern science and its technologies affect the majority of mankind in a negative or oppressive way, if at all. Science ignores, rather than addresses itself to, the richness and range of human potential. Knowledge is being replaced by hardware, not so much because hardware is superior to knowledge, but because it is more profitable. Unfortunately, the production and maintenance of the myriads of machines and technologies is linked to the threatening world crises in resources and environments. Technology as we know it cannot be expected to correct its own ills. These must be replaced with wisdom and practices that are fundamentally restorative rather than destructive.

An alternative science must seek to act on behalf of all people by searching for techniques and options that will restore the earth and create a new sense of *communitas* along ecological lines. Many talented people are working in the cities on urban problems, trying to make the cities liveable and human . . . but very few are interested in making the countryside and farmlands liveable by providing viable alternatives to the present rural destruction. Tools and techniques for individuals or small groups, however poor, must be created to enable rural dwellers to work towards recapturing and extending their biological and social diversity. This new science must also link social and scientific purpose with the aim of creating a reconstructive knowledge that will function at the basic levels of society. If it did address itself to social and environmental microcosms, people everywhere would be able to craft their own indigenous biotechnic systems, gain control over their own lives, and become more self-sufficient.

The ideal is to find ways of living that will help alleviate oppression at all levels, against the earth as well as against people. Ecology and personal liberation together have the potential to create environments within which people can gain increasing control over the processes which sustain them. This philosophy, call it 'New Alchemy', in seeking modes of stewardship attempts to fuse ethics with a scientific commitment to microcosms because in caring for the immediate, a dynamic may be born that will ultimately lead to a saner tomorrow.

Centers for new world research

The New Alchemy Institute has established a few small independent centers in a variety of climates and environments, including the tropics. In this way we hope to induce a high degree of diversity into research and approaches to land stewardship. However, there does run within the organization a common thread, namely a holistic view of the task ahead. No research is undertaken in a vacuum. Energy is linked to food production, food production to the larger questions of environment and *communitas*. Where possible, wastes, power, gardens, aquaculture, housing and surrounding ecosystems are studied simultaneously. In the foreseeable future all elements of the systems will be linked in a variety of ways so that the most viable living environment can evolve. Thus a holistic view becomes possible at the level of the social microcosm.

The New Alchemy farm on Cape Cod in Massachusetts typifies our research approach to the rural problems of tomorrow. The fundamental strategy has been to integrate an array of low-cost, yet sophisticated and efficient biological and solar energy systems. This has created a productive and self-contained microcosm.

With respect to our *preliminary* model at Cape Cod, windmills, solar heaters, intensive vegetable gardens, field crops and fish cultures are linked together in mutually beneficial ways.

The wind generator A wind generator is a streamlined windmill which generates enough power to run an electric generator. They were popular in rural areas during the 1920s and 1930s, before the advent of rural electrification. Our wind generator, which cost very little, was assembled primarily from scrap auto parts.[30] However, it is by no means perfected, and a great deal still needs to be learned about producing electricity inexpensively from the wind. Recent designs and new gearing systems, discoveries of solid-state power converters, efficient storage batteries and air-foil blade designs, coupled with a dwindling supply and increased cost of fossil and nuclear fuels are making wind generators increasingly practical as an alternative energy source.

Fish ponds Below the windmills, at the entrance to the gardens, are two small solar-heated aquaculture mini-farms. One is covered with a dome having a clear plastic skin and curved surface to trap the sun's heat and store it in a 'tropical' pond.[22–24] The other covered pond, of more conventional design, uses a solar heater for additional warming of the water. Both ponds are maintained at about 80 °F throughout the late spring and summer months. Within the 25-foot-diameter pools, *Tilapia*, a tropical fish of high food value, is raised. These fishes derive their feed primarily from massive algae blooms whose growth is stimulated in waters warmed by the sun and enriched by small amounts of animal manure. We have cultured edible-size *Tilapia* in as brief a time as ten weeks.

Other food sources will come from research involving the production of high-protein insect-food in polluted waters. In order to accomplish this, insects with an aquatic larval stage are being reared in large numbers in the tiny ponds. These provide an ecological food source for *Tilapia* and other fishes.[25] The insects presently being cultured are midges or Chironomids, tiny non-biting, mosquito-like insects which commonly swarm on summer evenings. The larval stage, normally found in the bottom muck in ponds, is cultured on burlap mats suspended in the fertilized ponds. The problems of food production and water purification are interconnected at the point of fertilization. At the present, in order to obtain high yields, animal manures are used as fertilizer. The ponds are, in fact, polluted to increase production. While growing, the larval midges help purify the ponds. They accomplish this by feeding on microscopic organisms, whose populations are increased by the manure, and perhaps also by direct assimilation of nutrients in the enriched waters. At this stage the insect-rearing ponds use only manure, but in the future there are plans to shift some of the culture over to human sewage, thereby linking sewage purification with the rearing of insects for fish culture.

The sun and the wind are coupled in the backyard fish-rearing systems to optimize productivity. It is a self-sufficient approach to the rearing of aquatic foods and there is little in the way of capital involved. It requires only labor and a large array of ecologically-derived ideas, many of which have yet to be completely elucidated.

Household purification system Human sewage is being partially purified in one practical experiment. At a house near by is a small glass-sided A-frame structure which was built at an approximate cost of $60. It is used to elevate temperatures over a series of pools which purify household sewage and wastes, through the culture of aquatic plants, live-bearing fishes, and insects of a variety of species. The produce from the household waste purification system is fed in turn to a flock of chickens. The wastes, partially purified by the living organisms, are subsequently used for irrigating the lawn and tree crops. Sewage, ordinarily an expensive and awkward problem for society, becomes a beneficial source of energy when dealt with on a small scale. New animal feeds are found and local soils enriched.

Intensive vegetable gardens The birthplace of much of our agricultural research is the gardens below the ponds. Several experiments intended to help find ways of culturing plants and animals without using expensive and harmful biocides have been initiated. One large project, involving several hundred collaborators throughout the country, is a systematic search for varieties of vegetables that may have some built-in genetic resistance to insect pests. Most modern plant breeders have assumed that pesticides are an inevitable tool in agriculture; consequently, knowledge is scanty concerning vegetable varieties with an intrinsic ability to resist pest attacks. In another research project the efficacy of interplanting vegetables with herbs and flowers that have a suspected ability to trap or repel pests is being tested, along with techniques for performing reliable yet simple experiments in highly productive vegetable gardens.[26–28] Each of the experimental gardens, irrespective of the research taking place, is treated as a miniature ecosystem, and many of the biological processes are monitored to determine aspects of diversity and 'stability' in each of the systems.

Integrating gardens and fish ponds Ideas for future research projects are being tested in the gardens. For example, one experimental plot is being used to look into the value of using nutrient-laden water from the small fish ponds for irrigating crops. Some fish species, when cultured in high densities, apparently secrete a fatty substance that tends to reduce evaporation. Consequently pond water containing moisture-conserving substances as well as nutrients may be highly useful for irrigating crops, especially under arid conditions. Early laboratory trials with lettuce and parsley indicated that the water from tanks containing fish has a 'hermetic' quality which conserves moisture around the roots of the plants. Field trials in 1973 demonstrated the agricultural value of using aquaculture wastes. Lettuce yields were increased up to 112 per cent over controls.

Already we can begin to envisage closely linked aquatic and terrestrial food systems suited to regions where water is seasonal and limited. Vegetation for food, and for shelter from the sun, could be nurtured from water stored and enriched in aquaculture ponds. Many of the earth's arid regions may one day sustain small communities within micro-environments that are biologically complete without the need to import large amounts of food, energy and capital.

Ecologically derived structures The investigations of a small group of people, at a single New Alchemy center, are coming together most completely in a project initiated in 1973. A direct involvement in process has drawn us towards the idea of creating living structures which are ecologically derived and reflect all that we have learned. Our initial approach to such housing is to have the structures evolve directly out of the ongoing aquaculture, waste, greenhouse, solar and wind energy research. On a microscopic scale such a strategy seems to make good sense, as the threads of each person's investigations are spun together to create a structure which mimics nature and perhaps will enable us to live in her rather than apart from her. These structures will be self-regulating and eventually provide inhabitants with shelter and a wide variety of aquatic plant and animal feeds as well as vegetables and fruits.[29] Such systems have the potential to provide the majority of food needs as well as housing for their inhabitants. Only the essential grains would need to come from outside.

The Ark

Our first structure, just started, we call the 'Ark'. It is a solar-heated greenhouse and aquaculture complex adapted to the rigorous climates of the north-east. If suitable internal climates can be maintained, we will eventually attach living quarters to the structure. The prototype will include a sunken greenhouse, an attached aquaculture pond and a diversity of light and heat conservation and distribution components. It will be an integrated, self-regulating system requiring the sun, power for water circulation, waste materials and labor to sustain its productivity. The electricity to drive the circulation pump will be provided by a windmill. The heat-storage/climate-regulation component will be a 13,500-gallon aquaculture pond. Solar heat will be trapped directly by the covered pond and by water circulating through the solar heater. The attached greenhouse will be built below the frost line and will derive its heat from the earth, direct sunlight and from the warmed pond water passing through pipes in the growing beds within the structure.

The intensive fish-farming component will be comparable to those already pioneered by New Alchemists. Several crops of *Tilapia* fish will be cultured throughout the warm months and a single crop of perch and trout during the cooler seasons. The aquaculture system may prove productive enough to underwrite the construction and maintenance costs of similar food-growing complexes in the future.

The greenhouse will be used to raise high-value vegetables and greens fertilized by wastes from the aquaculture pond. If our solar-heated 'Ark' should prove successful then ecologically derived, low-energy agricultures may thrive in northern climates.

Beyond ourselves: a people's science

So far, while building our models, we have learned that incredibly little is known about devising and caring for small-scale systems for communities that are both ecologically complete and restorative of environments. The contemporary colossal sense of scale, combined with the fragmentation of knowledge by the scientific establishment, has effectively blocked the development of an alternative for the future that is humble and yet ecologically wise. There are as many mysteries to be explored in the workings of the wind, the sun and the soil on a tiny plot of ground as exist in the grandiose schemes of modern science. The totality of the human experience becomes available to each of us as we begin to learn to function at the level of the microcosm.

We live under the spectre that there may not be enough time to solve the problems facing us. A few people working at a handful of centers cannot alone affect the course of human events. The elitism underlying contemporary science must be eliminated and a reconstructive science created. Knowledge should become the province of many, including all those struggling to become pioneers for the twenty-first century. If responsibility and diversity are to be established at the level of the individual, then individuals with a wide array of backgrounds and experiences should take part in the discovery of the knowledge and techniques required for the transformation ahead. A lay science, addressing itself to problems at basic levels of society, could restore diversity to the human sphere and establish an involvement for many in the subtle workings of the world around them.

In order to help effect scientific change, New Alchemy has instigated a lay science research program to study problems of importance to ecological pioneers. It is our hope that if many people begin to study earth-kindly skills, a genuine alternative to the industrial dynamic could begin to spread throughout society.

The lay research program was initiated in 1972. It dealt with a number of problems of importance to homesteaders and farmers. The research projects were announced and described in the pages of *Organic Gardening and Farming Magazine*. It was our belief that the drive to create and experiment is strong in many people, and the first year's experience has to a degree borne us out. From this start, a new science may evolve, created by the same people who use its findings to mold the course of their lives. This libertarian view may obtain its own scientific and technological foundation, one to which anyone can have direct access.

It is too soon for us to have developed much experience in guiding a lay science that will create its own independent dynamic. If we are at all successful, individuals and groups will within a few years branch out and explore the questions that seem most relevant to them and their own lives. Indigenous centers for learning through direct involvement in the process of reconstruction will spring up, providing an alternative to the colonization and fragmentation of knowledge by the universities.

Already it is apparent that a new science is evolving on a world-wide scale, and it will continue to grow. There are common threads weaving the tapestry that underlies the lives of the new pioneers and scientists; among these are a strong sense of the human scale, a desire to comprehend the forces of *communitas*, a passion for ecology and its teachings, which imply ethics and awakened sensibility and morality. These are forces in their own right, and though pitted against the shadow of technological man destroying man and nature, and a science operating in a moral vacuum, they may still represent the beginning of a hopeful path along which we may one day travel.

REFERENCES

1 Bookchin, M. (1968): *Ecology and Revolutionary Thought*. Anarchos 1.
2 Commoner, B. (1970) in *The Humanist*, Nov.–Dec.
3 Platt, J. (1969): 'What we must do' in *Science* **162**, 1115.
4 Boerman, A. H. (1970): 'A world agricultural plan' in *Scientific American* **223** (2).
5 Brown, L. R. (1970): *Seeds of Change*. Praeger, New York.
6 Commoner, B. (1970): 'Soil and fresh water – damaged global fabric' in *Environment* **12** (3).
7 Paddock, W. C. (1970): 'How green is the Green Revolution' in *Bio Science* **20** (16).
8 Todd, J. H. (1970): Editorial in *The New Alchemy Institute Bulletin* **1** (Box 432, Woods Hole, Mass. 02543).
9 Malone, C. R., A. G. Winnett and K. Helrich (1967): 'Insecticide-induced responses in an old field ecosystem' in *Bulletin Environ. Contam. Toxicol.* **2** (2).
10 Rodale, R. (ed.) (1961): *The Challenge of Earthworm Research*. Soil and Health Health Foundation, Emmaus, Pennsylvania.
11 Harnson, H. L., *et al.* (1970): 'Systems studies of DDT transport' in *Science* **170**, 503.
12 President's Science Advisory Committee (1967): *The World Food Problem* **1**. Also: Anon. in *Chem. Eng. News* **49** (2), 1971.
13 Reitz, L. P. (1970): 'New wheats and social progress' in *Science* **169**, 952.
14 Chedd, G. (1970): 'Hidden perils of the Green Revolution' in *New Scientist* **48**, 724.
15 Bardach, J. E.: personal communication.
16 Salaman, R. N. (1943): *The Influence of the Potato on the Course of Irish History*. The tenth Findlay Memorial Lecture, University College, Dublin, 27 Oct. Brown & Nolan Ltd., Dublin.
17 Gruchow, N. (1970): 'Corn blight threatens crop' in *Science* **169**, 961.
18 Pilpel, N. (1970): 'Crumb formation in the soil' in *New Scientist* **48**, 732.
19 Levi-Strauss, C. (1966): *The Savage Mind*. University of Chicago Press, Chicago.
20 Fromm, E. (1970): *The Revolution of Hope: Toward a Humanized Technology*. Harper & Row, New York.
21 Darling, F. F. (1951): 'The ecological approach to the social sciences' in *Amer. Sci.* **39** (2).
22 McLarney, W. (1971): 'An introduction to aquaculture on the organic farm and homestead' in *Organic Gardening and Farming Magazine*, Aug., pp. 71–6.
23 Todd, J. H. and W. O. McLarney (1972): 'The backyard fish farm' in *Organic Gardening and Farming Magazine*, Jan.
24 McLarney, W. (1973): *The Backyard Fish Farm Working Manual*. Reader's Research Project No. 1, New Alchemy Institute. Rodale Press, Emmaus, Penn.
25 McLarney, W., S. Henderson and M. Sherman: *The Culture of Chironomids* (in the press).
26 Todd, J. H. and R. Merrill (1972): 'Insect resistance in vegetable crops' in *Organic Gardening and Farming Magazine*, March.
27 Merrill, R. (1972): 'Companion planting and ecological design in the organic garden' in *Organic Gardening and Farming Magazine*, April.
28 Merrill, R. (1973): *Designing Experiments for the Organic Garden: a research manual*. Reader's Research Project. New Alchemy Institute.
29 Todd, J. H., R. Angevine and E. Barnhart (1973): *The Ark: an autonomous fish culture – greenhouse complex powered by the wind and the sun and suited to northern climates*. New Alchemy Institute, Woods Hole, Mass.
30 Barnhart, E. (1973): 'A windmill for generating electricity' in *Journal of the New Alchemists* **1**, 12–15.

Self-sufficiency: what is it? Why do it?

JOHN AND SALLY SEYMOUR

How many a poor immortal soul have I met well-nigh crushed and smothered under its load . . .

THOREAU

What does being self-supporting mean? Robinson Crusoe, if we except his raft-loads, got pretty near it, and many an African tribesman, or Indian *ryot*, is not far away. I have lived in African and Indian villages, and have seen a very high degree of self-sufficiency in both, and also a very high degree of happiness and true contentment. In every North Indian village of any use there is a man who knows how to go out into the country and cut down a *pipal* tree, and with it make a plough to sell to his neighbour in return for wheat or rice or other goods or services. There is a village miller, a *dhobi* or washerman, a *tonga-wallah* or driver of a hackney-cart, carpenter and blacksmith, potter, and the people spin their own cotton to give the yarn to the village weaver to weave their cloth. If a man wants to build a house he and his neighbours get to work and build it and that is that. Except at harvest nobody works very hard.

There is one man in each village, though, or very often not *in* the village but *of* the village, who does absolutely no good at all, and who is a terrible burden on his fellow villagers, and that is the *zamindar* – the landowner. He probably consumes more of the wealth of the village than all of the other villagers put together, and in return for this he does absolutely nothing at all. Remove the *zamindar* and at one stroke you more than double the wealth and well-being of every other villager.

The Central African village has no *zamindar*, in fact it has no landowners at all. The concept of landownership is completely alien to the African tribesman. The *village* owns, or at least controls, such of the surrounding forest as it can hold from others, and the villagers till the land in common, each man tilling what seems to the Headman of the village a reasonable amount, and paying nobody any rent for it. The Headman tills (or at least his wives do) the same amount as anybody else, and everybody has enough, and could have more if he wanted it.

Here, unless there is a famine (and in twelve years in Africa I never saw one), everybody gets enough to eat, and people who do not hanker after the flesh-pots of the white man live a very good life indeed.

Teach these people to read, though, and you immediately get a completely different situation. The children grow up no longer content with village self-sufficiency. They must have books, and books cannot be produced in the village (although I have seen paper being made in an Indian village in a mill; the chief constituent was a cow walking round in a circle providing the power), they wish to see the other parts of the world that they now become aware exist, they long for the sophisticated clothes, the machines, the gadgets and the other things that can only be produced by a city-based civilization. The Indians have two useful words: *pukha* and *kutcha*. *Pukha* means with a civilized finish on it. *Kutcha* means rough – made in the village without outside help. The man who has learnt to read, and been to town, comes back and wants a *pukha* house – one that makes use of glass and cement and mill-sawn timber and other materials that cannot be produced in the village: his old *kutcha* house is no longer good enough for him. He also wants white sugar instead of *gorr*, which is the unrefined sugar of his own sugar-cane, tea instead of buttermilk, white flour instead of his own wholemeal. He – and eventually his whole village with him – are forced into a money economy, crops are grown for sale and not for use, the village becomes part of the great world-wide system of trade, finance and interchange. In Africa what happens is that the young men of the village are forced to go and work in the white man's mines.

Now, the sort of self-sufficiency which I wish to treat of in this book is not the old, pre-industrial self-sufficiency: that of the illiterate peasant or hunter who has never heard of anything else. That kind of self-sufficiency is, for better or for worse, on the way out. What I am interested in is *post*-industrial self-sufficiency: that of the person who has gone through the big-city–industrial way of life and who has advanced beyond it and wants to go on to something better.

If the findings of the National Academy of Sciences and the National Research Council of the United States are correct (see their report *Resources and Man* – W. H. Freeman and Co., San Francisco), we will be forced into this kind of self-sufficiency whether we like it or not. For, according to these findings the fossil fuel supply of the earth will be exhausted long before we can possibly develop atomic or solar power to take the place of more than a tiny fraction of the motive power that our big-city civilization requires to make it work, and there are, apparently, insuperable obstacles to the really widespread global development of atomic power. After all, the existing electricity-producing power stations of the earth, no matter how they are driven, could not power a tiny fraction of the road, sea and air transport of the world, and if the latter ground to even a partial halt the whole great fragile edifice of global interdependence would collapse.

If this does not happen though, and if – as most people are in the habit of thinking – 'they' find a way to keep a hundred million motor cars roaring along the roads after the oil has dried up (whoever 'they' are), there is still a case for far more self-sufficiency of communities and individuals. If there is fast and cheap land transport it is not necessary for a jeweller to live in Birmingham, a potter in Stoke-on-Trent or a cutler in Sheffield. Such craftsmen can live, if they wish, right out in the country, and practise their crafts in their own homes. Their raw materials can be got to them cheaply, and cheaply they can send their finished articles away. With unlimited cheap transport the whole need for crowding people into industrial cities fades away, and more and more city people will leave the big cities (which will become more and more unendurable anyway as more and more ignorant people try to crowd *into* them) and set up their workshops in pleasant places, and many of these people will eventually get the idea of being at least partially self-supporting.

There is no good economic reason why they should be self-supporting: a craftsman living in the country need not even grow a cabbage if he doesn't want to – he can simply produce enough of the produce of his own industry to buy the food he needs. But a surprising number of such craftsmen find that they *want* to be at least partially self-supporting. A surprising number of the more intelligent people who have passed through the big-city–industrial stage are reacting against it: they *want* to advance to a more interesting and self-sufficient kind of life. After all, specialization may be economic, but it is terribly *boring*. I am a writer, but if I wrote enough hours a day to buy everything I and my family need I would write myself into the ground. I would quickly become bored and unhealthy. As it is, I write for half my working day, and during the rest of my time work mostly out of doors, growing and producing much that we eat and use, thus keeping happy and fit. Economics is a great science, but it falls down flat on its face when it tries to equate all good with *money*. It is inefficient, any agricultural economist will tell you, for me to hand-milk a cow. But what if I *like* hand-milking a cow? What is the economist going to say about that? Has any economist ever tried to measure the 'efficiency' of playing golf? And what if a couple of gallons of milk a day derive from my activity of hand-milking a cow? Does that make it in any way less 'efficient' than if I spent the time playing golf? When economists try to measure things like that they quickly get themselves into very deep water.

So more and more people, in all the highly industrial societies, are trying partially to opt out of the big-industry set-up and become less specialized and more self-sufficient. These people are not anachronistic, or ignorant or stupid, but are in fact drawn from the most intelligent and self-aware part of the population. The list of 'intentional communities' in the United States of America is long and getting longer with an increasing momentum. In this country there are several hundred such communities, and the army of 'hippies' and 'drop-outs' wandering about the roads like the pilgrims of old contains many individuals who would *like* to be self-supporting, but haven't the faintest idea how to set about it.

For the last eighteen years Sally and I have been probably as nearly self-supporting with food as any family in north-west Europe. We have a very good idea of what it is like and what it involves, and therefore I feel qualified here to utter a solemn warning.

It is beyond the capabilities of any couple, comfortably, to try to do what we have attempted. If a married couple settled down on five or ten acres of good land, in the British climate, and devoted their entire time to being self-supporting in food, clothes and artifacts; and if they knew how to do it, and had the necessary stock and equipment, already paid for, they could succeed. They would be working just the fifteen hours a day, three hundred and sixty five days of the year, that is, if they were to maintain the standard of living, and variety of food and of living, that they could maintain in a town. They would be very *healthy* doing this, they would not be *bored* (because they would never be doing the same job for long and would be doing a great variety of tasks), but they might sometimes wish they could sit down.

Thoreau, when he lived at Walden and wrote his famous book about it, lived almost exclusively on beans, and he didn't work very hard at all. He spent a very large part of his time there wandering around in the woods, peering into the depths of his pool, thinking and dreaming and meditating. I think he was a very sensible and enviable young man indeed. But he didn't have a wife and a family to bring up. Personally, I would not be prepared to live for two years and two months (which is the time Thoreau spent at Walden) on beans. Sally certainly wouldn't either, and we would be very hard put to make the children do it. We have, in fact, lived for eighteen years on the fat of the land; we have probably eaten and drunk better than most other people in this country: our food has been good, varied, fresh, and of the very best quality. We have never been self-supporting – but we have been very *nearly* self-supporting. We have lived extremely well on a very small money income, and the tax-eaters have not done very well out of us. We have not contributed much to the development of the atom bomb, nor to the building of Concorde. When the latter breaks the sound barrier over our heads, and scares the wits out of our cows, we have to endure it, but at least we have the satisfaction of knowing that we haven't *paid* for it.

We started our life of partial self-sufficiency with no stock, no land, no tools, and no money at all. Therefore, we have always had to work at money-bringing jobs, Sally at potting and myself at writing; and we have had to do the self-supporting work in our spare time. We have both had to work harder than people should have to work. But supposing there had been a small handful of *other* effective 'drop-outs' in the vicinity? Supposing, instead of having to keep both cows and pigs, we had only to keep cows? And swapped milk for bacon? Whenever we have been near another 'self-supporter' we have immediately found our task lightened considerably. We could share tools and equipment, 'know-how' (I apologize for borrowing a word from the culture that I have opted out of), and partially specialize: for example, trade asparagus for globe artichokes, mutton for salt fish, pottery for wooden vessels.

This, you may say, is the beginning of specialization, and the beginning of the road back to Birmingham. I do not think it need be. I believe that if half a dozen families were to decide to be partially self-supporting, and settle within a few miles of each other, and *knew what they were doing*, they could make for themselves a very good life. Each family would have some trade or profession or craft, the product of which they would trade with the rest of the world. Each family would grow, rear or produce a variety of goods or objects which they would use themselves and also trade with the other families for their goods. Nobody would get bored doing their specialized art or craft, because they would not have to spend all day at it, but there would be a large variety of other jobs to do every day too. This partial specialization would set them free for at least some leisure: probably more than the city wage-slave gets, after he has commuted to and from his factory or office. A more organized community than this – such as the Americans call an intentional community, or the Israelis a *kibbutz* – might work even better. There is room for endless experiment. The New England village community of the eighteenth century, if you forget the witch-hunting, must have been a very good place to live in.

I can imagine, one day in the future, a highly sophisticated society, some of the members of which would live in towns of a humane size, others scattered about in a well-cared-for countryside, all interdependent and yet in some ways very independent, the towns contributing to the country – the country to the towns. This would not be a very mechanized or industrialized society, but a society in which the real arts of civilization are carried on at a high level, in which literature, music, drama, the visual arts, and the crafts that lead to the good life, are all practised and appreciated by all the people. This would not be 'going back', whatever that means. It would, if you like to think in terms of such imaginary progressions, be 'going forward', and into a golden age. Periclean Athens wasn't such a bad place, give or take a few slaves. If we could find a way to achieve the same result without slaves, we would have achieved something very worth while.

China: a new society in the making

DEREK BRYAN

At the 'Movement for Survival' seminar held at Imperial College, London, in 1972, one of the speakers said that the developed countries had set 'a standard of extravagant consumption that has become a model for the rest of the world' – a statement that, as far as China (i.e. at least one-third of the rest of the world) is concerned, is the exact opposite of the truth: the developed countries' standard of consumption is what the Chinese call a 'negative example'. Such conscious or unconscious omissions of China have for over twenty years been a commonplace in the thinking of the Western intellectual establishment and it is worth considering why this should have been so.

For over a century before the revolution of 1949, China – with the biggest population, longest recorded history and oldest surviving culture in the world – had been the sick man of Asia, a storehouse of wealth and resources to be plundered at will by the West and later also by Japan.

After 1949 old attitudes took a long time to change. It was always easy to find some excuse for leaving China out of account: it was a Russian satellite or was starving or was overrun by mad Red Guards – to mention only three of the mindlessly contemptuous clichés of the nineteen-fifties and 'sixties.

In the past year China has taken her place in the United Nations, and has started to play a full role in the world generally. But time-lags in our thinking persist and huge gulfs of blank ignorance remain to be filled.

To many concerned professionally with the subject, it is ironical to observe how Chinese ideas and policies which they have for years been trying to publicize are suddenly now being seriously discussed and even advocated in the West as if they were something completely new. This is strikingly true, for example, of what Janine and Robin Clarke call 'some utopian characteristics of biotechnic communities' (*Futures*, June 1972). And the new philosophy of life, where goals can be achieved without destroying the environment, advocated in 'A Blueprint for Survival' (*The Ecologist*, January 1972) in fact reflects what is already being put into practice by a quarter of the world's population.

From *Futures*, December 1972.

The historical perspective

Before China was set on her present road her revolutionaries had to overcome many obstacles. By the end of the nineteenth century the old social and political system lay in ruins. For millennia the farmers of China had toiled to produce enough to support their families – using traditional organic farming methods, returning all wastes to the soil. If they were fortunate, they and their families survived, but in many districts, to quote R. H. Tawney's well-known words:

> the position of the rural population is that of a man standing permanently up to the neck in water, so that even a ripple is sufficient to drown him (*Land and Labour in China*, 1932).

Yet everything over what the Chinese needed to exist – and often even that too – was squeezed, through rent, usury and taxes, to support the whole vast structure of Chinese society. Again and again reformers and revolutionaries came back to the question of the land as the basic problem that had to be solved if the masses were ever to enjoy a decent life. And again and again they failed to solve the problem. It was left to Mao Tse-tung to define the solution, and to show how it could be attained:

> A rural revolution is a revolution by which the peasantry overthrows the authority of the feudal landlord class. If the peasants do not use the maximum of their strength, they can never overthrow the authority of the landlords which has been deeply rooted for thousands of years.

These words were written in Mao's 1927 report 'On the peasant movement in Hunan'. Eighteen years later, after ten years of civil war and eight of resistance to Japanese invasion, he recounted the old Chinese fable of 'The foolish old man who removed the mountains', and drew the moral:

> Today, two big mountains lie like a dead weight on the Chinese people. One is imperialism, the other is feudalism. The Chinese Communist Party has long since made up its mind to dig them up. We must persevere and work unceasingly and we too will touch God's heart. Our God is none other than the masses of the Chinese people. If they stand up and dig together with us why can't these two mountains be cleared away?

By 1952, after another seven years of struggle, they *had* been cleared away. The old regime had been overthrown and the peasants had divided the land among themselves. The way was clear for the building of a new society, but what kind of society? Scores of millions of new peasant proprietors, relieved of the old burdens of rent and interest, could have become the most conservative class in history, and the basic problems of technical backwardness, shortage of fertilizer, lack of irrigation and danger of flooding, would all have remained. So, just as the peasants had been mobilized under communist leadership to resist the

Japanese invaders and then to overthrow the landlords, they now came together for the common good, first in mutual-aid teams working together at seed-time and harvest, then in producer co-operatives. In the first form of co-operative, rent was paid for the use of the individual's land, tools, and animals (if any) as well as a dividend on labour; when it came to the higher form of co-operative, the land, etc. was pooled, and dividends were paid on labour alone. But even these higher co-operatives were too limited in size and scope to operate on the scale required for the irrigation and flood prevention works; nor could they satisfy adequately the growing needs for better seed, tools, fertilizer, and consumer goods.

The completion of land reform (i.e. distribution of land among the peasants) in 1952 coincided with the end of the period of rehabilitation of the old economy after the years of war and revolution. From 1953 to 1957 large-scale, centralized modern industry was being built up in the towns on the Soviet model, and with Soviet aid. An inevitable result of this type of development (in which almost all state investment was going into industry, not agriculture) was that urban standards of living rose much faster than rural and the pull of the towns was strong. If the peasants were to wait on urban industry for all the farm machinery, fertilizer and consumer goods they needed, their needs would hardly be satisfied within a generation or even two, even if they could achieve increased purchasing power.

It was in this situation that, after a great debate up and down the country, the rural communities decided to do things for themselves. In the seven months from October 1957 to April 1958 over fifty million acres of land were brought under some form of irrigation – as much as in the whole of China's previous history. Over 15 million tons of fertilizer was collected from lake, river and canal beds, and vast areas (including important shelter belts against blowing sand in the arid north and north-west) were afforested. Thanks to these efforts, and to experiments in close planting, intensive cultivation and other measures, a tremendous increase in crop yields was achieved in 1958; the People's Communes were formed the same year.

These organizations, each formed by a number of co-operatives joining together, had over-all responsibility not only for all the agriculture in their area, but for local industry, which they started and owned, for commerce, education, welfare, the militia, and local government. For the first time the policy of self-reliance, well-tried during the years of fighting against Chiang Kai-shek and against Japan, was put into practice throughout the whole country. The Chinese peasants would never be the same again. They made many mistakes but for the first time in history they knew they were no longer at the mercy of the elements and could begin to control their own destiny.

The Great Leap Forward of 1958 was followed by the three bad years, 1959–61, when drought in the north and floods in the south caused catastrophic crop failures. This was the time Khrushchev chose to 'bring

China to her knees' – as he thought – by suddenly withdrawing all Soviet aid and technicians. The effects of the blows of nature combined with those of man were very serious but, in the Chinese phrase, a bad thing was turned into a good thing. The communes not only survived, they ensured that nobody starved as countless millions had starved again and again in the past. Moreover, China learned that it was a mistake to rely on any single friend, however apparently genuine, and her technicians learned not only how to do what their Soviet colleagues had been teaching them but very often to do them in ways more suitable to Chinese conditions. The Soviet blow was in fact a great stimulus to technical progress in China.

In 1962, and every year since, harvests have been good, thanks to the irrigation, flood control and other work initiated in 1957 and since continued and expanded by the communes.

Advance was never steady and uninterrupted; each successive stage was achieved only after struggles between opposing policies. The Chinese categorize all these struggles as being between the socialist and capitalist roads, taking different forms at different times. Three of the clearest and most significant pairs of opposites are:

1 Individual peasant family farming/collective farming.
2 Centralized, bureaucratic administration/local initiative and self-reliance.
3 Selfish interests of members of privileged elites/unselfish pursuit of collective interest.

The first of these battles was fought and basically decided in the mid-'fifties. The second seemed for a time to have been won in 1958 but had to be fought again in the 'sixties and will always have to be fought. The third, which came to the fore in the Cultural Revolution, is likewise a continuing battle.

Indicative growing points

All this is the political background against which the development of Chinese society today and its likely future course of development have to be viewed. In 1971, I was back in China for the first time since 1959. We travelled widely for five weeks, in the north, north-west, east and south, and the most significant thing we observed was the innumerable growing points in society. The Chinese, clearly, are not rejecting the concept of economic development but it is development of a very different kind from that which has generally been held up as a model. Food is abundant and often excellent, produced by methods still largely based on the traditional organic farming, improved with the aid of modern scientific knowledge and a relatively small input of chemical fertilizer. Clothing is practical and adequate or more than adequate. There is plenty of attractive new housing in the communes, built by the peasants themselves with the aid of their friends. But there is still a long way to go to ensure that everyone has good housing, especially in the big cities. The policy is not to expand existing cities any further, nor to build new ones.

We visited a remarkable commune at a place called Tachai, a name that is a household word in China. In 1964, Chairman Mao said, 'In agriculture, learn from Tachai'. The Tachai production brigade (former co-operative, now division of commune) is a community of about 500 people, in an extremely poor mountain area, who formerly lived in great poverty. By dint of sheer hard work, collective organization with good leadership and a combination of the old traditional farming methods with modern science, they have reclaimed their barren hillsides, constructed terraced fields and gradually – despite floods, wash-outs and every kind of setback – succeeded in raising grain production to 6, 7½ or even 9 tons per hectare, against the national average of about 2 tons. At the same time they have built up the fertility of the soil to a depth of 6, 9, 12 or even more inches. To see what the people there have achieved, and then to see how people a thousand miles or more away *are* learning from them, is a deeply impressive experience.

Tachai is the agricultural model; 'in industry, learn from Taching', says Chairman Mao.

Taching is a new oilfield, where large-scale construction started in 1960, after the first well had been opened the year before. It is unique because, although it is a big modern industry using advanced techniques – many created by workers on the spot – the workers' families are very largely engaged in agriculture. The entire Taching basin is organized as a single municipality, consisting of many scores of residential areas connected by highways, with free bus services. It is situated on pasture and waste land; most of the oil pipelines have been laid underground. A certain proportion of the land has been opened up and cultivated; the over-all plan is to preserve the pasture as far as possible so as to avoid any danger of creating a dustbowl. Nevertheless, many thousands of families of the oil-workers have organized themselves into agricultural production teams so that the region is now self-sufficient in vegetables and has a growing output of grain. Small factories make use of waste products from oil production and the various residential communities have their own educational, medical, and other social services.

In short, Taching is not only a great modern industrial enterprise but is totally integrated in its own countryside – a large-scale industrial-farming community of a new type.

Taching is the supreme example of what the Chinese call 'walking on both legs', i.e. using both traditional and modern methods. The term also includes the policy of simultaneous development: of industry and agriculture; of central and local industry; of small, medium and large enterprises. It is well illustrated by the present development of local industry, which term covers enterprises run by provinces, administrative districts, municipalities, counties and communes: i.e. everything not run by the central authorities. A single city may contain industries run by the centre, by the province and by the administrative district, as well as its own. But at present the main emphasis in local industry is at the county level; more than half of China's 2000 counties have all five key industries: small machinery, fertilizer, cement, iron and steel, and coal mines; the rest of the counties have some but not all of these five. Small power stations, iron and other mines, are also widespread. The technical level in many cases may be relatively unsophisticated but quality of output is satisfactory. In both chemical fertilizer and cement, small plants account for about half of national production and expansion is very rapid, as it is also in pig iron.

As productivity goes up and consumer goods become more varied and more abundant, the importance of material in relation to non-material incentives, both for peasant commune members and for industrial workers, goes down. Material welfare and consumption alike are rising but China is not becoming a consumer society. Standards of food, clothing and housing are not, and never can be, uniform throughout the country but there is no urge in China to 'keep up with the Joneses'. There never will be any question of a car, a washing machine or a TV for every family, even when there is the industrial capacity, as in a generation or two there will be.

Indeed, one may venture to forecast that, as the economy makes further progress, the proportion of increased production devoted to raising the Chinese standard of living will decline and China's capacity and surpluses will be devoted even more than is already the case to helping other peoples in the world along the path of self-reliant development.

A new kind of human being

The pattern of China's economic development, of which the foregoing gives some indications, is one leg on which China is advancing towards a truly socialist society and it is obviously very different from the Soviet model. The other leg is the pattern of relationships among individuals, and between individuals and the community. It may be summarized by saying that the Chinese are setting out to demonstrate that the maximum fulfilment of the individual is to be found through his pursuit of the collective interest. Two quotations illustrate the point. John Gurley, of Stanford University, writes:

> Perhaps the most striking difference between the capitalist and Maoist views concerns goals. Maoists believe that while a principal aim of nations should be to raise the level of material welfare of the population, this should be done only within the context of the development of human beings, encouraging them to realize fully their manifold creative powers. And it should be done only on an egalitarian basis – that is, on the basis that development is not worth much unless everyone rises together; no one

> is to be left behind, either economically or culturally. Indeed, Maoists believe that rapid economic development is not likely to occur *unless* everyone rises together. Development as a trickle-down process is therefore rejected . . . (*Center Magazine*, Santa Barbara, May 1970.)

That probably would be more widely accepted today than when it was written. And a UN consultant economist, Curtis Ullerich, says:

> Unlike the capitalist West, China is not building an economy-oriented society. In spite of the enormous prominence given to 'production', in education, information and public life in general, Chinese society does not make the economy the main goal of national life but rather subordinates it to transcendent targets . . . (*Journal of Contemporary Asia*, Vol. 2, No. 2, 1972.)

I have quoted above the slogans 'In agriculture, learn from Tachai', and 'In industry, learn from Taching'. There is a third, 'The whole country, learn from the People's Liberation Army', which links agriculture and industry and goes further. Its meaning is summarized in the conclusion of the Peking *People's Daily* editorial of 1 August 1966, written at an early stage of the Cultural Revolution:

> Every field of work should be made into a great revolutionary school where people take part in industry and agriculture, in military as well as civilian affairs – such is our programme.

Another editorial in the same paper two months later said:

> The new world needs a new man to create it. In a certain sense, communism is absence of a private concept, it is for the public. We must foster and form a new communist man, wholeheartedly for the commonweal . . . This kind of man is . . . a man with no selfish interests, heart and soul for the people . . . (quoted in *Broadsheet*, London, January 1967).

This vision of the all-round man may be utopian but what strikes almost every visitor to China today above everything else is the way in which a new kind of human being, creative and intelligent but unsophisticated, an individual but a member of a strong and wise community, is becoming typical of young people in China.

China's attitude to pollution and the environment

Not unexpectedly China's policy, as expounded at the recent UN conference at Stockholm, has been widely misunderstood or misinterpreted in the West but not in the Third World. Even though they may be opposed to nuclear testing by China, Third World countries know that she is a bastion of support for their main concern, i.e. that their own development should not be hampered by measures initiated under the banner of conservation by precisely those affluent nations chiefly responsible for world pollution and the plunder of the resources of the world as a whole.

China dissociated herself from the final declaration of the conference because it was not the expression of a consensus, failed to mention the political causes of environmental pollution, failed to denounce imperialist wars and war crimes (as in Vietnam), and failed to demand the prohibition and destruction of biochemical and nuclear weapons and the renunciation of their use.

A key aspect of her point of view was pithily expressed in the maxim quoted by China's chief delegate Tang Ke, 'We must not give up eating for fear of choking'. The balanced character of her socialist development works towards the most economic use of all materials; waste, a prime cause of pollution, is reduced to a minimum. And, in Tang Ke's words, 'our government is now beginning to work in a planned way to prevent and eliminate industrial pollution'. In China such a policy, like any other, involves the education and mobilization of the whole people with an effectiveness inconceivable in the 'advanced' industrial societies of the West and Japan, where profit is the mainspring.

It should also be noted that the widely quoted sentence from the English version of Tang Ke's speech, 'The possibility of man's exploitation and utilization of natural resources is inexhaustible', is a seriously misleading rendering of the original Chinese which, literally translated, reads: 'Mankind's opening up and utilization of natural resources is constantly extending'. The phrase 'constantly extending' does not connote 'inexhaustible', and 'opening up' is far from 'exploitation'.

It is capitalism and imperialism that 'exploit' natural resources, as they exploit people, wherever they can. The Chinese believe that sooner or later all peoples will protect their environment in the only secure way, by overthrowing the sytem that plunders and pollutes it.

Part Six

THE HUMAN FUTURE

*From the politics of the 600 million to the politics of the one . . . the step that has defied all politicians of all ages. The gas and the atom. The whole is not the sum of its parts, and even less is the part an arithmetic fraction of the whole. Theodore Roszak: 'What, after all, is the ecological crisis that now captures so much belated attention but the inevitable extroversion of a blighted psyche? Like inside, like outside. In the eleventh hour, the very physical environment suddenly looms up before us as the outward mirror of our inner condition, for many the first discernible symptom of advanced disease within.'**

But how should all this be put into words? Many have tried. Many, too many, have sought their refuge in the reductionist style of psychological analysis which should have been not their means but their target. To probe, to lay bare, to strip away superficial coverings, to reveal the inner man. These have been the preoccupations of our eminent experts in human relations. And the new culture, springing from the rich compost of the flower children of Haight-Ashbury, has been no less deceived, confusing Encounter Groups with encounter, Love with affection, and sex with everything. The counter-culture, conceived with the Beat Generation and the Vietnam war as parents, might have known better. Having rejected the reductionism of its parent generation towards the material world, it might have foreseen that to apply that same philosophy not to the inanimate world but to human society might be to replace evil with worse. And yet of course it did not appear so. It seemed only as if the young were sensibly diverting the attention of men away from consumerism and back to human beings and human life.

But this is the cross-roads at which we (or they) now stand. The gist of this book has been the story of the fight to replace the technocratic nightmare with a human future. A decade ago none could have foretold the inroads that would have been made by the mid-1970s. The technocracy, of course, blunders on – but not a little disturbed by calls for participation, by political apathy and a growing awareness that a large segment of the population appears to be slipping slowly away towards some more elusive goal.

It is, then, all the more tragic that so many lessons have yet to be learnt. To a

* From *Where the Wasteland Ends* (Doubleday, and Faber & Faber).

student of these affairs, it seems scarcely credible that the good sense and sure taste of the counter-culture could, for example, have swallowed that particularly invidious form of behaviourism known as Skinnerism and to have founded a community called Walden II (after one of Skinner's books). Or that people who have read and taken inspiration from Thoreau's original Walden could choose to live in such bureaucratized work camps as the Walden II communities where life is more rigidly imposed than even it is at Du Pont or ICI. Of course, it is customary for the academic critic to insert such negative points in his otherwise glowing report to give the impression of having preserved an impartial objectivity. But this is no minor point, nor is it impartial. I believe that a large part of the counter-culture has in fact taken the wrong turning on a critical road. And whether it will find its way through the confusion of the human potentials movement, growth centres and allied phenomena, which owe more to an over-ripe rationalism than to true compassion, is far from clear. Trust and acceptance do not demand total psychic access. Nor, perhaps, would trust any longer have meaning in the face of such openness. But trust is the substance from which we must forge all human relationships. Any short-cut to that must be seen as just another technocratic fix, albeit one which appears more benevolent than most.

But we should start with the concept of plenty. Both Murray Bookchin and Philip Slater have argued that the attitude of the generations to scarcity and plenty are what fundamentally distinguishes them – the old generation clinging fiercely to the idea of insufficiency, the new accepting plenty and hence leaving themselves open to the acceptance of novelty and experience. Strange, in a way, this contrast with attitudes to ecological abundance, where the old culture claims there will always be a way to provide the energy and materials, and the new stresses the Earth's natural limitations. Yet the contrast is only superficial, for the trick lies in how one defines 'less' and 'more'. For the other generation, there always seems to be less because it is assumed people always want more; the young always find more because they know people need less. And, for them, the important things – like love and smell and happiness, sunshine, people and the seasons – are not rationed. The more you see, the more there is.

From the outsider looking in to the insider looking out. Gary Snyder, the poet of the beat generation, celebrates rather than analyses the new generation, for him a totally expected and understandable phenomenon dating not to the beats of 1950s America but to the world-wide Palaeolithic age, when it is assumed men were informed more by their real sensibilities than they are now. Perhaps they were. Either way, Snyder's is a poetic evocation of all that is best in the counter-culture. In crossing the i's and dotting the t's we should not forget the dream.

Back to Bookchin, for two reasons. The first, lest we forget that the dream must shape reality. The second, lest we forget that the counter-culture is more than an escape to rural Eden. And Bookchin's admiration for the young's attempt to reshape the impossible urban environment of Berkeley is quite proper. Indeed, one of the strengths of the movement is that it seeks its improvements for city and country alike. Perhaps, like Mao, it aims eventually to eliminate the difference, as is apparent from some of its nomenclature. An eco-house in London is known as Street Farm, a rural commune in the States as Drop-out City. So be it, and much healthier than the attitude of the elders who in this century sought to define country living out of existence, and through its urban insistence brought about so many of the problems of urban-industrialism. And just at the time when the new technologies of communication could have made the country a better place for people to live than ever before. The greatest folly of the nuclear age?

From Judson Jerome we can learn experience. A middle-aged professor of something or other, Jud entertained me once at his urban home just before he took the move to a rural commune (and not long before I did). Though I returned, he for all I know is still there and has been the first to record the triumphs and heartaches of the new life in a way which neither obscures the real issues nor resorts to a language too new for us to comprehend. He calls it a mirror-life. Perhaps his book will be the Lewis Carroll of later generations.

I end with Theodore Roszak for his writing has probably turned more heads than anyone else I know. As my admiration for him as a person and a writer knows no bounds, I will not contain him with a few facile phrases. His is the sure voice of a new vision.

Passage to more than India

GARY SNYDER

'It will be a revival, in higher form, of the liberty, equality, and fraternity of the ancient gentes.'

LEWIS HENRY MORGAN

The Tribe

The celebrated human Be-In in San Francisco, January of 1967, was called 'A Gathering of the Tribes'. The two posters: one based on a photograph of a Shaivite sadhu with his long matted hair, ashes and beard; the other based on an old etching of a Plains Indian approaching a powwow on his horse – the carbine that had been cradled in his left arm replaced by a guitar. The Indians, and the Indian. The tribes were Berkeley, North Beach, Big Sur, Marin County, Los Angeles, and the host, Haight-Ashbury. Outriders were present from New York, London and Amsterdam. Out on the polo field that day the splendidly clad ab/originals often fell into clusters, with children, a few even under banners. These were the clans.

Large old houses are rented communally by a group, occupied by couples and singles (or whatever combinations) and their children. In some cases, especially in the rock-and-roll business and with light-show groups, they are all working together on the same creative job. They might even be a legal corporation. Some are subsistence farmers out in the country, some are contractors and carpenters in small coast towns. One girl can stay home and look after all the children while the other girls hold jobs. They will all be cooking and eating together and they may well be brown-rice vegetarians. There might not be much alcohol or tobacco around the house, but there will certainly be a stash of marijuana and probably some LSD. If the group has been together for some time it may be known by some informal name, magical and natural. These households provide centers in the city and also out in the country for loners and rangers; gathering places for the scattered smaller hip families and havens for the questing adolescent children of the neighborhood. The clan sachems will sometimes gather to talk about larger issues – police or sheriff department harassments, busts, anti-Vietnam projects, dances and gatherings.

All this is known fact. The number of committed total tribesmen is not so great, but there is a large population of crypto-members who move through many walks of life undetected and only put on their beads and feathers for special occasions. Some are in the academies, others in the legal or psychiatric professions – very useful friends indeed. The number of people who use marijuana regularly and have experienced LSD is (considering it's all illegal) staggering. The impact of all this on the cultural and imaginative life of the nation – even the politics – is enormous.

And yet, there's nothing very new about it, in spite of young hippies just in from the suburbs for whom the 'beat generation' is a kalpa away. For several centuries now Western Man has been ponderously preparing himself for a new look at the inner world and the spiritual realms. Even in the centers of nineteenth-century materialism there were dedicated seekers – some within Christianity, some in the arts, some within the occult circles. Witness William Butler Yeats. My own opinion is that we are now experiencing a surfacing (in a specifically 'American' incarnation) of the Great Subculture which goes back as far perhaps as the late Paleolithic.

This subculture of illuminati has been a powerful undercurrent in all higher civilizations. In China it manifested as Taoism, not only Lao-tzu but the later Yellow Turban revolt and medieval Taoist secret societies; and the Zen Buddhists up till early Sung. Within Islam the Sufis; in India the various threads converged to produce Tantrism. In the West it has been represented largely by a string of heresies starting with the Gnostics, and on the folk level by 'witchcraft'.

Buddhist Tantrism, or Vajrayana as it's also known, is probably the finest and most modern statement of this ancient shamanistic–yogic–gnostic–socioeconomic view: that mankind's mother is Nature and Nature should be tenderly respected; that man's life and destiny is growth and enlightenment in self-disciplined freedom; that the divine has been made flesh and that flesh is divine; that we not only should but *do* love one another. This view has been harshly suppressed in the past as threatening to both Church and State. Today, on the contrary, these values seem almost biologically essential to the survival of humanity.

The Heretics

'When Adam delved and Eve span,
Who was then a gentleman?'

The memories of a Golden Age – the Garden of Eden – the Age of the Yellow Ancestor – were genuine expressions of civilization and its discontents. Harking back to societies where women and men were more free with each other; where there was more singing and dancing; where there were no serfs and priests and kings.

Projected into future time in Christian culture, this dream of the Millennium became the soil of many heresies. It is a dream handed down right to our own time – of ecological balance, classless society, social and economic freedom. It is actually one of the possible futures open to us. To those who stubbornly argue 'it's against human nature', we can only patiently reply that you must know your own nature before you can say this. Those who have gone into their own natures deeply have, for several thousand years now, been reporting that we have nothing to fear if we are willing to train ourselves, to open up, explore and grow.

One of the most significant medieval heresies was the Brotherhood of the Free Spirit, of which Hieronymus Bosch was probably a member. The Brotherhood believed that God was immanent in everything, and that once one had experienced this God-presence in himself he became a Free Spirit; he was again living in the Garden of Eden. The brothers and sisters held their meetings naked, and practiced much sharing. They 'confounded clerics with the subtlety of their arguments'. It was complained that 'they have no uniform . . . sometimes they dress in a costly and dissolute fashion, sometimes most miserably, all according to time and place.' The Free Spirits had communal houses in secret all through Germany and the Lowlands, and wandered freely among them. Their main supporters were the well-organized and affluent weavers.

When brought before the Inquisition they were not charged with witchcraft, but with believing that man was divine, and with making love too freely, with orgies. Thousands were burned. There are some who have as much hostility to the adepts of the subculture today. This may be caused not so much by the outlandish clothes and dope, as by the nutty insistence on 'love'. The West and Christian culture on one level deeply wants love to win – and having decided (after several sad tries) that love can't, people who still say it will are like ghosts from an old dream.

Love begins with the family and its network of erotic and responsible relationships. A slight alteration of family structure will project a different love-and-property outlook through a whole culture . . . thus the communism and free love of the Christian heresies. This is a real razor's edge. Shall the lion lie down with the lamb? And make love even? The Garden of Eden.

White Indians

The modern American family is the smallest and most barren family that has ever existed. Each newly-married couple moves to a new house or apartment – no uncles or grandmothers come to live with them. There are seldom more than two or three children. The children live with their peers and leave home early. Many have never had the least sense of family.

I remember sitting down to Christmas dinner eighteen years ago in a communal house in Portland, Oregon, with about twelve others my own age, all of whom had no place they wished to go home to. That house was my first discovery of harmony and community with fellow beings. This has been the experience of hundreds of thousands of men and women all over America since the end of World War II. Hence the talk about the growth of a 'new society'. But more; these gatherings have been people spending time with each other – talking, delving, making love. Because of the sheer amount of time 'wasted' together (without TV) they know each other better than most Americans know their own family. Add to this the mind-opening and personality-revealing effects of grass and acid, and it becomes possible to predict the emergence of groups who live by mutual illumination – have seen themselves as of one mind and one flesh – the 'single eye' of the heretical English Ranters; the meaning of sahajiya, 'born together' – the name of the latest flower of the Tantric community tradition in Bengal.

Industrial society indeed appears to be finished. Many of us are, again, hunters and gatherers. Poets, musicians, nomadic engineers and scholars; fact-diggers, searchers and re-searchers scoring in rich foundation territory. Horse-traders in lore and magic. The super hunting-bands of mercenaries like Rand or CIA may in some ways belong to the future, if they can be transformed by the ecological conscience, or acid, to which they are very vulnerable. A few of us are literally hunters and gatherers, playfully studying the old techniques of acorn flour, seaweed-gathering, yucca-fiber, rabbit snaring and bow hunting. The densest Indian population in pre-Columbian America north of Mexico was in Marin, Sonoma and Napa Counties, California.

And finally sexual mores and the family are changing in the same direction. Rather than the 'breakdown of the family' we should see this as the transition to a new form of family. In the near future, I think it likely that the freedom of women and the tribal spirit will make it possible for us to formalize our marriage relationships in any way we please – as groups, or polygynously or polyandrously, as well as monogamously. I use the word 'formalize' only in the sense of make public and open the relationships, and to sacramentalize them; to see family as part of the divine ecology. Because it is simpler, more natural, and breaks up tendencies toward property accumulation by individual families, matrilineal descent seems ultimately indicated. Such families already exist. Their children are different in personality structure and outlook from anybody in the history of Western culture since the destruction of Knossos.

The American Indian is the vengeful ghost lurking in the back of the troubled American mind. Which is why we lash out with such ferocity and passions, so muddied a heart, at the black-haired young peasants and soldiers who are the 'Viet Cong'. That ghost will claim the next generation as its own. When this has happened, citizens of the USA will at last begin to be Americans, truly at home on the continent, in love with their land. The chorus of a Cheyenne Indian Ghost dance song – 'hi-niswa' vita'ki'ni' – 'We shall live again'.

Passage to more than India!
Are thy wings plumed indeed for such far flights?
O soul, voyagest thou indeed on voyages like those?

Community and city planning

MURRAY BOOKCHIN

The 1960s opened an entirely new era in the modern definition of the city, or, more precisely, of a humanistic community. It is a noteworthy fact that this era acquired little of value from the work of the professional city planners, who continued to sink deeper into shallow problems of design and technical expertise; rather, its inspiration came from the countercultural values and institutions formulated almost intuitively by young people who were breaking away from suburbia and the regimentation of the multiversity. In the communes of drop-out youth and in activist upsurges such as People's Park in Berkeley, far more than design criteria were formulated. However naïvely, new values for human sociation were posed that often involved a total break with the commodity system as a whole. The full implications of this movement – a movement that has yet to find its own confidence and its way through the maze of mod and pop culture – have not received the attention they deserve from the 'urbanists'. For the values of this culture, carried to their logical conclusion, pose the problem of developing entirely new communities in a harmonized, ecologically balanced society.

The young people of the 'sixties who tried to formulate new values of sociation – values that have since been grouped under the rubric of the counter-culture – unquestionably comprised a privileged social stratum. They came, for the most part, from affluent white middle-class suburbs and the better universities of the United States, the enclaves and training

From *The Limits of the City* (New York: Harper & Row, 1974), pp. 124–34.

grounds of the new American technocracy. To adduce their privileged status as evidence of the trifling nature of the movement itself and casually dismiss it, as so many writers have done, sidesteps a key question: why did privilege lead to a rejection of the social and material values that had spawned these very privileges in the first place? Why didn't these young people, like so many before them in previous generations, take up the basic values of their parents and expand the area of privilege they had inherited?

These questions reveal a basic change in the material premises for radical social movements in the advanced capitalist countries of the world. By the 'sixties, the so-called 'First World' had undergone sweeping technological changes – changes which opened a new social perspective for the era that lay ahead. Technology had now advanced to a point where the values spawned by material scarcity, particularly those values fostered by the bourgeois era, no longer seemed morally or culturally relevant. The work ethic, the moral authority imputed to material denial, parsimony, and sensual renunciation, the high social valuation placed on competition and 'free enterprise', the emphasis on a privatization and individuation based on egotism, seemed obsolete in the light of technological achievements that offered entirely contrary alternatives to the prevailing human condition – freedom from a lifetime of toil and a materially secure social disposition oriented toward community and the full expression of individual human powers. The new alternatives opened by technological advances made the cherished values of the past seem not only obsolete and unjust but outrightly grotesque. As I have pointed out elsewhere, there is no paradox in the fact that the weakest link in the old society turned out to be that very stratum which enjoyed the real privilege of rejecting false privilege.

Which is not to say that the technological context of the counter-culture was consciously grasped and elaborated into a larger perspective for society as a whole. Indeed, the outlook of most middle-class drop-out youth and students remained largely intuitive and often became easy prey to the faddism nurtured by the established society. The erratic features of the new movement, its feverish metabolism and its quixotic oscillations, can be partly explained by this lack of adequate consciousness. And quite often many young people fell victim to cheap exploitation by commercial interests. Large numbers of them, exultant in their newly-discovered sense of liberation, lacked a significant awareness that complete freedom is impossible in a prevailing system of unfreedom. Insofar as they aspired rapidly to replace the dominant culture by their own example and by moral suasion, they failed. But insofar as they began to see themselves as the most advanced sector of a larger movement to revolutionize society as a whole, the counter-culture lives today in alternating ebbs and flows as the mainstream of a historic enlightenment that may eventually change every aspect of social life.

The most striking feature of the new movement is the emphasis it places on personal relations as the *locus* of seemingly abstract social ideals – the attempt it makes to translate freedom and love into existential realities of everyday life. If freedom in its fullest sense is a society based on self-activity and self-management, a society in which every individual has control over her or his daily life, then the counter-culture may be justly described as the attempt to produce that very self, free of the values spawned by hierarchy and domination, that will yield liberated social forms of management and activity. That this degree of freedom can be definitively achieved only after sweeping revolutionary changes in society has already been emphasized; but young people were quite right in sensing that existential personal goals must be defined and striven for even today, within the realm of unfreedom, if future revolutionary changes were to be sweeping enough and not to bog down in bureaucratic modes of social management. This focus added an essential psychological element to abstract social doctrines that were formulated by traditional radical theorists. Accordingly, in its most advanced and theoretically conscious forms, the counter-culture reached directly into and sought to radically change the lived relationships between people as sexual beings and as members of families, educational institutions, and work places. One must return to the writings of the early anarchists, whose appeal was often very limited, to recover the moral and psychological dimensions this approach added to socialist theories of the 'sixties, most of which had become so denuded of humanistic qualities that they were little more than economistic strategies for social change.

This personalistic yet socially involved approach yielded an increasingly explicit critique not only of doctrinaire socialist theory, but also of design-oriented city planning. Much has been written about the 'retreat' of drop-out youth to rural communes. Far less known is the extent to which ecologically-minded counter-cultural youth began to subject city planning to a devastating review, often advancing alternative proposals to dehumanizing urban 'revitalization' and 'rehabilitation' projects. Generally, these alternatives stemmed from a perspective toward design that was radically different from that of conventional city planners. For the counter-cultural planners, the point of departure for any design was not 'the pleasing object' or the 'efficiency' with which it expedited traffic, communications, and economic activities. Rather, these new planners concerned themselves primarily with the relationship of design to the fostering of personal intimacy, many-sided social relationships, non-hierarchical modes of organization, communistic living arrangements, and material independence from the market economy. Design, here, took its point of departure not from abstract concepts of space or a functional endeavor to improve the *status quo*, but from an explicit critique of the *status quo* and a conception of the free human relationships that were to replace it. The design elements of a plan followed from radically new social alternatives. The attempt was made to replace hierarchical space by 'liberated space', to use an expression that was very much in the air.

Among the many plans of this kind to be developed in the late 'sixties and early 'seventies, perhaps the most impressive was formulated by an *ad hoc* group of people in Berkeley from People's Architecture, the local Tenants' Union, and members of the local food co-operative or 'Food Conspiracy'. The plan shows a remarkably high degree of radical social consciousness. It draws its inspiration from the 'People's Park' episode in May 1969, when drop-out youth, students, and later ordinary citizens of Berkeley fought for more than a week with police to retain a lovely park and playground which they had spontaneously created out of a neglected, garbage-strewn lot owned by the University of California. The park, eventually reclaimed by its university proprietors at the cost of a young man's life, many severe injuries, and massive arrests, is at this writing a parking lot and paved soccer field. But the memory of the episode has waned slowly. To the young Berkeley planners, 'People's Park was the beginning of the Revolutionary Ecology Movement'. The thrust of the plan, entitled *A Blueprint for a Communal Environment*, is radically 'counter-cultural'. 'The revolutionary culture', declares the *Blueprint*, 'gives us new communal, eco-viable ways of organizing our lives, while people's politics gives us the means to resist the System.' The *Blueprint* is a project not only for reconstruction but for struggle on a wide social terrain against the established order.

The plan aims at more than the structural redesigning of an existing community; it avows and explores a new way of life at the most elementary level of human intercourse. This new way of life is communal and economically divorced as much as possible from commodity relationships. The design gives expression to a basic goal: 'Communal ways of organizing our lives help to cut down on consumption, to provide for basic human needs more efficiently, to resist the system, to support ourselves and overcome the misery of atomized living.' In this single sentence, the social and private are thoroughly fused. Design is assigned the function of articulating a new life style that stands opposed to the repressive organization of society.

Shelter in the *Blueprint* is redesigned to 'overcome the fragmentation of our lives . . . to encourage communication and break down privatization'. The plan observes that with 'women's liberation, and a new communal morality, the nuclear family is becoming obsolete'. Accordingly, floor plans are proposed which allow for larger multi-purpose rooms which promote more interaction – 'such as communal dining rooms, meeting spaces and work areas'. Methods are suggested for turning roofs and exterior upper walls into communicating links with neighbouring houses as well as between rooms and upper stories.

'All land in Berkeley is treated purely as a marketable commodity', observes the *Blueprint*. 'Space is parcelled into neat consumer packages. In between rows of land parcels are transportation "corridors" to keep people flowing from workplace to market.' The *Blueprint* proposes the dismantling of backyard and sideyard fences to open land as interior parks and gardens. Platform 'bridgeways' between houses are suggested to break down the strict division between indoor and outdoor space. The purpose of these suggestions is not merely to bring nature into the urban dweller's horizon, but to open intimate avenues of communication between people. The concern of the plan is not merely with public plazas and parks, but with the immediate neighborhoods where people live their daily lives. Indeed, with magnificent insouciance, the plan tosses all considerations of private property to the winds by suggesting that vacant lots be appropriated by neighborhoods and turned into communal space.

Half the streets of Berkeley, the plan notes, could be easily closed off to stimulate collective transportation experiments and reduce traffic congestion in residential areas. This would 'free *ten times* more land area for public use than we now have in park acreage. Intersections could become parks, gardens, plazas, with paving material recovered and used to make artificial hills.' The plan recommends that Berkeley residents should walk or bicycle to places whenever feasible. If motor vehicles must be used, they should be pooled and maintained on a communal basis. People should drive together to common destinations in order to reduce the number of vehicles.

Community services will make a 'quantum leap' when 'small groups of neighbors mobilize resources and energy in order to cement fragmented neighborhoods back together and begin to take care of business (from child care to education) on a local level and in an integrated way'. In this connection, the *Blueprint* suggests that men and women should rotate the use of their homes for child care centers. First-aid skills and knowledge of more advanced medical techniques should be mobilized on a neighborhood basis. Finally, wastes should be collectively recycled to avoid pollution and wastage of resources.

At its core, the plan advances a refreshingly imaginative program for ruralizing the city and fostering the material independence of its inhabitants. Communally worked backyard gardens could be created and food cultivated organically. Here, the plan enters into the specifics of composting, mulching, and the preparation of seedlings. A 'People's Market' could be established 'which will receive the organic products of rural communes and small farmers, and distribute them to the neighborhood [food] conspiracies. Such a market place will have other uses – craftspeople can sell their wares there.' The plan sees the 'People's Market' as a 'solid example of creative thinking about communal use of space. Its structure will be portable, and will be built in such a way as to serve neighborhood kids as play equipment on non-market days.'

The *Blueprint* creates no illusion that this ensemble of reconstructive ideas will 'liberate' Berkeley or other communities. It sees in the realization of these concepts the first steps toward reorienting the individual self from a passive acceptance of isolation, egotism, and dependence on bureaucratic institutions to initiatives from below that will recover communal contacts and face-to-face networks of mutual aid. Ultimately, society itself will have to be reorganized by the great majority who are now forced into hierarchical subservience to the few. Until these sweeping changes are achieved, however, a new state of mind, buttressed by working community ties, must be fashioned so that people will be able to fuse their deeply personal desires with higher social ideals. Indeed, unless this fusion is achieved, these very ideals will remain abstractions and they will never be realized at all.

Many of the *Blueprint*'s technical suggestions are not new. The notion of roof openings to link houses together are obviously borrowed from Pueblo Indian villages, the urban gardens from medieval communes and precapitalist towns generally, the pedestrian streets and plazas from the Renaissance cities and earlier urban forms. In the context of an increasingly bureaucratic society, however, the *Blueprint* is unique in deriving its concepts from radically new life styles and reinforcing them in a single ensemble by many traditional design notions. Doubtless, quite a few of the design proposals in the plan can be assimilated piecemeal to new construction projects without having a significant impact on conventional ways of life. This has been the fate of many radical ideas and art forms in the past. But the *Blueprint* is true to itself insofar as it is not merely a structural plan. The authentic content of its proposals is the kind of life in which its design elements are rooted. The premise of the plan, in advance of any design, is a culture counter to the prevailing one – a culture that emphasizes community rather than isolation, the sharing of resources and skills rather than their privatized possession and accumulation, independence from rather than dependence upon the bourgeois marketplace, loving relations and mutual aid rather than egotism and competition. The planners, whether they were freely conscious of their historic antecedents or not, were presenting their vision of urban life in Hellenic terms. The truly human city, to them, is a way of life that fosters the integration of individual and society, of town and country, of personal and social needs within a framework that retains the integrity of each. A new synthesis is to be achieved which makes the fulfillment of individual and urban needs complementary to the fulfillment of social and ecological needs.

The new consciousness

JUDSON JEROME

Except that we be born again, it sometimes seems, there is no hope that we can pass through the looking-glass into the new world order to which communes point the way. Before me are piles of file folders pertaining to such things as drugs, meditation, diet, ceremony and ritual, music, crafts, art, extrasensory perception, and new religious cults. Something is happening – something with an over-all unity in spite of the diverse range of influences from ecology and cybernetics to astrology. Jungian and Reichian psychology, yoga, Zen, and Christianity revived – a new culture made up of the remnants of several old ones, piled on counters at the thrift shop. One may see it especially on country communes, where life is informed by the seasons, the needs of plants and animals and people, by a rigorous economy, and the relative isolation and intimacy of the members, these disparate streams combining into a coherent vision and style of life characterized by a casual, familiar, undemonstrative awareness of human participation in the universe, an awareness which, after all, involves little mystic ecstasy, few drug-assisted revelations, or even regular baths of alpha waves, but carries one into new ranges of experience, illumines a new sense of self, and is sensitive to the network of relationships linking individual to group and group to environment in balanced systems.

These conclusions are warranted by the evidence we have from communes, and yet seem too abstract, if not pretentious, for the kinds of experience from which they arise. I am fearful of being misled myself or misleading others in matters so critical. Too many messiahs in recent years have announced the apocalypse and an imminent transcendence of humankind into an era of new awareness, whereas in essential ways, day by day, the world and people go on much as they have in the past. The risks I and others have taken in committing ourselves to the values of the new culture are too great to permit pursuit of the *ignes fatui* of desperate belief. Meanwhile, as we recognize daily on our own commune, there are bills to be paid – not only those in dollars for groceries and mortgage and gas, but bills for our past conditioning, our insecurities, our distrust, and bills for our present divergence from the norms of the surrounding society. Anarchism and the new consciousness are chic topics for academic discourse, but do they work – with real people in real situations? The grand rewards such as delivering humankind from oppression and saving the planet from despoliation beckon like fantasies; but are there sufficient rewards to sustain us in practice, to get us through dark nights of doubt, to meet our practical needs? Is there sufficient verification along the way to assure us we are not wandering in the desert of madness?

The first discovery of the new consciousness is that we are linked – as were the black and white prisoners in the film *The Defiant Ones*. Before those two men were able to break the cuff chains they wore and free themselves of one another, they not only overcame their mutual hostility and learned to co-operate intuitively (since one could not move without the other), and even used their chain as a tool (e.g. as one lowered another into a warehouse), but they also developed a positive affection and concern. When the chain was finally broken the pair tried to hop a freight. One got onto a boxcar successfully, but the other, wounded, lagged behind, running desperately, and the white hand and black hand stretched toward one another, reaching for help and to be helped, genuine love melded with mutual dependence. Their strength derived from their weakness. Those parts of self which society had repressed and which had become atrophied were reawakened. Human bondage was not weakness nor even unfortunate necessity, but an aspect of human completeness. To be linked is to be whole.

The second discovery is that the more bound we are to one another, the freer we are to be different. Again and again the experience of communes has shown that once basic allegiance is established, individuals are *more* able than formerly to disagree to disapprove, to judge attitudes and behavior of others. Members of a mutually committed group are not only free to but impelled to criticize one another because of group survival instinct, and serious failures of one member cripple the group.

Such interaction can be purely utilitarian, like that of mountain climbers on the same rope. There have been instant communes on life rafts in the middle of the Pacific, in villages struck by flood, in foxholes under bombardment. When communal living is voluntary, however, the dependency is enhanced by love, and utilitarian interests are enriched by a dimension of genuine, positive desire for each to help each be fulfilled. This is most easily seen in child-rearing. A parent may correct a child because he projects his own reputation upon him, thinking the child's behavior reflects himself. He may do so for practical reasons – e.g. demanding that the child not waste food, damage property, hurt others. He may – as in farm families – want to develop a strong, capable worker in the common enterprise. But there is, in addition to such motives as these, a strong instinctual desire that the child achieve his fullest potential, for the child's own sake, even when that means tolerating or encouraging behavior that is costly, painful, even heartbreaking. Wise mothers often 'correct' a son's dependency, even when the mothers find that dependent behavior extremely gratifying to themselves.

In communes the correction may have the same intent, but often is in the opposite direction: the members have to teach one another how to be dependent, knowing how repressed is the need of dependency in American society. But, conversely, group consciousness does not produce conformity, but actively fosters growth, change, and differentiation. In the courtship period lovers are reluctant to notice differences; they take delight in common interests. Imagine! We are both stamp collectors, both like swimming, both like to cook! As the relationship matures, the opposite tendencies come into play: diversity of talents and interests makes the corporate unit stronger, more capable, more engrossing, and the emphasis is upon how its members complement (rather than compliment) one another. The communal ideal is that each be able to perform as many functions as possible, so that no one is 'essential' as a specialist, and each can take over for another, each radiating the fullest possible spectrum of self-fulfillment.

Some might think that the security of love would lull a group and lure it into the swamp of indolence. One of the myths of capitalism is that people need incentives to grow and change, that without fear of failure or promise of reward, the human condition is to remain inert, static. But in an organic view of life the natural impulse of people is to grow, change, to rectify error as a stalk seeks sunlight, to seek self-actualization through symbiotic relationship with other self-actualizing and very diverse individuals (as healthy flowers require healthy bees, and vice versa). Mechanistic controls and constraints interrupt this process. Conformity, or repression of self, results from surrendering inner motives to external expectations. A farmer does not 'grow' (an odd verb in the transitive, as is 'heal') his corn by stretching it on a rack, but by fertilizing its roots and clearing the way for it to develop. Given the right conditions an ecosystem will establish itself as a heterogeneous plenitude in which each component thrives.

Three indices of poor communal health, usually apparent instantly to a visitor from the outside (though the members themselves may have let the conditions grow upon them without noticing) are excessive conformity, apathy, and valuelessness. One leads to another. Fear of deviation, in self or others, is paralyzing. Soon nothing gets done. Nobody cares. Anything goes – the rebellious other face of conformity. As in many kinds of psychic disorder, the symptoms may be defended tenaciously. At one of the free-land communes a visitor returned to his car to find it being pillaged by a resident. When the visitor objected, the resident said, 'All property belongs to the people, man. The stuff in this car is no more yours than mine.' The visitor established his claim to the contents of the car with the threat of physical violence, luckily being bigger than the would-be thief. When a commune succumbs to such an ethos, the only redress is escape or violence. The commune quickly dissipates or reverts to a kind of primitivism tolerable to very few. The atmosphere is oppressive, sullen. The members feel unable to speak out and helpless to change conditions that bother them. Often it is the conduct of one or two members which is bumming out the others, but (often bolstered by philosophical justification of diversity and freedom) those causing the trouble are increasingly defensive about and even domineering in behavior that others object to, like children begging for limits. But no one feels free to criticize, because to do so would raise the horrendous question of rejection. In these situations, as when our factory is paralyzed, the only hope is for a change in consciousness. But how can that be brought about?

Recognition of the need for transcendent awareness is both intuitive and intentional in communes. Terms such as 'change of consciousness' and 'consciousness raising' became current in political activities, spreading over to women's liberation, black and chicano identity, gay liberation, and other strands of the movement in the late 'sixties. Consequently, there has been an effort to take thought and thereby add a cubit to one's stature – and to some degree it seems to work. Again, though the analogy was rarely explicit, the techniques of consciousness changing were reminiscent of those of anarchist affinity groups of earlier decades, now strengthened by experience in encounter groups. Intense, intimate mutual- and self-knowledge provide a base from which people can move on, with a conscious awareness of purpose and direction, attempting to internalize values which will result in new behavior patterns. A fine balance has to be maintained between indiscriminate acceptance of where one and others are on the one hand, and excessive pressure, or mind-fucking, on the other. Marxists, particularly, denounce the apparent pacification of encounter groups, in which a brotherly understanding emerges (e.g. between militant blacks and police) that obliterates 'objective' differences of interest. At the other extreme, the hippie mentality sometimes resists all change in the name of freedom to do one's thing. Wherever one is at is right. A crude conversion process was recognized in protests and mass demonstrations, when peppergas and clubs changed (as well as battered) many heads, resulting in instantaneous radicalization. Confrontation was often sought strategically, not for the effect it had upon the establishment, but for the way it drew liberals over the line into radical consciousness.

The contradictions and frustrations of all such methods of changing values have led many to abandon them. Simultaneous with efforts to bring about intentional change by developing awareness of human brother-and-sisterhood through persuasion and political action there has been a more intuitive movement in the same direction as people experienced consciousness change through the use of drugs and exploration of new religious forms. Never having taken a psychedelic drug (aside from a few experiences with cannabis), I am in some ways poorly qualified to comment on the importance of such drugs in the movement. In other ways, ironically, in view of the prevailing scientific criteria of objectivity, that fact may serve as a credential.

The social effects of the drug culture are as important in changing consciousness as are the effects of drugs upon inner awareness. Through involvement with drugs many – particularly many young people – first became significantly outlaws. The punishments for drug traffic were outrageous in the 'sixties – in some states exceeding those for any other crime. (Incidentally, there is some correlation between strict enforcement of harsh drug laws and paucity of communes by states, e.g. Texas has many characteristics which would foster rural communes, but the laws used to be more stringent there, and many fewer communes emerged there than in, say, Colorado and New Mexico.) One after another learned that crime does, indeed, pay – in a coin of incalculable value: the experience of transcendence. A web of trust emerged, with a sharp, almost fearful distinction between those in and out (cf. the status of the saved and unsaved on the eve of the apocalypse in Johannine strains of Christianity – as opposed to more rationalistic Pauline strains). If someone in this context is cool, he may be instantaneously accepted as an intimate family member – with all his oddities. One becomes accustomed to deviant behavior from the experience of being in strange mental places and of accompanying others on their trips. He learns that the distinctions between sanity and insanity are relative and based on conveniences of the alien society (hence, in part, the popularity of the writings of the psychoanalyst R. D. Laing and of Thomas Szaz).

This tolerance is symbolized by the growing popularity of astrology. If a person is an Aquarius or a Taurus, or if the moon is in Cancer, certain peculiarities must simply be accepted as beyond rational control. (To some extent this parallels assumptions of scientific determinism, in which personal responsibility is mediated by social background, conditioning, and other factors external to individual will.) A person's trip is to be respected as sacred – provided he doesn't lay it on others. The exotic and peculiar become celebrated as ends in themselves. As Quakers and Shakers in earlier days identified with labels rendered in ridicule, so the term *freak* was accepted with approval by those who took pride in their divergence from social norms. Straights sometimes accuse freaks, with some justice, as having merely invented a new kind of conformity, but I have heard freaks extend their appreciation even to archetypal conservatives in the straight world, as one marveled at an extremely reactionary rationalistic professor: 'I think it's really neat the way he has it together, the way he thinks, dresses, his emotional responses, his politics.' This was not sarcasm. Judgment is truly suspended, except insofar as strong individuality and sincerity are admired.

Do those who use astrological categories actually believe that celestial bodies so minutely affect human behavior? Some do, some don't, and in the new culture it hardly matters. Compare this attitude with common acceptance of the *I Ching* as a basis for making a decision. One meditates about a problem or question, then casts yarrow sticks or coins to lead him to a hexagram and its interpretation, usually with astounding relevance to one's concerns. Does he 'believe' in the *I Ching*? There is really nothing to believe in. The book itself says take it or leave it. Above all, in this culture one learns there is more in heaven and earth than is dreamt of in philosophy. One's stance is modest before the burning bush.

The orthodoxies have all failed, however oppressively they continue to wield their sterile power. What we have left to go on is our inner sense of necessities of ourselves in this moment, which includes an awareness of the need of others as they need us. It is possible that no theory derived from cultural history can help us adapt to the future, so rapid are the new demands, but cybernetics and systems analysis and servo-mechanisms provide what may be a groundwork for a theory of communities in the future. Meanwhile theoretical controversy drones on like a wire in the wind. Our problem is, can we figure out who will take out the garbage?

As I write, the tractor out by the factory begins chugging. A belt to its power takeoff turns the cutoff saw, which sections the logs, to be cored on the bandsaw, to be nailed and painted and sorted and labeled and packed and trucked. Topher, at six, likes to sort and label. He takes pots off the drying rack, measures them with a tape to determine their size, puts on two labels with a pneumatic stapler, and puts the pots on the appropriate shelf for packing. He was afraid of the sound of the machinery some months ago, but has grown accustomed. Recently he and I were the only ones left out there, and I told him I was leaving. 'I'll work alone', he said, going on about his stapling. 'I have a few more pots to finish up.' I thought of child-labor. Topher has no sense of toil – not even that making pots is necessary to survival. It is a privilege. It is fun. It feels good – both the work and the appreciation he gets from others. Polly, thirteen, started the tractor, and now is helping Robb, a twenty-four-year-old former teacher, handle the large logs on the cutoff saw. I wonder in what other context is it possible for people like Topher and Polly and Robb and me to work together, feeling useful, feeling each day the challenge to personal growth and the strengthening of affectionate bonds.

On an experiential level it seems so simple – and yet to imagine an anarchism built on such principles will require prophets of a radically new world-view. They are emerging, and their vision is being pieced together. Prophets of this disposition do not predict the future so much as they intuit the meaning of the flow of time. The world they describe is one of open-ended possibilities. They are more inclined toward the steady state than the big bang theory of cosmology. They are more of the persuasion of Heraclitus than of Parmenides – i.e. more inclined to imagine the universe in perpetual flux, perpetual evolution, than to see change as the play of illusion upon a ground base of fixed principles. History tells them only of the past, not of the future, not of the essential or determined. Ethologists have attempted to define human nature in terms of its evolution from primitive forms of life, asserting that what we can be is circumscribed by what we have been. But to the new prophets, such scholarship tells us the task of transcendence, not its limits: even our celebrated territoriality is no more definitive than body hair. As the ever-renewed universe leaks its energy to the void, life pulls it into new order, a negentropic force (i.e. a force of negative entropy), forming the formless, anew and anew as forms petrify, in what Norbert Weiner called 'enclaves of order'. Some scientists have described consciousness as nothing but a rear-view mirror, a sort system for the past disappearing behind us. But in the world-view I am describing it is also an awareness of the *élan vital* welling under us, the wisdom of the surfer making the infinite, instantaneous, subrational choices that maintain balance and direction in accord with our sense of the movement of overwhelming evolutionary power, guessing the future on the basis of our gross yet definite sympathy with the intention of the wave.

This may not be a new consciousness at all, but a prehistoric intuition. The speculation surrounding cave paintings that look remarkably like men in space suits has given rise again to theories that some of early man's sophistication (e.g. the mathematical precision of Stonehenge) may derive from extraterrestrial visitation. More simply, we may imagine that the organisms which became human at an earlier stage had primitive awareness, like the communication in a cloud of gnats flying in formation over evening water, which has been lost in our specialized, cerebral development. Current experiments with polygraphs attached to plants suggest that there may be a network of consciousness linking cellular life throughout the universe, a network in which, anomalously, human beings can only participate through the laborious use of electronic instruments, so effective is our cerebral consciousness in jamming the vibrations transmitted to and by our other cells. Whether it be through drugs, or yoga, or meditation, or biofeedback mechanisms or other means of extending awareness, we seem to be on the verge of regaining a capacity to relate to natural processes from which we have been excluded, like black sheep returning to our Edenic home.

Nature, except for humankind, lives in anarchy. Not lawlessly, of course: indeed, it seems that only humankind can violate its implacable laws. But in that environment which we despoil and from which we so desperately shield ourselves, there are no constitutions or hierarchies, no officials, no roles (that world is not a stage), no schedules, no duties – though there are imperative loyalties requiring the mother tirelessly to feed her young, the mate to defend the bower, the species to maintain itself, even by stratagems as destructive to individuals as lemming migrations. In that anarchy, tragedy is linked to bounty irrevocably as winter to autumn, and affirmation to negation with the mindless persistence of March shoots pushing through rotten snow. In political terms anarchy means the abnegation of power, but that belies the reality. Rather it is adoption of the greatest power available, riding the wave of nature's dynamics, identifying with insuperable forces. 'Politics', Buckminster Fuller once said, 'is of the machine age, obsolete.' If we can find a way to unleash the new anarchism, with its promise not of chaos but of the supreme orderliness and dependable rhythm of nature, it will make politics unthinkable as warfare is made by the possibility of nuclear holocaust.

Finding a way to unleash it is a slow, sensitive task, like that of bank thieves with sanded fingers sensing the muted fall of tumblers that lock in the mystery. A paradigm for the task is the lesson of love. If I desire you, I must recognize that sexual pressure may be exactly what will drive you away. If I love *you* and not a reflection of myself, I must want you to be what you are, not shape you to my wishes. That may mean I must learn to be glad if you love another, if you choose to leave me. And those hard lessons must be learned in the midst of intense passion, not through diminishment of feeling, but through its increase, by learning to care enough not to destroy.

The world beyond the looking-glass will seem much like the one we leave – or at least the one on blueprints produced by humane intelligence. Only the motives will be reversed, and the fruit looking just like perfectly manufactured wax will, strangely, be real, edible, perishable. The factory will run – without pressure, without wages, its profits absorbed by the community as unceremoniously and uncompetitively as air is breathed and water drunk. People will make pots as they prepare and eat a meal, sleep, make love, sweat, defecate – as something that must be done, that one can learn to like to do.

Or so we hope. For those of us who have lived long on the wrong side of the glass, adjustment to the reversed world will no doubt always be somewhat self-conscious and awkward, like immigrants who even after many years in their new home still dream and count in the old language. For Topher it may be different – if we have wisdom and love enough to let him become, and to learn a little from him.

Where the wasteland ends

THEODORE ROSZAK

When I was at college (the middle 'fifties) I learned the death of God like a data point in freshman survey courses. I took exams on 'contrasting concepts of the absurd – time limit twenty minutes'. I was taught to admire the latest refinements Beckett and Ionesco had wrought upon the existential vacuum. Modern man, I dutifully noted, is in search of a soul, and the age is an age of longing. But sophisticated minds must know better than to expect that search and that longing to find gratification. There might be private strategies of consolation (like Santayana's cultivation of an aesthetic religiosity), but the first fact of public life was alienation – and alienation was here to stay. Except perhaps in economic affairs. There a strong left-wing commitment permitted one to speak of eliminating the worker's 'alienation' from the means and fruits of production – a much reduced Marxist usage of the term, which, of course, had nothing to do with the spiritual life. Of the needs of the spirit one simply did not speak; the very word was without a negotiable meaning in educated company. This, I rapidly learned, was the most intellectually intolerable aspect of personality and accordingly the most repressed. One might discourse in luscious detail about one's sex life in fact and fantasy; but how gauche, how offensive to introduce anything even vaguely religious into serious conversation – unless with a fastidious scholarly detachment . . . as a point of fact . . . about other people . . . in other times and places.

But what was all this clever confabulation with the alienated life but the cultural expression of urban-industrial social necessity? For the sake of the artificial environment, the soul *had* to die. The transcendent impulse that cried out in me for life and a dignified space in the world *had* to stay jailed up in my head as personal fantasy. Either that or be gunned down on sight for subversive activity. God – any god who was more than a presidential platitude – had become an enemy of the new industrial state. This was why secular humanism had become the orthodox intellectual style of the age; why Marxism had become the orthodox radicalism. Neither took issue with science or technics or the psychological mode

Reproduced by permission of Doubleday & Co. Inc., and Faber and Faber Ltd., from *Where the Wasteland Ends* (1972).

they demand. Neither broke with the artificial environment. Both served the needs of technocratic politics.

How long could this principled repression of the visionary energies go on? How long before there came a generation which realized that a wasteland is no place to make one's home?

No doubt there are ways and means to ameliorate, at least temporarily, the most dangerous excesses of urban-industrialism and the technocratic politics it breeds. But for the disease of single vision there can be no *ad hoc* reform, no quick technological fix. And it is single vision that underlies the despair, the anomie, the irresponsible drift, the resignation to genocide, the weakness for totalitarian solutions, which make radical, enduring change in our society impossible. Until we find our way once more to the experience of transcendence, until we feel the life within us and the nature about us as sacred, there will seem to us no 'realistic' future other than more of the same: single vision and the artificial environment for ever and ever, amen.

That is why the politics of our time must reopen the metaphysical issues which science and sound logic have for the last two centuries been pleased to regard as closed. For to expound upon social priorities or the quality of life without confronting those issues is the very folly of alienation. It is, once again, the half person prescribing the whole person's needs. But it is *experience* that must reopen those issues, not academic discourse. We must learn once more to discriminate experientially between realities, telling the greater from the lesser. If there is to be a next politics, it will be a religious politics. Not the religion of the churches – God help us! not the religion of the churches – but religion in the oldest, most universal sense: which is vision born of transcendent knowledge.

'Be realistic. Plan for a miracle', reads a hip maxim of the day. What miracle? The Buddha once said there is only *one* miracle. He called it 'the turning about in the deepest seat of consciousness'. *Paravritti*. The sharp reversal – like coming out of a crash dive at the last minute. Not a turning-back of the clock – which is never possible personally or socially – but a saving return from the depths. The prophet's return from the speaking solitude of the wilderness. Ishmael's return from the demonic voyage. The return of the mad from their secret self-annihilation. A *wise* return, which brings back the full experience of the outward journey.

The apocatastasis: the great restoration. Since its earliest days Christian thought has been haunted by this strangest and most beautiful of all heresies. Where does it come from? Out of the old mystery cults and the orient, by way of Plato perhaps. A memory of the great cycle in which history turns like a wheel around the hub of eternity. The teaching speaks of another world that is destined to inherit from this fallen creation and which is, in fact, paradise regained. And between the two worlds, the fire of perdition is no more than the interval of terrible instruction that burns the soul's gold free of its dross. Hell having been universally harrowed, even Satan and his reprobate band (so the heresy teaches) will turn from their infernal obsessions and find their way to original unity.

In the Gnostic myth, the apocatastasis is the illumination in the abyss by which the lost soul, after much tribulation, learns to tell the divine light from its nether reflection. So a new reality replaces (or rather *embraces*) the old and draws the fallen spirit up, wiser than if it had never fallen. For us, this means an awakening from 'single vision and Newton's sleep', where we have dreamt that only matter and history are real. This has been the bad, mad ontology of our culture, and from it derives that myth of objective consciousness which has densified the transcendent symbols and persuaded us to believe in the reality of nothing that cannot be weighed and measured – not even our own soul, which is after all a subtle dancer. So long as that myth rules the mind, not even the most humanely intentioned among us will find any course to follow but roads that lead deeper into the wasteland. But the mind freed of that myth may begin to find a project as vast as repealing the urban-industrial dominance not only feasible but necessary.

It would be preposterous to think that anything I write here, anything that any one person says or writes, demands or pleads for, could bring about the apocatastasis. Such a spiritual regeneration happens of its own mysterious accord or not at all. And of course it is happening. The fact that these words find their way into print now – as they could not even ten years ago – is a manifestation of that happening. Though whether the reversal will happen soon enough and on a sufficient scale there is no telling. That is the cruel edge of the adventure.

The signs of regeneration can be seen all about us in the heightened appetite for experience, the often indiscriminate passion to explore every forgotten reality of the self and nature. Listen, and you can hear that appetite eating away at its exotic diet of dreams, ecstasies, old mysteries, and quaint personal awakenings; you can detect it in the mode of the music, in the tones and gestures of ordinary people, in the rhythms of their breathing. The outlaw young in their counter-culture, the restive middle Americans in their Growth Centers have become a participating audience for all the long-neglected artists, psychologists, and philosophers of the Extraordinary.

And this is – potentially – the beginning of the end for the old Reality Principle and the artificial environment that strives to become its perfect embodiment. Gradually the realization dawns that *all* the realities men and women have known are real, each being the discovery of a human potentiality. The scientist's reality together with the mystic's, the technician's together with the poet's. Even the madman's reality is real, and not only to the mad. For have we not, in the twentieth century, found our way back to the mythic and visionary origins of culture in large part by following the mad through their dark, internal country? 'Breakdown', R. D. Laing has observed, 'may also be breakthrough', a tortuous return to the source of the transcendent symbols. Here is one of the strangest adventures of our time: the rediscovery by psychoanalysis of universal truths beneath the wreckage of personal nightmare and neurosis.

It is as Robert Duncan has said: we are gathering together a new symposium where all are invited to participate.

> To compose such a symposium of the whole, such a totality, all the old excluded orders must be included. The female, the proletariat, the foreign, the animal and vegetative; the unconscious and the unknown; the criminal and failure – all that has been outcast and vagabond must return to be admitted in the creation of what we consider we are.

In the new reality game, all these pieces are on the board, and any conception of Reason or Sanity that demands a smaller, more conveniently manageable field of play will be overturned. Too many have now learned the Reason which represses any part of the Whole is only insanity's mask.

To be mad, as the world judges, is to be trapped in a narrow and lonely reality. To be sane, as the world judges, is to be trapped in a reality no less narrow, but heavily populated. But there is also the higher sanity, which is neither the going consensus nor the latest compensatory excess. Its health is freedom from all traps; its sign is the knowledge of many realities. All realities are real; but sanity's reality is vaster, more various, more vividly experienced in all its sectors, and more judiciously ordered. It is a spectrum, and not a single color worn like a uniform and flown like a crusading banner. The higher sanity can taste of all realities, but respects the ontological priorities.

Here and now, as we restore the orders of reality, we are in the stage of closing up all the traditional dichotomies of western culture which have served as the bulwarks of the old Reality Principle. Spirit–flesh, reason–passion, mad–sane, objective–subjective, fact–value, natural–supernatural, intellect–intuition, human–non-human . . . all these familiar dualisms which have divided the spectrum of consciousness vanish as we create the higher sanity. The dichotomies are healing over like old wounds. Even science, in its awkward single-visioned way, has been led to continuities that baffle traditional assumptions. It can no longer draw hard lines between matter and energy, organic and inorganic, man and lower animal, law and the indeterminate, mind and body. What is this but a final cold reflection of the visionary Whole, the Tao, the One, at last appearing in the alienated mind where it reaches the end of its tether?

In the society generally, this closure of the dichotomies appears as a ransacking of all the excluded human traditions. It is as if the repressed collective unconscious of our culture were being turned inside out before our very eyes. Everything once forbidden and outcast now makes its way into paperback editions, comic books, poster art, pop music. A dizzying spectacle. A necessary stage. Easy enough to ridicule the excesses. They are apt to be with us for some time to come. Perhaps there will always be people undergoing at some interval in their lives the same ungainly traumas of liberation, desperately trying this and that. There will surely always be fourteen-year-olds coming along the way, absolute beginners. But the fair questions to ask are: how did the traumas resolve themselves . . . where are the fourteen-year-olds ten years later . . . what was learned by the failed experiments? These exotic samplings and improvizations – even where they abandon caution – are essential to the personal and cultural search for wholeness. Though of course the whole, as a disciplined creation, must finally become more than a chaos of possibilities. Just as the finished painting must be more than the well-heaped palette.

Only one dichotomy will remain, the inevitable distinction between more and less. There must always be this tension between those who would have sanity be less than the whole, and those who would have the whole. Where this book, for example, has taken issue with single vision, it has been with the *exclusiveness* of 'Satan's mathematic holiness'. Not, in turn, to exclude it, but to find it its proper place in a science of rhapsodic intellect. Between those who are still locked in the box of the Reality Principle and those who have escaped it there will always be the tension of disagreement. For Jack In-the-Box will insist there is nowhere to be but where he is. Jack Out-of-the-Box will know otherwise. It is the inevitable contrast of sensibilities between the free and the imprisoned mind – and only the *experience* of more will ever overcome anyone's allegiance to less.

To argue as I do that urban-industrialism is a failed cultural experiment and that the time is at hand to replace it with the visionary commonwealth amounts to a strict denial of the secularized myth of progress as we have learned it from our forebears of the Enlightenment. That is a bitter pill. It declares many generations of hardship and effort to have been a catastrophic mistake. For those who are not in touch with other, more fulfilling realities, such an admission is bound to seem an intolerable humiliation. But I hope I have made clear that I am not, as has become so much the morbid fashion among western intellectuals since the *fin de siècle*, rejecting the pursuit of secular progress in favor of wholesale cynicism. Such cynicism, being legitimately unacceptable to society at large as a basis for life, has only increased the desperation with which the millions cling to that myth despite their inadmissible misgivings. We must remember Blake's warning.

> Man must & will have Some Religion: if he has not the Religion of Jesus, he will have the Religion of Satan & will erect the Synagogue of Satan, calling the Prince of the World, God, and destroying all who do not worship Satan under the name of God.

True enough, no one who is not lying himself blind to the obvious can help but despair of the well-being that a reductionist science and power-ridden technology can bring. Nothing humanly worthwhile can be achieved within the diminished reality of such a science and technics; nothing whatever. On that level, we 'progress' only toward technocratic elitism, affluent alienation, environmental blight, nuclear suicide. Not an iota of the promise of industrialism will then be realized but it will be vastly outweighed by the 'necessary evils' attending.

But there is another progress that is not a cheat and a folly; the progress that has always been possible at every moment in time. It goes by many names. St Bonaventura called it 'the journey of the mind to God'; the Buddha called it the eightfold path; Lao Tzu called it finding 'the Way'. The way *back*. To the source from which the adventure of human culture takes its beginning. It is *this* progress which the good society exists to facilitate for all its members.

The higher sanity will find its proper politics when we come to realize in our very bones that we have nothing to add to the splendor of the Old Gnosis and can make no progress 'beyond it'. We can do no more than return to it, borrow from it, reshape it to suit the times. This is to recognize that all the resources of the spirit human beings have ever needed to work out their destiny have always been with them . . . *in* them . . . provided; all they have needed to be beautiful and dignified, graceful and good. *In this sense*, there is nothing to do, nowhere to get. We need only 'stand still in the light'. This is something that must be emphasized not only to the technocrats with their ingrained contempt for traditional wisdom, but also to the young media-freaks and acid heads with their bizarre passion for an electrochemical epiphany. For they seem not to realize how pleased Westinghouse, Du Pont, and RCA would be to wire them up for skull-flicks and throw the switches. Anything to keep the public grateful and distracted.

Technologically speaking, there is indeed a course of history, obviously linear and cumulative. Its measure is increase of material power and, within a discipline of the sacred, that historical potentiality must also be unfolded. But the Old Gnosis needs no history; it is whole in every moment of time. The Romantics, in their struggle against single vision, thought they saw such a timeless self-fulfillment in the delights of infancy. Certainly they, with most artists, found it in their work, in the stasis that comes of capturing a symbol's transcendent meaning.

But such symbols are with all of us everywhere and at all times; not only in the language and imagery of our cultural making, but in every most ordinary moment, every least scrap of the world around us, in the rhythms of our own body, in the lights and airs that fill the sky, in the things and creatures with which we share the earth. It is the presence of transcendent symbols instructing, nurturing, brightening life at every turn that makes the world at large a magical object and human culture a whole from its most technologically primitive origins to the present time. Here we find what can alone give meaning to our historical project: the eternity that seeks its reflection in the mirrors of time.